938. . . and the Consequences

Studies in Austrian Literature, Culture, and Thought

1938...and the Consequences

Questions and Responses

Interviews

by

Elfriede Schmidt

Translated by

Peter J. Lyth

ARIADNE PRESS

Translated from the German *1938 . . . und was dann?*
©1988, Österreichischer Kulturverlag

Library of Congress Cataloging-in-Publication Data

1938-- und was dann? English.
    1938-- and the consequences : questions and responses: interviews
\ by Elfriede Schmidt : translated by Peter J. Lyth.
      p.   cm.--(Studies in Austrian literature, culture, and thought)
    Translation of : 1938-- und was dann?
    Includes bibliographical references.
    ISBN 0-929497-34-1
    1. Austria--History--1918-1938--Sources. 2. Anschluss movement,
1918-1938--Sources. 3. Antisemitism--Austria--History--20th
Century--Sources. 4. Interviews--Austria. I. Schmidt, Elfriede.
II. Title. III. Series.
DB97.A17 1991
943.605'1--dc20   91-25375
                                 CIP

Cover Design: George McGinnes

Copyright©1992
by Ariadne Press
270 Goins Court
Riverside, California

". . . whoever destroys a single life from Israel is considered by Scripture as if he had destroyed an entire world; and whoever preserves a single life from Israel is considered by Scripture as if he had preserved an entire world. . . A man mints many coins from one mold and they are all alike, but the King of kings, the Holy One, Blessed be He, minted all men from the mold of Adam and not one is like another. Therefore, everyone is obligated to say, For my sake was the world created. . ."

—MISHNAH SANHEDRIN 4:5
TALMUD

TABLE OF CONTENTS

Comment of the author:

I will ask such questions as, what has happened during the more than fifty years since the *Anschluss* in 1938? What are the reactions in foreign countries today, for example, in Germany or the United States? Interviews with two well-known personalities are appended here in this connection. As those interviewed earlier, they offer their own opinions, with which the author does not necessarily agree in all respects. But such voices must not be ignored. We must respect the diversity of views.

Foreword

It was a Friday evening, March 11, 1938. *Radio Wien*, the Viennese radio station, had canceled its regularly scheduled program and was playing solemn music. Listeners were told to stand by for an important announcement. Then the Austrian Chancellor, Kurt Schuschnigg, came on the air. In a strained and tired voice he told his countrymen that, faced with an ultimatum from Hitler, he had resigned. Within hours German troops poured across the border, while homegrown Austrian Nazis took over the reins of government. On March 13 hundreds of thousands of Austrians cheered Hitler in Vienna as Austria was incorporated into the German Reich.

It was a critical turning point. Whatever Hitler had done up to that point in defiance of the Treaty of Versailles he had done within Germany. Now for the first time he had crossed the border and annexed an independent country—and the world stood by.

It was a turning point in another respect as well. Hitler had come to power in January 1933 on a rabidly anti-Jewish political platform. But except for a few anti-Semitic street demonstrations shortly after his assumption of power, the focus of Hitler's anti-Jewish program had been on the dismissal of Jews from certain job categories: governmental service, the legal profession, academia, prominent positions in the art world, etc. More than five years after the Nazi take-over, hundreds of thousands of Jews were still in Germany, hoping that they could weather the storm.

The events in Austria after March 11, 1938 ended that illusion. Jews would be picked up in the streets and publicly humiliated. They would be arrested for no reason other than that they were Jews. Segregation was imposed in the public schools. As the weeks and months passed, the anti-Semitic measures became increasingly oppressive and brutal. They gradually spread from Austria to Germany proper. The gas chambers of Birkenau could not have been reasonably foreseen in light of the dismissal notices received by Jewish government officials and professors in Germany in 1933. They could have been foreseen in light of the treatment accorded to Jews throughout Austria from March 12, 1938 onward.

Elfriede Schmidt has sensitively and thoughtfully given us a collage of the traumatic experiences suffered in 1938 by Austrian Jews and by those other residents of Austria who were not prepared to hail the country's new masters. It also provides insight into the attitudes of those who looked the other way as their fellow-citizens were brutalized and tells us about those who actively participated in such brutalization. The series of eyewitness accounts in *1938. . . and the Consequences,* prompted by appropriate questions from the author, enables us to understand a period of Austrian history which some wish to send down Orwell's memory hole.

—Richard Schifter

Why I Have Conducted These Interviews

Time and again I have asked myself how it was possible for such an inhuman regime as National Socialism to establish itself in Austria with the cooperation of so many Austrians.

In the summer of 1987 there was the so-called "Remembrance Action for the Austrian Resistance" in front of St. Stephan's Cathedral in Vienna. Its purpose was to ensure that history is not forgotten through the concealment and suppression of the facts.

I listened quietly to a lot of people there. Once I spent several hours and heard things like, "people never liked the Jews. . . they murdered God, didn't they? They're in a world conspiracy and now they want to turn our President into a war criminal." The saddest experience for me, however, was seeing an elegant lady attack a man supported by a cane, who with great calm and self-control was trying to explain the purpose of the Remembrance Action.

He recalled what he himself had suffered fifty years earlier and said: "Never again should an Austrian have to go into a concentration camp." He himself had suffered in such a camp. Simply because he was a Jew, it had been right to mistreat and torture him. People should remember how terrible it was then, how many resistance fighters were executed. He hoped that people would learn from history.

Then the elegant lady interrupted him: "You could have emigrated! You didn't have to stay, did you? Why didn't you get out soon enough? Nobody told you to stay! It was your own fault, wasn't it? The concentration camps weren't so bad anyway, otherwise you wouldn't be here!"

Her cold, finely made-up eyes, the inhuman words of this seventy-year-old "lady" with the Viennese accent struck me deeply. I had to say something. Why? Was it "collective shame" that I experienced in the presence of this poor man who had suffered so much?

I was ashamed for this woman.

An elderly couple with a foreign accent drew me discreetly to one side. "We come from Sweden and didn't believe what we read in the papers. Now we've heard it for ourselves. We've stood here for hours and we just can't believe it—and after the Holocaust. We are leaving immediately and are never coming back to Austria." I had a long talk with this couple because I didn't want them to generalize and extend what they had heard there to include the whole Austrian people.

"We have a lot to learn from one another to correct the lack of understanding that has built up over the centuries," said former President Rudolf Kirchschläger.

Unfortunately, the Stephansplatz discussion has not been an isolated event. Other remarks and statements by various personalities have distressed me with their lack of humanity, such as Michael Graff's comment that "so long as it's not proven that he [Waldheim] strangled six Jews with his own hands, there's no problem" (*L'Express*, 13 November 1987). Or the extremely anti-Semitic letter of the Deputy Mayor of Linz, Dr. Hödl, who later declared in an interview that of course, he wasn't an anti-Semite!

"Many people have become troubled that in the political atmosphere of the last few years, the theme of anti-Semitism has reappeared in our midst. There is particular concern at the ease and lack of sensitivity with which the old wounds of anti-Semitism are reopened in the course of party-political debate. Four decades after Auschwitz, we as Austrians and Catholics are once more confronted with phantoms that we thought had been laid to rest." With these eloquent words Cardinal König spoke out for reconciliation between Christians and Jews—why can't he reach the hearts of some people?

May the conversations and recorded life stories presented in this book contribute to a new understanding of the period, and bring about a state, in which the old can relate to the young just how it was and what atrocities can flow from blind political fanaticism. What was done to these poor people—in our own neighborhoods—should be understood by all. It is a process which cannot be completed overnight, but must take place at home, in the schools, in the workplace.

Friedrich Heer—whose daughter Johanna I had the privilege of interviewing—begins his book *Gottes erste Liebe* with the following inscription: "This book, written by an Austrian Catholic, is dedicated to the Jewish, Christian, and non-Christian victims of the Austrian Catholic Adolf Hitler."

In memory of this great Austrian historian I bring this preface to a close. May my work be taken as a modest contribution—a stone in the mosaic of dialogue between Christians and Jews.

—Elfriede Schmidt

Acknowledgements

In producing the English version of my book *1938. . . und was dann*? I have received help from many people and I would like to take this opportunity to express my gratitude. Peter J. Lyth has done a great deal more than simply translate the German text; he has been a source of encouragement from the onset. Professor Donald G. Daviau and Jorun B. Johns have been understanding editors and publishers. The Styrian Government headed by Josef Krainer has supported the book from the beginning of the German version and has covered the costs of some of my trips to the United States. Eleasar Weissbrot assisted with the editing. Ronald Lauder in New York made a generous contribution to the costs of the translation. Austrian Airlines helped with the expense of my many trans-Atlantic flights, and the Austrian Embassy arranged my lectures on the Anschluss to Washington audiences. The Austrian Institute in New York invited me to give readings from the original German version.

Roland D. Graham, an attorney in Minneapolis, gave me invaluable advice and insight concerning publication of the book. His judgment and continuing support remained vital.

I would also like to mention those people who kindly placed advance orders for the book, thereby facilitating its publication: Landeshauptmann von Burgenland Johann Sipötz, Konsul Kurt Brühl, Generaldirektor Wilhelm Thiel, Frau Daisy Bene, Generaldirektor Rudolf Pieber, Dr. Gerfried Förster, Dr. Wido Stracke, Kommerzialrat Franz Preminger, Christa Mayer Rieckh, Kommerzialrat Peterheinz Gebell, Dr. Klaus P. Heiss. And many thanks to Mrs. Adaire Klein, Coordinator at the Library & Archival Services at the Simon Wiesenthal Center in Los Angeles. Last but not least, I would like to thank Dr. Peter Lux in Germany for his assistance with some parts of the translation when I could not reach my translator Peter J. Lyth in Israel.

To my children, Hansi and Yvonne.
Their love is the motivation for my work.

Introduction

The Road to Anschluss: A Brief History of
the Austrian Republic 1918-1938
Peter J. Lyth

The Austro-Hungarian Empire that broke up with the end of
the First World War was an altogether weaker structure than the
German Reich. Not only was it strained by the large number of
different races and ethnic groups within its borders, but in terms
of economic development it was also generally backward. When
the Austrian Republic was created from its small German-
speaking rump in 1918, many Austrians did not consider that the
new state was even viable and felt that the moment had arrived
for union with Germany, the so-called Anschluss. On 12
November 1918 the Austrian parliament actually declared German
Austria to be part of the new Weimar Republic, and in Berlin
Gustav Stresemann, later to become Germany's leading statesman,
offered to give up his initial opposition to Weimar if union with
Austria could be achieved.[1] The Anschluss which finally took
place twenty years later in 1938 was, therefore, neither new in
conception nor the exclusive goal of Hitler and the National
Socialists. It had been the dream of Pan-Germans on both sides
of the border for decades before 1914, and even the Austrian
Social Democrats saw a merger with socialist-led Germany as
their best hope for the future.

But in 1918 this was not to be. The victorious Western Allies
had no intention of allowing the defeated Germany to end the
war with more territory than when she began it, and the Treaties
of Versailles and St. Germain made Austria's independence inviol-

---

[1]See the appropriate "Staatsgesetzblatt für den Staat Deutschösterreich,"
reprinted in English translation in W.C. Langsam, *Documents and Readings
in the History of Europe Since 1978* (Chicago, 1951), p. 657, and Henry A.
Turner, *Stresemann and the Politics of the Weimar Republic* (Princeton, 1963),
p. 37.

able and forbade any kind of union between the two states.

Initially the outlook for Austria looked dismal. War debts and reparations, a collapsing currency, and new tariff barriers thrown up around her borders, all contributed to the difficulties of the young republic. Economic factors had been generally ignored in the break-up of the Empire, and each "successor state" had whatever resources happened to be in the territory allotted to it. Former trading patterns and industries were disrupted, so that, for example, the Austrian textile industry found itself with its spindles in Czechoslovakia and the weaving looms in Vienna. Having established Austria, however, the Great Powers had a certain obligation to keep it on its feet. The League of Nations helped with economic assistance, particularly after the hyperinflation of 1922, and eventually a League loan was organized and Austria's finances placed under international control. This regime lasted until 1926 during which time the expenditure of the state was cut and taxes raised. The currency was stabilized and a new unit, the Schilling, introduced.[2]

Part of Austria's problem was that it had a head larger than its body. Practically a third of the country's seven million inhabitants lived in Vienna. The former imperial capital was an enormous city for such a small country, and it now had a multitude of superfluous bureaucrats, their numbers swollen as the "successor states" dismissed and repatriated the Austrian civil servants in their territory. For this army of unemployed white-collar workers the government had to provide relief, which it did by printing money, thus aggravating the currency depreciation.

Vienna was the stronghold of the Austrian Social Democratic Party, dominated by worker's councils. By contrast in the rural Austrian hinterland the peasant population was Catholic and conservative, and not surprisingly exhibited a strong antipathy towards "Red Vienna" and its left-wing politics. The city was also undoubtedly Jewish. According to one source, "it is safe to say that by 1914 the industry and trade of Vienna were to overwhelming extent in Jewish hands."[3] Moreover, Jews were heavily

---

[2]W. Arthur Lewis, *Economic Survey 1919-1939* (London, 1970), pp. 21-22.

[3]Arthur J. May, *The Hapsburg Monarchy 1867-1914* (Cambridge, Mass., 1960), p. 177.

represented in the professions, journalism, and the civil service. Many Viennese Jews were recent arrivals from Galicia and other eastern provinces, and they stood out from the rest of the population by their language, clothing, and general way of life.

The result was an anti-Semitism that grew swiftly in commerce and the universities, indeed, everywhere where Jews were numerous and visible. Among Austrian students and their *Burschenschaften*, Pan-German sentiments mixed readily with anti-Jewish prejudice. Many were influenced by the anti-Semite and Pan-German parliamentary deputy, Georg von Schönerer (1842-1921), one of the spiritual fathers of National Socialism. Another important figure at this stage was the popular Christian Social mayor of Vienna, Karl Lueger (1844-1910), whose anti-Semitism was more opportunistic than Schönerer's (he remarked: "I decide who is a Jew and who is not"), but whose political acumen was certainly rated more highly by one young Austrian of the time. Adolf Hitler had been born in the border town of Braunau am Inn in 1889, and it was in Lueger's Vienna that he received his political education.[4]

In the postwar years two large and mutually hostile political parties emerged in Austria: the conservative Christian Socials and the Social Democrats. The Christian Social Party was led throughout the 1920s by the ascetic priest, Ignaz Seipel, who was also Chancellor for much of the period. The Social Democratic Party had a leadership divided between moderates like Karl Renner and his friend the Mayor of Vienna, Karl Seitz, and revolutionary Austro-Marxists like Otto Bauer, champion of the *Anschluss* movement after 1918, and Julius Deutsch, organizer of the Socialist *Schutzbund* militia.

While the Christian-Socials drew their strength from the rural provinces, the socialists had their stronghold in Vienna, where the municipality built a large number of badly-needed workers' dwellings, the rents for which it subsidized with levies on other city householders. For the enemies of socialism these apartment blocks were ideological citadels in the class war, as well as military strong points in a future civil war.

The beginning of the crisis came in 1927. In July, workers

---

[4]F. L. Carsten, *The Rise of Fascism* (London, 1967), pp. 32-41.

in Vienna had rioted and burned down the Palace of Justice upon learning that a group of Free Corps fighters, accused of murder, were to be acquitted.[5] To the horror of the Austrian middle-classes a nationwide general strike was called. This was defeated by the mobilization of the *Heimwehr* (Home Guard), a collection of right-wing militia that grew up in Austria during the 1920s with the support of the Italian dictator Benito Mussolini and the tacit agreement of Seipel's government. The *Heimwehr* stood for Austrian nationalism. But though fascist in character, it was a fierce rival of the Austrian Nazi Party. Divided between "clerical" and Pan-German wings, it exhibited an old style reactionary conservatism closer to Franco's Spain than Mussolini's Italy.[6]

After 1930 the world economic depression revived Anschluss sentiment in Austria. Proposals were made for a Customs Union between Austria and Germany as a first step towards full political amalgamation. Once again the Western Powers, mainly at French insistence, vetoed it for fear of allowing Germany to become too powerful.[7] In 1931 a major financial crisis hit the capitals of Europe and a series of bank failures took place beginning with a collapse of the great Creditanstalt in Vienna. The ensuing policy of exchange and trade controls adopted by the Austrian government only served to bring further economic misery, so that by July 1932 industrial production was 43% below the 1929 level and 25% of the work force was unemployed. While exports collapsed, the overvalued Austrian Schilling allowed a steady stream of imports into the country. Repayment of foreign debts ground to a standstill and the government's fiscal policy collapsed as tax revenue dried up. In the following years there was some recovery, but it was very slow in pace and lagged noticeably behind that of neighboring Nazi Germany. At the time of the Anschluss in 1938

---

[5]The Free Corps (Freikorps) were independent militias formed in Germany and Austria after the First World War. Composed largely of veterans of that war, their purpose was to combat Bolshevism and frontier encroachments, e.g., by the Poles (in Germany) or the Yugoslavs (in Austria).

[6]For a detailed account of the *Heimwehr*, see C. Earl Edmondson, *The Heimwehr and Austrian Politics, 1918-1936* (Athens, Ga., 1978).

[7]F. G. Stambrook, "The German-Austrian Customs Union Project of 1931: A Study of German Methods and Motives." in Hans W. Gatzke, *European Diplomacy Between the Two Wars 1919-1939* (Chicago, 1972), pp. 94-125.

unemployment in Austria was still 17%.[8]

Economic depression with its lost jobs and bankruptcies formed the background to the tumultuous events that rocked Austria in the early 1930s, sealing its fate as a democratic nation. This is not to say that the depression alone was responsible for its surrender to National Socialism; the older democracies in Britain and France did not collapse in the face of similar adversity. However in a country with shallow democratic roots and hardly a decade of independent existence, the economic crisis provided an endless supply of ammunition for those on the political right who sought to destroy the Republic.

In November 1930 the *Heimwehr's* new leader Prince Starhemberg led the organization to a disastrous defeat in the federal elections of that year, with the result that some members now turned to more violent means of gaining power. In September 1931 the leader of the more radical Pan-German wing, Walter Pfrimer, led a "March on Vienna," which ended in debacle when the other *Heimwehr* leaders refused to support him. The attempted coup had a brief success in the southeastern province of Styria, where the capital Graz was surrounded for a while, but everywhere else it was a failure. Pfrimer and a number of others were put on trial, and like Hitler and his followers in the 1923 Munich Beer Hall Putsch they received very mild treatment from the courts. Thereafter support for the *Heimwehr's* brand of Austrian nationalism diminished as the more potent Pan-German ideology of the National Socialists gained ground, especially in Styria.[9]

In May 1932 the young Christian Social Minister Engelbert Dollfuss became Chancellor. The following year he created the "Fatherland Front" as a political umbrella organization with the object of rendering the old parties superfluous. The republican constitution was suspended, parliament abolished, and a corporate

---

[8]Derek H. Aldcroft, *The European Economy 1914-1980* (London, 1980), pp. 107-109.

[9]The Styrian *Heimwehr*, or *Heimatschutz* as it was locally known, was the largest, best organized and most radically Pan-German of the Austrian Heimwehren. It also most closely resembled the National Socialists, and its members deserted to the Nazis with few regrets. See Bruce F. Pauley, *Hitler and the Forgotten Nazis: A History of Austrian National Socialism* (Chapel Hill, N.C., 1981), pp. 75-77.

state based largely on Papal Encyclicals was established. The "Fatherland Front" reached a strength of around three million members by 1937, but, as a state party created "from above," it commanded little real support; people tended to join in order to protect their jobs. Like the Nazi Party it was organized on the "leadership principle" and even had a similar insignia, a kind of doublesided swastika called the *Kruckenkreuz*. However, Dollfuss was a bitter opponent of the Austrian Nazis and in June 1933 he banned the party altogether after the country had endured a sustained Nazi bombing campaign.

Meanwhile the Austrian Social Democrats, despite their strength (the Left was not split as in Weimar Germany), made no attempt to oppose the new regime until 1934, and by then their vacillation had allowed Dollfuss to effectively destroy the basis of working-class institutions. Eventually there was resistance from the *Schutzbund* in Linz and Vienna, but it was too little and too late. Most of the fighting in the three-day civil war of February 1934 took place in working-class districts like Floridsdorf in Vienna, where Dollfuss ordered the bombardment of the workers' apartments. In less than a week the Army had crushed the uprising and the *Schutzbund* leaders were hanged.

The effect of the civil war and the destruction of the Social Democrats was to remove the one organized force that might have been able to defend Austria from Hitler's aggression.[10] In fact some former socialists now joined the outlawed Austrian Nazis, rather than submit to Dollfuss's "clerical fascism." The civil war played right into Nazi hands by providing them with a major propaganda coup: they were able to point to the shooting of Austrian workers by Dollfuss's forces, and mock his dependence on Mussolini and the despised Italians.

Within months of putting down the threat to his authority from the left, Dollfuss lost his life facing an attack from the right, when in July 1934 he was murdered by Austrian Nazis in another abortive coup attempt. This precipitous action seems to have been carried out by a local leader, Theo Habicht, without Hitler's full knowledge of the details and in the midst of a bitter dispute

---

[10]F. L. Carsten, *The First Austrian Republic, 1918-1938: A Study Based on British and Austrian Documents.* (Gower, 1986).

between rival factions within the Austrian party.[11] Mussolini, who was actually awaiting the arrival of his friend Dollfuss and already had the Chancellor's wife with him as a guest, was enraged by the news of the assassination and immediately ordered four divisions of the Italian Army to the Brenner Pass to guard against any possible invasion of Austria by the Germans.

The failure of the *Putsch* showed that the Austrian Nazis could not bring about the Anschluss single-handedly, as long as Italy was opposed. For Hitler to have supported the Austrian Nazis in 1934 would have meant war with Italy and this was impossible. Instead he disowned the conspirators immediately, and changed his tactics to one of slow infiltration of the Austrian government and bureaucracy, and its isolation from possible allies.

With the death of Dollfuss the Chancellorship passed to Kurt von Schuschnigg, who continued the former's authoritarian regime as well as he could. Instead of confrontation with the reorganized Nazis, he chose to try to undermine them by imitating those features of German National Socialism which he thought would prove popular and lure the more moderate Nazis into the "Fatherland Front." Abroad he worked hard to keep Italy's friendship, but this proved increasingly difficult as Mussolini's overseas adventures, in particular the invasion of Ethiopia and the support of Franco in the Spanish Civil War, meant that the Duce had less time for the problems of his northern neighbor. With the relationship between Nazi Germany and Fascist Italy strengthened by the formation of the Berlin-Rome Axis in 1936 and the accession of Italy to the Anti-Comintern Pact in 1937, Austria became diplomatically isolated.

For Schuschnigg there seemed little alternative to some kind of arrangement with Hitler. This materialized in the "Gentleman's Agreement" of July 1936. The Austrians consented to grant an amnesty to the thousands of Nazis who had been interned after the *Putsch* and promised to pursue a policy suited to her status as a "German state," while Germany acknowledged Austria's independent sovereignty. It was a temporary breathing space for Schuschnigg, but nothing more.

---

[11]Pauley, *Hitler and the Forgotten Nazis*, pp. 122-137.

In the remaining months before the Anschluss the Austrian Nazis around the figure of the Viennese lawyer Arthur Seyss-Inquart systematically penetrated the "Fatherland Front" and Schuschnigg's administration, while the rival group around Josef Leopold unleashed a new terrorist campaign. Then on 12 February 1938 Schuschnigg was summoned to Hitler's Alpine retreat at Berchtesgaden. There, surrounded by his generals, the Führer harangued the Chancellor and gave him an ultimatum: admit Nazis to his cabinet or there would be an immediate invasion by the German Army. Schuschnigg gave way; shortly afterwards Seyss-Inquart became Minister of the Interior, a fateful step because it meant that the Nazis gained effective control of the Austrian police force.

Schuschnigg made a last-ditch attempt to save Austria with a plebiscite in which the people were asked if they were in favor of "a free and German, an independent and social, a Christian and united Austria," a list with such a wide range of desiderata that it was bound to gain the assent of all but the most dedicated Nazi. Although at this stage the army, administration, and police were thoroughly infiltrated with Nazis, Hitler saw the plebiscite as a serious threat to his plans and demanded that it be called off. When it was rescinded on 11 March, Schuschnigg's resignation was immediately called for, and Seyss-Inquart became Chancellor. One of his first acts was to sanction the sending of a telegram to Berlin requesting that German troops enter Austria "to restore order."[12]

The following morning the Wehrmacht rolled across the frontier. On 13 March Hitler arrived triumphantly in Vienna, where he announced to an ecstatic crowd in the Heldenplatz that the historic reunion of Austria and Germany had taken place. The enthusiasm, brought about by the genuine belief of many Austrians that the years of civil strife and economic misery would now be brought to an end, did not last long. On the heels of the invading German troops came another army of administrators, in-

---

[12]In fact, the Nazis already controlled the whole country and the streets were comparatively quiet. Seyss-Inquart, who still hoped for a Nazi takeover without a German invasion, did not send the famous telegram to Hermann Göring. This act was performed by Wilhem Keppler, Hitler's liaison man in Vienna. Pauley, *Hitler and the Forgotten Nazis*, pp. 207-215.

cluding the Gestapo, who took over every branch of public life so that Austria was very quickly reduced to the status of another German province—the *Ostmark.*

The immediate result of the Anschluss was a wave of terror launched against Jews, Socialists, and any other opponents of the new order. All the brutal characteristics of the police state, built up gradually in Germany since 1933, appeared literally overnight in Austrian towns and cities. And it was under these conditions that Schuschnigg's plebiscite was eventually carried out on 10 April, yielding a 99% vote in favor of union with Germany.

In retrospect it is clear that Hitler's attitude to the Anschluss was both racial and political. Austria's acquisition was a necessary precondition for the realization of his plans in the East and at the same time its important German-speaking population would be brought "home into the Reich," the *Großdeutsch* solution that Bismarck had failed to accomplish in 1866, but which he, Adolf Hitler, would now bring about. But the Anschluss was also an important milestone on the road to war in the late 1930s. Without Austria any German move against Czechoslovakia would have been more difficult if not impossible. The Czech position in its conflict with Hitler over the Sudeten Germans in the autumn of 1938 would have been much stronger if the country had not been strategically and politically outflanked six months earlier.

The policy of appeasement by Britain and France towards Hitler, and in particular the failure to improve Anglo-Italian relations and announce support for an independent Austria at the critical juncture undoubtedly contributed to the ease with which Hitler was eventually able to bring about the Anschluss. It is said that Mussolini did not even answer the telephone when a desperate Schuschnigg sought his help on the eve of the German invasion. By contrast, he sent Hitler "his regards," accepting the situation "in a very friendly manner." For this the Führer was eternally grateful: "Please tell Mussolini I will never forget him for this. . . never, never, never, whatever happens. . . As soon as the Austrian affair is settled, I shall be ready to go with him, through thick and thin. . . ."[13]

---

[13]Quoted in Alan Bullock, *Hitler: A Study in Tyranny* (Harmondsworth, 1962), p. 431.

With the end of Italian patronage, Austria's other potential allies faded away. In Britain the authoritarian Catholicism of the Dollfuss/Schuschnigg regime had no popular support and the government of Neville Chamberlain was not about to choose Austrian independence as the issue on which it would stand up to Hitler. The French had vigorously opposed Austro-German union since 1918, but by 1938 the degeneration of the Third Republic had progressed so far that they were content to follow the British lead in foreign policy. In both countries there was a strong sense that a union of the two German states was inevitable sooner or later and a feeling, typical of the period, that it was not worth risking a war over.

"... A lesson of how one can lose one's home and never find it again. No matter how happy one can be in other places ..."

Interview with *Leon Askin* on May 6, 1988.

Mr. Askin, for fifty years you have lived in America. In 1938 you had to leave Austria because you were a Jew. Your screen career began in 1953 in the film "The Robe" with Richard Burton. Thereafter you appeared in more than sixty films with stars like Doris Day, Danny Kaye and in the Billy Wilder film "One, Two, Three" with James Cagney. You entertained millions of Americans with the successful TV series "Hogan's Heroes." If you look back today what are your memories? What has influenced you?

If I talk to you—an Austrian—then of course I think of the year I had to leave Austria in a hurry. I can remember it as if it happened yesterday and I will tell you about it:

One afternoon about three o'clock I was walking with a friend. We had been talking about a new cabaret that we wanted to do: he would do the first half, I would do the second, or the other way around. About 3:30 I told him that I had to go to the

Grand Hotel (yes, in those days there was a Grand Hotel). I had to see an Austrian-American writer who later wrote the script for my film with Tony Curtis and Jack Lemmon.

Well, I saw this writer and we talked till about 4:45 and then I had to go. When we got to the elevator, the elevator boy said, "Have you heard? Schuschnigg has resigned. Seyss-Inquart is Chancellor. . ."

The words were hardly out of the boy's mouth before my companion embraced me, and with the words "we'll see each other again somewhere in this world," he vanished.

I got in the elevator and went out onto the Ringstrasse. I didn't recognize it anymore: everywhere there were swastikas and storm troopers marching and singing the Horst Wessel Song, "the streets belong to the brown battalions etc." Yes, that was Friday evening as the Messerschmidts flew over the city.

What did you do then?

I went home as fast as I could, but not with the intention of staying there. I ate dinner quickly, then the lady from next door came and told us that Schuschnigg had been brought to the Hotel Metropole—that was the Gestapo headquarters at the time. I went into town and stayed with a girlfriend. I telephoned to Paris—one could still do that at this stage—and said that I would be coming there. I had been there before and that is actually where I did go.

"Emigration must be a skilled matter." By that I mean that one should not try and leave on the first day of a Putsch because all the borders are closed. That's the way Fritz Grünbaum got killed, because he wanted to get away immediately, and many others died on the Czech border because they wanted to get out straight away.

On Saturday I stayed overnight with friends and I heard on the radio that Hitler was in Linz: "hurrah! hurrah!"

On Monday I rushed to the French Embassy to get a visa and got one straight away. My Carte d' Identité, which I already had, and which confirmed that I had a residence in Paris, made it possible for me to get a visa for the trip to France, and at the same time I was able to get an exit visa from the police.

So, how did I eventually get away? I went home again and quickly burned some books which would have been compromising for my parents had they been found. Then I said goodbye to my mother, whom I never saw again, and, accompanied by my father and brother, I set off for the city. I said goodbye to my father in the Petersplatz; my brother came with me to the station where I boarded the train for Paris.

Did you get to Paris without incident?

No. In Innsbruck I was taken off the train and taken to the local police headquarters. There I had to undress and they searched everything: my clothes, my case, but they didn't find anything.

Then they asked me if I was the same gentleman who had written a terrible anti-Nazi cabaret of the time.

"No," I replied, "that was a little red-haired chap whom I know."

This was really a dangerous situation for you, wasn't it?

Yes. Well, then a miracle happened. A "hiasl" (a country yokel) appeared, he was from the Tirol, and he said, "if you give me cigarettes and money, I'll get you to the station; the train leaves in fifteen minutes". . . so, he took my case and I really did make that train.

I got to Zürich but no-one wanted me there so I travelled on to Paris. I was interned there and eventually in 1940, I left for America.

So now you have it—what you want to know. And you also want to know, I suppose, what happened to my mother? Well. . . I only have to mention the gas chambers of Lublin and Minsk. . . do you want more? No.

How did you life continue from then?

I lived in Paris for a while, where I wrote film scripts and then I went to the USA, first to Washington, then to New York and finally to Hollywood, where I've been ever since.

What sort of relationship do you have to Austria today? Do you miss Austria?

Fifty years later? My relationship to Austria? What should I tell you? All I can do is sing:

> Dieses schöne Reich
> Einem Garten gleich
> ist mein Heimatland
> mein Österreich.

I was born there, grew up there, grew up there, in K-gasse, in T-park, I know every street in Vienna. Vienna is in my blood and I can't deny it. As I said when I got my medal, "I am an American citizen, but I can't forget my roots."

Do I miss Austria? Am I homesick? Not exactly. You can't miss a country that took your parents to the ovens. But I do have a tremendous affinity to Vienna and Austria because that is where I was born and you can't wash that away—that's the right expression, wash away. I went to school in the Kalvarienberggasse. And I had many friends in Vienna: Professor Kraus, Hans Weigel, Paul Blaha, Klaus Maria Brandauer—a long list, I could go on. And I should not forget György Sebestyén, who is unfortunately no longer with us.

Do you feel that things have changed regarding anti-Semitism in Austria?

Changed? When was Austria not anti-Semitic? There has always been a latent anti-Semitism in Austria. In recent times it was simply polarized. But changed? No.

How do you see the present situation in Europe? Since the fall of the Iron Curtain and the union of West Germany with the GDR? Do you think about 1938 in this context?

I think of the remark my history professor in Vienna once made: history is crazy! And it's crazy again. No-one would have imagined that the Communist system in Russia or East Germany or Poland would collapse. And no-one can predict what will happen in the future. I just think we should remember every historical event, and 1938 was a dreadful, I should say terrible, historical event. For me personally. Probably for the whole European history. . . but even terrible events pass away.

Would you have stayed in Austria if 1938 had never happened?
Of course!

I'll finish our interview with these words: A lesson of how one can lose one's home and never find it again. No matter how happy one can be in other places. . .

"... what the *Anschluss* would mean in terms of humiliation, expropriation, and torture. .."

Interviews with *Helmut Bader* on 18 and 30 September, 27 October and 28 November 1987, in addition to numerous letters.

Dr. Bader was born in 1915. He lived until 1938 in Graz and was a member of the Jewish student fraternity Charitas. He lives today in Los Angeles.

You were in Graz in 1938, you loved this town and were driven out of it because you were a Jew. Were you already aware of anti-Semitism?

The assumption that anti-Semitic remarks, riots, and insults began in Graz only with the *Anschluss* in March 1938 is of course completely wrong. Graz always had a strong German Nationalist population; particularly in the academic professions in Graz there was a racist anti-Semitism, closer to Schönerer's than the clerical variety of Lueger.[1]

---

[1]Georg von Schönerer (1842-1921), one of the spiritual fathers of National Socialism, was a renowned anti-Semite and the most prominent of the Pan-German leaders in the Austro-Hungarian

Do you have memories from your schooldays?

For most of the time from 1925 to 1933 I was the only Jew at the High School on Tummelplatz and that's where I heard for the first time the swear-word "Pig Jew" (*Saujud*). With Hitler's success in Germany after 1930 the teachers were radicalized as much as the students. Most of them declared themselves openly to be Nazis. In consequence anti-Semitism grew stronger, although I must say that in my class it was not directed against me personally, since by this stage I had friends there as well as enemies. One of my schoolfriends from those days has remained a good friend to this day. The professors were generally very anti-Semitic and were not above making anti-Semitic remarks, but they were completely fair in marking my grades. That applies to the University too.

Where did you study? What was it like at the University?

I studied between 1933 and 1935 in Vienna and from 1935 to 1937 in Graz. I became a doctor of law in November 1937. At Graz University, in contrast to Vienna, there weren't many anti-Semitic incidents. On the other hand as long as Jews were still allowed to visit coffee house and nightclubs, before the *Anschluss*, there were fights almost every weekend, which began with anti-Semitic pestering, and in which I was often involved.

What was the atmosphere like in Graz at the end of 1937 and the beginning of 1938?

The atmosphere was completely poisoned even before the *Anschluss*; after Schuschnigg's meeting with Hitler in Berchtesgaden in February 1938, it was quite clear to me and other young Jews in Graz that there was no future for us in Graz or in Austria. On the other hand no one could imagine what the *Anschluss* would mean in terms of humiliation, expropriation, and

---

Empire. Karl Lueger (1844-1910) was the popular Christian Social mayor of Vienna, who made the famous remark that he himself would determine who was a Jew and who was not.

torture, not to mention the concentration camps and gas chambers. The older generation of Jews did not realize the danger. They hoped that Austria's independence would be preserved by Schuschnigg under the protection of the Western Powers and Mussolini, and at an advanced age they were obviously not prepared to give up livelihoods that they had worked hard to build up.

You told me that you maintained good contact with Schuschnigg when you were in the USA. How did he see the situation for the Jews?

Dr. Schuschnigg, who was a close friend of mine in the USA after the war, believed that he could rescue Austria's independence and told me that he regretted not warning the Austrian Jews sufficiently in advance.

Did you work after your studies in Graz?

From November 1937 to 13 March 1938 I was clerk to the regional court for civil cases in Graz in the Radetzkystrasse, and I was working for my doctorate in political science at the University. The judges were all official members of the Fatherland Front.[2]

What was the day of the *Anschluss* like? Do you still have memories of it?

---

[2]The Fatherland Front (Vaterländische Front or VF) was a political "umbrella" organization created by Dollfuss in 1933 with the object of rendering superfluous the old parties, including his own Christian Socials. It was a fascist state party created from "above" in the manner of those set up in Hungary, Romania, and Spain (Primo de Rivera's Unión Patriótica), and not a grass-roots movement growing from below like Mussolini's Fascists or Hitler's National Socialists. The Front reached its maximum strength— around three million—in 1937 under Schuschnigg, although it commanded little popular support and people tended to join to protect their jobs, etc. It was organized on the "leadership principle" like the Nazi Party and even had a remarkably similar insignia—the *Kruckenkreuz*, a kind of double-sided swastika.

On the day of the *Anschluss* I found out that most people had already belonged illegally to the NSDAP[3]. The day after the German invasion I went to court and found all the judges and officials wearing swastikas and swastika armbands, which didn't surprise me but which did surprise my parents and relatives. I was immediately called to the office of the court supervisor, who told me that I was relieved of my duties at once. I was not given any reason.

After the *Anschluss* the situation for the Jews was extremely dangerous, although there were fewer disturbances than in Vienna. There was no police protection for Jews against insults and even physical injury. Jews, if they were recognized on the street, were often spat upon and rudely insulted. Signs were put up in hotels and shops—"Jews Not Allowed." Officials of Jewish organizations were immediately arrested and held for weeks. In my case, whenever I saw friends and acquaintances, they almost always looked away to avoid having to speak to me.

Did all your former friends and acquaintances behave the same?

A notable exception is the friend I mentioned before. The first time after the *Anschluss* that I went to the University, where I was very well known, he was standing on the ramp in uniform, and, as I came by, he put his arm—with the swastika armband— around my shoulder and spent a few minutes in this position with me, just to prove that nothing in his feelings toward me had changed. There is another example: my father went every day for decades to the same barber to get a shave. Then after 13 March the barber wouldn't let him in his shop on the Gleisdorfer Gasse anymore.

Were there also economic sanctions?

There were immediate economic measures. Jewish employees were fired, in Jewish businesses highly-paid commissioners were

---

NSDAP = National-Sozialistische Deutsche Arbeiter Partei (National Socialistic German Workers' Party), the Nazi Party.

brought in, who would not let the owners into the shop, which of course led to losses. My parents owned a large property, a convalescent home in Stifting; in June five trucks with about thirty SS men arrived and the property was commandeered. A *Gestapo* man supervised it and put a commissar in and forbade my parents any further entry. A similar fate awaited my mother's family, which was one of the oldest Jewish families in Graz and owned the oldest furniture business in the town. They were completely dispossessed.

Can you remember the *Kristallnacht* in Graz?

The *Kristallnacht* on 9 November! My mother was in the hospital after a serious operation. My father and I were alone in the apartment on the Technikerstrasse, where he also had his surgery. At about three o'clock in the morning there was a knock and two policemen in civilian clothes were at the door with orders to arrest us. In most cases these arrests, which involved the entire male Jewish population, were carried out by SA thugs who used the opportunity to beat people up. With us, however, this was not the case; the elderly official declared that he refused to carry out the order to arrest Dr. Artur Bader (my father was a very popular doctor in Graz). So I alone was taken to the police station and two days later began the trip to *Dachau*.

How long were you in Dachau?

I left *Dachau* in December 1938 with the first group that was released. The reason was that I had registered in Graz for an illegal transport to Palestine and luckily at the medical inspection before the release they didn't find any wounds or other signs of beatings on my body.

I spent one night at my parents' apartment and the next day traveled to Vienna, where the transport was a Danube river steamer that left from the Reichsbrücke. The steamer sailed down to the Black Sea, and there the refugees were put on a Greek freighter that was already completely overflowing. Sanitary conditions on the ship were appalling, and the ship itself was hardly seaworthy. We sailed through the Dardanelles into the Mediterranean, and in about six weeks we were off the coast of Palestine.

Since there was the danger that the ship would be discovered by English coastal patrols, we transferred to small boats sent by the Jewish Haganah. I swam the last 200 meters to land.

What happened to the refugees?

The refugees were brought in buses to Tel-Aviv. The economic situation was extremely precarious. There was simply not enough food to go around for the thousands of refugees. I worked for two months in the country on a chicken farm and then some time building roads. From April 1939 to the beginning of 1940 I was an auxiliary policeman with the English Mandatory Government, although I was in the country illegally.

What happened to you after the outbreak of the War? What happened to your relatives?

After the outbreak of war I volunteered for the British Army. In those days there were Jewish units being formed that were eventually brought together in the Jewish Brigade in 1943. I served in Palestine, Egypt, and then with the Brigade on the Italian front. At the end of the War I was at Tarvis. I was the first "English soldier" in Graz in May 1945 at a time when the town was still under Russian occupation. The Brigade was then transferred to Germany, Belgium, and Holland, as part of the British Occupation Forces. During this time I visited my parents twice in Switzerland.

My father had been *Judenbehandler* (medical attendant to Jews) in Vienna from 1939 to 1942. In 1942 my parents were sent to *Theresienstadt.* In February 1945, just before the end of the War, a thousand concentration camp inmates, including my parents, were allowed to go to Switzerland after American Jews had paid Himmler a ransom of $1,000 per head for their release.

Did you remain in Palestine after the War? Didn't you want to return to Austria?

I worked in an office of the Mandatory government. There I got to know my future wife (we got married in 1949 in Graz).

The economic situation in Palestine was still extremely difficult. For example, it was impossible to find accommodations. It was clear to me that I would not be able to support my elderly parents, who were completely penniless, in Palestine. Particularly because my father's health was very bad, I decided with great reluctance to go back to Austria.

My only brother had been shot as a hostage by the Germans in Belgrade in 1942.

In October 1947, in other words before the founding of the State of Israel, I left Palestine, although I had the intention of returning as soon as I had cleared up the situation with my parents. However I saw soon that I couldn't leave them alone and that I would have to make some sort of livelihood for them in Graz. My parents returned from the refugee center in Switzerland and moved into the apartment of my grandparents in the Gleisdorfer Gasse, where my father, as soon as his health permitted, returned to his medical practice.

What sort of work did you do in Graz?

At the beginning of 1948 I entered court service. In the first months I served as translator and liaison for High Court President Dr. Zigeuner to the English military authorities. After I passed my judge's exams I served as a political investigating judge and from 1951 councilor at the State Court for Civil Cases.

What happened to your relatives? Did you lose many? When did you go to the United States?

In November 1950 my father died. My father's family was completely wiped out. The survivors of my mother's family were in America, and so in 1953 we emigrated to America.

Were you successful in America?

In January 1953 we arrived in Los Angeles. I worked at first in a bank. From 1954 I worked at night and studied by day for an American doctorate (of political science). In 1957 I got my Ph.D from the University of Southern California.

I taught in numerous colleges and universities in Los Angeles and retired in 1980 as a full professor.

Graz was very quickly made *judenrein* (clear of Jews): you emigrated to Palestine after your stay in Dachau, and your father was one of the so-called ten permitted "Jewish Medical Attendants" in Vienna. Can you tell me something about that?

Adolf Eichmann, who was head of Jewish Affairs with the Vienna *Gestapo* at the time, gave him a so-called document of appointment as doctor, according to which my father was subject to the many degrading provisions such as:

1) "Before taking up your duties and after. . . . . you must register personally or in writing every change of address. . . with the health office and the Commissioner for Jews appointed by the Reich Doctors Chamber, and produce this document of appointment.

2) Your practice should be conducted according to prevailing medical provisions.

3) You are under the control of the Health Authority. You must also follow the orders of the Commissioner for Jews, in particular those which concern the place where you are working. Announcements about your activity in the newspapers are only permitted with his permission.

4) You are not permitted to call yourself a doctor or carry a medical title (e.g., Sanitätsrat).

5) You must wear a badge showing a yellow Star of David in a circle on a blue background. This sign is also to be affixed to letters and prescriptions. On the badge and the papers there should also be added, so that they can be clearly seen, the words, 'Only for the medical treatment of Jews.'"

Returning to May 1945: you told me that you were the first "English soldier" in Graz in May '45. At that time Graz was still occupied by the Russians wasn't it?

What I wanted to tell you will take a bit longer: you must understand that a certain uneasiness, even reluctance, must be overcome before I can relate this story—which is a true story, something that happened to me personally decades ago. But I have taken this decision.

The story took place at the end of May 1945, in other words just a few weeks after the unconditional surrender of the German Reich. I was a non-commissioned officer in the British Army. My unit, the first battalion of the Jewish Brigade, which had been formed from volunteers in Palestine, had participated in the Italian campaign as part of the British Eighth Army and was at this point on the border between Styria and Carinthia in Austria. As a special mark of honor the soldiers of the Brigade carried on the right arm of their uniforms a yellow Star of David, exactly in the same form and size as the sign which Jews under the Nazi regime were forced to wear as a sign of shame. We had already known since the Yalta Agreement that Styria and Carinthia would be part of the British occupation zone; but parts of Styria were actually conquered by the Russians. In the short time since the cease-fire they had not yet retired into their zone in Lower Austria and the Burgenland. The Styrian capital (Graz) was therefore still under Russian control.

This meant that I was just two hours' drive by car from the place of my birth, from which I had been driven seven years before.

I wanted to use the opportunity to see the town again from which I had to flee years before. My battalion commander and I had doubts about entering an area still occupied by the Russians, since relations between the Russians and the Western Allies at this stage were tense. In the end we procured a small armored vehicle, and seven soldiers gathered together—partly out of friendship, partly out of a desire for adventure, and partly out of curiosity —and set off on the trip. The driver was a man at least six feet tall, with broad shoulders, blue eyes, and blond hair, who came from Berlin and had a real Berlin accent. Although he came from an old German rabbi family, you would have thought him a classic Siegfried from the stage at Bayreuth.

It was a beautiful spring day, the wonderful Carinthian countryside was in full bloom, everything was quiet and peaceful until we got close to the city. Twenty kilometers from the town there was a barrier across the road; to the side was a house on which a huge Soviet flag was displayed; there was even the obligatory portrait of Stalin. The sentry was astounded to see an English military vehicle. He immediately raised his rifle and said "njet," and indicated with signs that one could not proceed any further.

Now there was another surprise for him: among the soldiers in English uniform there was somebody born in Russia, who explained the situation to the sentry in perfect Russian. An officer appeared. When it was explained to him in his mother tongue that it was the great hope of one of these English soldiers to visit his parents' home after many years, and when it transpired that the Russian-speaking "Englishman" and the officer both came from the same region of the Soviet Union, he became very friendly. On his own authority he gave permission for the "Englishmen" to visit the town for two hours. In a short time we were at the edge of the town.

I tried to take the shortest way to the center. That was more difficult than I had imagined, since on the edge of the town near the bombed-out station whole rows of houses had been destroyed and some streets simply did not exist anymore. However, I found my way. Despite the fine weather the streets were deserted; now and again I saw a few Russian soldiers. It was about 11 in the morning. The few people to be seen on the streets slipped by the piles of stones and houses; mainly old men, absolutely no women. One noticed that they were starved and, above all, fearful. The bright sunshine could not outshine this fear.

Soon we reached the main street where the two best coffee houses in town had stood next to each other. The last time I had seen them, seven years before, they were full of happy, well-fed people, and swastikas hung from every window. In front of the entrance to the first one there had been a sign with huge letters: "Jews forbidden entry." The other one did not want to take second place and had erected a sign saying: "Jews and dogs are forbidden entry." On the way to my parents' house I remembered Hitler's visit to the town. Swastikas had waved from every house, every window had at least one flag. Thousands marched through the streets in the uniforms of the different military units and the Hitler Youth. Thousands more stood on the sidewalks and cheered the Nazi bosses. They sang the Horst-Wessel Song over and over again, and raised their arms in the Nazi salute, and shouted again and again "Deutschland erwache, Juda verrecke" (Wake up Germany, Death to Jews).

Now it was different in the streets of the town. In the present empty misery one could hardly imagine the earlier enthusiasm.

Of my parents' house there were just four walls remaining; the high school I had attended for eight years was burned out. The atmosphere was so depressing that we'd soon had enough and after just an hour we started to go back. On the way I noticed that we were driving past the house of my old Latin professor. The street was not destroyed. I remembered him well. Perhaps he was still alive. I stopped the truck at the next corner and told my comrades that I would be back in a few minutes. There was no one on the streets. The front door was barred, but since I knew that my former teacher lived on the ground floor I knocked on the window, and after a short while it was opened. The old man looked out fearfully. When he recognized his student he immediately let me into the apartment, embraced me, and broke into tears. Then his wife appeared and the two old people cried together. They had two sons who had both fallen on the Russian front. They told me about the terror of the occupation, and their fear of the Russian soldiers who were indiscriminately both cruel and good-natured. It was time to say goodbye.

As I came out of the house a quarter of an hour later, the street had changed completely. Windows were open and people were coming out of the houses, not only old men, but young women with children. Around the truck there were about a hundred people gathered, and as I came closer I heard how they shouted happily, "The English are here! Thank God! The English are here!" Then I saw the blond driver climb on the roof of the truck and point his pistol at the yellow Star of David painted there and shout at the crowd in pure Berlin dialect, "Don't be so stupid! Can't you see: We're not English, we're Jews!" And then came the cry, as if from one throat, "The Jews are here, thank God, the Jews are here!"

"... guilty of the death of German soldiers. .."

Interview with *Vera Bauer* on 11 December 1987.

Mrs. Bauer was born in 1929 and works today as a medical technical assistant. She spent 1938 in Graz, where she still lives today.

Do you have memories from 1938 or the years before?

In 1938 I was in the third grade at elementary school, and we had a teacher who left us in March 1938—in other words after the *Anschluss*. I can remember clearly that this teacher described to us children what "wonderful times were coming." There would be an end to unemployment. I told my father about it and he said that there might be an end to unemployment, but that it would be because of war.

I want to make it quite clear that there were people then who understood the connection between ending unemployment by preparing for war and the consequences thereof.

In September 1939 I went to the high school in Felix-Dahn-Platz, where I met the teacher from my elementary school again; she was now a history professor. I was amazed to see her here in the high school, knowing that she was just an elementary school teacher!

I want to make it clear that I was confronted with illegal National Socialism and its everyday routine even as a child. These memories have stayed with me until this day.

And now I would like to tell you another little story that took place in 1985.

There was a group of young people in their thirties, among whom I was also present, and the War was discussed. I told them about a time when we high school kids had to collect money for the Winter Relief (a Nazi charity) and I had collected the lowest amount and it was entered in my school report. One of the young men present—he was an officer in the Austrian Army (and this was in 1985!)—told me that I was "guilty of the death of German soldiers in Russia," since through my lack of effort on the home-front I had stabbed the fighting soldiers in the back. I stopped the conversation immediately. To this day I am sad that the portrayal of history by the Austrian Army glorifies war.

You wanted to tell me about your father! What happened to him?

My father was an Austrian by conviction!
He was a real Austrian patriot!
He loved his country. His Austria!

Many years before the *Anschluss* he got to know unemployment pretty well. But he never submitted to the Hitler regime. He was an opponent and he found out soon enough about the criminal Nazi regime.

On 7 October 1943 he was beheaded for his Austrian patriotism.

My mother, Mrs Franziska Motschnik, will tell you more; she suffered a terrible break in her life on this day. (See pages 183ff.).

". . . We lost all our relatives in unknown concentration camps. . ."

Conversations with *Ilse Biro* on 24 August and 25 October 1987.

Mrs. Biro was born in 1904 and is the widow of the Graz lawyer Dr. Ludwig Biro. She died in the autumn of 1988.

Was the year 1938 very important in your life?

1938 was decisive for me—for my life. Immediately after the invasion of the German troops my husband was locked up three times, and—it sounds paradoxical—that was our "good fortune" because in this way we were warned—mercilessly warned—and became aware of the extent of the situation. Because of this we were able to leave Austria before the *Kristallnacht*. We had to give up our apartment immediately after the invasion and, of course, let our servants go. Already around 20 March our home was searched and naturally the office too. They installed a non-Jewish colleague in my husband's place.

My husband was no longer allowed to go to court, he was "permitted" to work on the inglorious "Aryanization" contracts. . . it was terrible. My husband saw "what was coming" even before 13 March. Unfortunately we could not prepare our-

selves financially. Our "Aryan" friends still helped us after 13
March. . . our child we sent to friends in the country for safety.

At the end of October 1938 we fled to Maribor (Yugoslavia).
A Nazi friend had gotten us accommodations, and we stayed there
until the beginning of March 1939. Then out of fear of discovery
we fled on to Zagreb. It was a complete underground life! Continual fear. . . continual hiding . . . the Jewish community helped
us with money, it supported us and finally paid our passage to
Israel. We had an English visa, but we could not get to England
because the Swiss had refused us a transit visa. Then in the spring
at last we left for Israel. . . it was unspeakably sad and painful to
leave our parents and above all not to know when we would ever
see them again. Up until 1940 at least we had written communication by means of cover names and addresses. Then in 1940
suddenly all contact was lost. . . all this was in Yugoslavia.

In Israel we stood before the great unknown! I immediately
got a job as waitress, so at least we had our meals free. Then my
husband got work and with enormous difficulty studied "British
Law" through correspondence courses from England. All the time
the three of us lived in one small room. Later my husband was
able to resume his profession as a lawyer in Israel, but we both
wished, even during the worst years of the War and even if we
had lost all our relatives in unknown concentration camps, to
return to Austria as quickly as possible. We were always patriotic
"Austrians," heart and soul.

**Mrs. Biro, you and your family knew, among others, the Nobel
Prize winner Otto Loewi.[1] Can you tell us about him?**

My husband and I were friends of Loewi. We did a lot in the
cultural field together. Everybody who was acquainted with Loewi
knew of his knowledgeable love of art. His great love for the

---

[1]Otto Loewi was born on 3 June 1873 in Frankfurt, an only son with
two sisters. He went to school in Frankfurt and studied medicine in Strassburg. He was even in a fraternity. He was a physiologist and pharmacologist
and from 1909 professor at the University of Graz. In 1936 he received the
Nobel Prize for medicine. In 1938 he emigrated to England. In 1939 he was
at the University College of Medicine in New York. See Otto Loewi, *Ein
Lebensbild in Dokumenten,* (Berlin/
Heidelberg/New York, 1968).

stage, for music and art couldn't stop him, however, from dedicating himself to the study of internal medicine.

In 1895/96 he presented his dissertation on the "Quantitative Effects of Prussic Acid, Arsenic, and Phosphorus on the Isolated Frog Heart," and then in Frankfurt he extended his knowledge of analytical and inorganic chemistry. . . In 1900 he did his Habilitation on "Investigations into Nuclear Metabolism" and continued working in this area. In 1902 and 1903 he traveled to England to extend his knowledge of physiological methods. In 1905 Loewi went to Vienna and enjoyed the marvelous cultural life in the city. In 1909 he was appointed to the chair of pharmacology at the University of Graz.

Did Loewi have difficulty with his profession in Graz because he was a Jew?

I can remember that he had difficulties at the beginning. But he was a very outstanding personality: through his human and professional qualities he very soon commanded respect and was able to carry on. In addition he had German nationalist sympathies, and in the First World War he was an enthusiastic supporter of the Fatherland.

In his lecture "Our Attitude towards England and Its Importance for Later," which he gave in Graz in June 1915, his German nationalist feelings were clearly expressed. He said, for example, that it was worthwhile "learning English, but the acquisition of the language did not mean that we should use it more than occasionally." Yes, Loewi was very patriotic and defensive about his Fatherland. Up to their entry into the First World War, the English were "not a subject of our common thoughts and feelings," but after the beginning of the War it was different. Then it was necessary to surrender ourselves "in flesh and blood against them—against the English." Under the influence of the War impressions became deeper. He felt that his "Fatherland" had been attacked and that there was "no success without a national loss." That was his view during the First World War!

What was it like in 1938? Was he politically persecuted then?

It was scandalous! The same man who in October 1936 received the Nobel Prize for Medicine and Physiology with Sir Henry Dale, was suddenly arrested—two and a half years after that great honor!

Did the arrest come as a surprise to him?

He lived for science. On 11 March 1938, just as on any other day, he was working industriously with his colleagues on an experiment, which was to be the last in a series. Suddenly he learned from a colleague that the Nazis had seized power. But as far as I can remember from what he said, he could not really grasp the full meaning of this news because he was so busy with his work. He was preoccupied with his latest discovery! He also heard Schuschnigg's farewell speech, but he still had not grasped the enormity of the situation—and the danger to himself.

At three o'clock in the morning, however, he knew what was happening: he was no longer a respected scientist and an honorable member of the human race, but someone who had been arrested! Some young men, with weapons, burst into his bedroom and demanded that he get dressed and come with them. A prison vehicle was waiting for him in the street, he was thrown into it and taken to the city prison. The same night his younger sons Victor and Guido suffered the same fate. His older children, Hans and Anna, were not in Austria at the time.

It must have been particularly tragic for him, because Loewi was so tied up with his work. He told us that he suffered every day he was under arrest and feared that he could be murdered before he had published the results of his last experiment. After repeated requests he was allowed, in the presence of an overseer, to send a letter to the *Naturwissenschaften*. His concern was that the world would be deprived of knowledge by his unexpected death! After he had written the postcard and was satisfied that it would be mailed, he didn't fear so much for his life. That was Loewi!

When was he released and how was his life after this humiliation?

He was under arrest for about two months. Three weeks later his sons were also released from prison. In the autumn of 1938 he went to London. The money he had received for the Nobel Prize he had to transfer—in the presence of the *Gestapo*—to a bank controlled by the Nazis. The Nazis took literally everything that the Loewis owned. They had to show "proof of poverty," and got a so-called "work permit." In 1941 his wife Guida was allowed to follow her husband, who by that time was already in the States.

How did Loewi cope with it?

Loewi could excite other people with his élan. He was impulsive, open-minded, and made friends quickly. That helped him very much, particularly in this difficult time. He had good instincts and behaved with simple people exactly as he did with learned scholars. He was a great man. He arrived in England without a penny. But he mastered his fate. Immediately after he left Graz in 1938, on his way to London, he worked in Brussels. There he learned that New York University wanted him as a "Research Professor of Pharmacology." He followed this up and went to the States.

When were you and your husband closest to Loewi?

We spent wonderful years together between 1928 and 1938. The Loewis lived in a well-kept villa in the Johann-Fux-Gasse in Graz. Frau Loewi was a wonderful hostess. Everyone who knew her admired her: she had a fine, educated manner and nobly coped with the later humiliations.

The fourth of every month—I remember it still after sixty years—the Loewis had an "at home." Only personal friends came and they were invited personally by Loewi. His cultural ideal had a real and unconscious basis, like his patriotism. Otto Loewi was wonderful company. He was never boring and because of his terrific sense of humor he was open to all sides of life. He was also tolerant and forgiving. He also had an enormous fund of knowledge and an excellent memory. Because of his versatility he was much loved. And I remember that he was also a good raconteur and loved music and art.

How could Loewi, who was no longer a young man in 1938, successfully start anew?

It was admirable the way he adapted to the violent changes in his circumstances. After they had fled the family had hardly anything. He was nearly seventy, but he got furniture from the Salvation Army and lived in a little apartment in New York. He had the ability to enjoy the exciting atmosphere of a real *Weltstadt* like New York with all its cultural offerings. The man had style and knew how to live.

How did Loewi view his old country after the War? Did you see him after the War?

In 1959 Loewi invited me to America. I had a wonderful time with him. We exchanged old memories and relived the past. We'd experienced a lot together. We also had kept in contact during the War. He wrote to us in Israel. My husband and Otto were good friends. They did not forget each other even during the worst years.

Loewi could forgive! He could forgive, without forgetting! It was in this sense that he accepted the numerous honors that he was given by Germany and Austria after the War. The authorities in Graz also wanted to honor him. He replied that although he had forgiven the humiliation he had suffered, he would never be able to forget it.

He took up all his old friendships again, at least with all those people who were not directly involved in those terrible events.

Are you still in touch with the family?

His wife Guida died on 31 July 1958, and, as I told you, I visited him in 1959. His children also live in the States.

Otto Loewi died at home in New York on Christmas Day 1961. His urn was buried in Woods Hole in 1962.

". . . That was 'our fulfillment of duty!'. . ."

Conversation with *Franz Danimann*, 10 November 1987.

Dr. Danimann was born in 1919 and was in Schwechat during 1938. He served as chairman of the Lagergemeinschaft Auschwitz and as an official of the Austrian League for Human Rights. He lives today in Vienna.

Doctor Danimann, in 1938 you were active in the illegal free trade unions and as an official of the Catholic Youth Front. Can you tell me something about 1938 as well as the years before? Was there anti-Semitism?

I came from an old Social-Democratic family. Anti-Semitism was foreign to us, but of course we knew that it existed among a part of the population and that the Nazis exploited it. And there were a number of other things that made it worse. In particular the mass unemployment, the political exclusion of the democratic Left in 1934, and the international encirclement of Austria by fascism after 1933. Our only truly democratic neighbors were Czechoslovakia and Switzerland.

Were you politically active before 1938?

Yes, I was already active before 1938 in the so-called illegal Left, which sought to regain the democratic rights that had been abolished in 1933/34 and to warn people about the "brown peril." Hitler had come to power in 1933, and it was clear to us that he represented a deadly threat to Austria. Also that he was preparing for war. We wanted to build a resistance movement that would encompass both the illegal Left and the those sections of the middle class that opposed fascism. In this regard I was active in 1937/38, above all in the illegal free trade unions, trying with my friends to win back democracy for Austria. It was a hard struggle, but, as a representative of the illegal left opposition said on the occasion of a visit by the Austrian Chancellor Dr. Schuschnigg: "You can't fight with your hands tied."

What happened then?

Well yes, it is well known what happened then. Hitler foresaw this resistance and invaded Austria militarily. Within a few days the shameful measures against Jewish citizens began.

I had a critical experience at this stage. I lived at that time in Schwechat, a suburb of Vienna, where there were a number of Jewish business people.

They were known as Jews but were well-respected among the populace. Immediately after 11 March 1938 they were driven onto the street by Nazi functionaries, given toothbrushes, and told "to clean the streets." The Nazi leader remarked mockingly that "the Jews would finally learn how to work." You could still see in the streets slogans like "For a Free Austria!" or "Our Motto: Red-White-Red!," which had been painted on shortly before for Dr. Schuschnigg's plebiscite. These slogans now had to be washed off. They were heart-breaking scenes. The victims were often old people, but despite the fact that they were forced to kneel down to do the work, they managed to retain their dignity.

I had no illusions about the "brown power," but I was still shocked. The reaction of the people around about varied. Some made fun and said "it serves them right. . ." Others turned away in disgust muttering that it was a *Schweinerei* (scandal) to do that with old people. . ." Others just stood and stared, although their expressions showed that they rejected what they saw.

Finally I could not restrain myself anymore, and I said to a Nazi who seemed to be in charge and whom I knew, "Aren't you ashamed, to harrass these people like this?" To which he replied,

"Ah, so you are a friend of theirs, are you? Well, for you we can find another toothbrush. Get down on your knees and start scrubbing!" I escaped by getting on my bicycle and riding off.

What did you feel about such scenes?

If I had had any doubts about continuing my illegal political activities, even under the more dangerous conditions that now existed, then those doubts were removed. You have to fight against such a regime if you have the chance—that is, if you want to avoid being guilty with the rest.

Of course it was very difficult because in the first few days communications were broken as many people were being arrested. People were taken from both the illegal Left and the so-called corporatist camp, so far as they were known to the *Gestapo*. And of course many Jews, some of whom had not previously been recognized as such.

The difference between illegal activity now and before was that whereas earlier you had risked your freedom and job, assuming you had one, now you risked your life. This was particularly so after the beginning of the war when the death penalty was meted out for comparatively trivial offenses.

When I talk about this in schools today the young people often say, "But that was suicide surely?" Well, for us it was a sort of fulfillment of duty. Certainly, many more people saw through the criminal Nazi system than actually fought against it. But then illegal conspiracies never assume a mass character for various reasons.

Did this have consequences for you?

At the end of February 1939 I was "sent up," that is, I was arrested. I was sentenced to three years imprisonment for "preparing treason" (I attribute this relatively mild sentence to the fact that the "crime" was committed before the outbreak of the War). After the prison term I was taken into "protective custody" and finally I was sent to *Auschwitz*, which up until then I had never even heard of—that was 23 April 1942. I can show you my inmate's number from *Auschwitz*: 32 635!

So you survived Auschwitz?! The place of such gruesome horror?

Yes, I was a witness to what one later called the "Final Solution." I was there at a place of mass extermination, which according to certain propagandists never existed. . .

How long were you in Auschwitz?

Over two and a half years. Until 27 January 1945.

How old were you then? And how could you have survived Auschwitz? How can anyone survive Auschwitz?

I was 23 then. I was young and pretty fit. But that was no guarantee that you survived. It was a question of luck. And a big help was the solidarity that existed among the political prisoners. In *Auschwitz* there was even an international resistance group, the *Kampfgruppe Auschwitz*, in which Austrians were very active—the names Hermann Langbein[1] and Ernst Burger should be mentioned in this connection. We were in close contact with Polish, Russian, and French prisoners. Occasionally one could save an individual's life, but the machinery of mass extermination could not be stopped.

Did you know about this mass extermination?

Yes. I happened to escape the "testing" of the gas chambers by accident.[2]

How do you mean?

---

[1]See Hermann Langbein, *Im Namen des deutschen Volkes. Zwischenbilanz der Prozesse wegen nationalsozialistischer Verbrechen* (Vienna, 1963), and other publications.

[2]Dr. Danimann kindly made available to the author an extract from the manuscript of his work *Finis Austriae,* in which he describes in detail the "testing" of the gas chambers.

You see, initially the prisoners were told that the gas chambers were really "convalescent blocks." One of the tests to see if the gas chambers worked took place in the summer of 1942 when the hospital was cleared under the pretext of preventing typhus fever. I was in the hospital at this time with typhus and actually wanted to get into the "convalescent block" myself, but I was put in a work detail instead. Three friends of mine, who were in the hospital but were getting better—Alois Sindl from St. Pölten, Franz Riegler from Mürzzuschlag and Graz, and Josef Nagel from Vienna-Floridsdorf—they were sent to the "convalescent block" to regain their working strength and they never came back. There were simply reports of their deaths. They belong to the first victims of the gas chambers at *Auschwitz-Birkenau*.

From this point on, transports from all over occupied Europe arrived at *Auschwitz*.

Hospital "convalescent blocks" as gas chambers?

There were several euphemisms used to avoid getting the victims alarmed.

During the "testing" I mentioned, 746 people were murdered. I was actually rescued by an orderly, who, in contrast to myself, knew what was really meant by "convalescent block." I was returned to the work detail, still half sick. My comrades helped me to survive the next few days.

The mass extermination continued from this time onwards without a break, and the gas chamber facility was enlarged several times. Besides Jews, the victims included Gypsies, Soviet prisoners of war, the disabled, and so on. The exterminations had absolute priority. They said that "wheels must roll for victory," but there always had to be enough wheels to transport people to *Auschwitz*. Even when the Nazi leadership knew that the war was lost—and there are documents to confirm this—the transports to *Auschwitz* continued without pause.

As late as May 1944 400,000 Hungarian Jews were sent to their deaths at *Auschwitz*, and in August 1944 the so-called Gypsy camp was wiped out.

If they could not have their "final victory," at least they were going to have their "final solution."

How do you see the situation fifty years after this terrible time?

I think we have to be a little self-critical here. After 1945, in the immediate postwar period, we allowed ourselves the illusion that the Nazi problem would solve itself as the old generation of Nazis died out. Of course we concentrated on the rebuilding of our country. We assumed that in a democratic Austria, with healthy economic and social policies, and the lessons of the past at hand, there would be no place for neo-Nazis, anti-Semitism, and similar poisonous ideas.

For this reason the young did not get proper instruction. And this was made worse by the fact that many parents preferred not to talk with their children about those times. So the "brown plague" of yesterday has not been confined to history. We are seeing again the old xenophobia and clichés about foreigners, and unfortunately there is now a whole generation that has not been taught the lessons of the past. There is a lot to catch up on.

What is your own contribution in this connection?

As an eye-witness, I am asked a great deal by the education authorities to give lectures in schools and take part in discussions. It's not the task of the witness to give history lessons, there are enough qualified teachers for that; instead he should simply tell how he personally experienced resistance, persecution, and the concentration camp, and how with luck and a few chance occurrences he survived it all.

Are young people interested?

In school classes they are as quiet as a mouse when you talk about the gas chambers—the *Auschwitz* gas chambers whose existence is still doubted by certain groups. These young people value the directness of the eye-witness report, and one notes how they are touched by the description of particularly tragic events.

However, one should remain down-to-earth and rational, since a report given in an emotional fashion may be very moving, but it inhibits the audience from asking questions. Examples should illustrate the inhumanity of the whole system, above all the "final solution of the Jewish question" in *Auschwitz-Birkenau*, etc.

The number of crimes that were punished with the death sentence was very wide indeed. Many people landed in the death cell because they had made a joke about the Nazi regime or had repeated news from a foreign radio station or had collected money for the persecuted—as you yourself learned from the widow of a resistance fighter who was beheaded (Mrs. Motschnik—see page 183).

What do you stress when you speak to young people?

It seems essential to me to point out that the victims of Nazism were not just its opponents and the "diverse groups of undesirable persons," which indeed were very large, but also, on account of the "total war," large sections of the population as well as people in the occupied territories.

Of course Hitler led his own beloved people into the greatest catastrophe of their history. There were 380,000 casualties in the Danube and Alpine provinces alone. And it should also be remembered that in the Budget we are still paying for pensions of war victims and widows.

Would you like to say something in conclusion?

Yes. We must fight prejudice and clichés. We all know the destructive role of anti-Semitism, extreme nationalism, and racism from our recent history.

Today we are experiencing once again a systematically stirred-up xenophobia, in which none of the so-called "arguments" bear close inspection. Similarly, there are attempts to construct a contrast between young and old, and between townspeople and country folk. . . there are plenty of examples. There is an atmosphere hostile to politicians, particularly of the "old parties." Even if you are critical of some of the excesses of the present political practices, the tendency to paint politicians in a completely negative light must be rejected. Politicians have a right to be judged according to their behavior and work. There is a very appropriate quotation from Marcel Reich-Ranicki, "Whether we contribute or just watch, whether we see ourselves as super-numeraries or prompters: politics is our fate."

Don't you ever detect a so-called "weariness with democracy"?

Yes, but despite all the criticism there is no alternative. It was Winston Churchill who said: "Many forms of government have been tried in this earthly vale of tears and will be tried in the future. Nobody believes that democracy is best, indeed, some people think it's the worst type of government possible—with the exception of all the others that have been tried over the years."

In conclusion I would like to say one more word about the "old parties": they are the guarantors of the state, they built up the Second Republic from the ruins, and they should be able to overcome any ossification in the interests of a living democracy.

". . . I know my opinion is not very popular. . ."

Interview with *Ernest Dichter* in New York on June 2, 1988 and June 5, 1988.

Professor Dichter you are the father of "Motivation Research." Your life is far more than just an unusual success story; it is a fascinating study of people and their often peculiar, sometimes hilarious, behavior, observed over a lifetime of "people-watching."

You were born in Vienna where you earned degrees in psychology and you later held professorships in Florida and New York. You also worked for CBS, for many advertising agencies and founded the world famous Institute for Motivational Research in 1946.

I want to go back to your childhood. Do you have memories from school days in Austria? Were you already aware of anti-Semitism in Vienna?

I remember our apartment in Vienna. It was a cold water flat without bathroom. The toilet was inside; we were lucky, most of the families had to share theirs with other tenants on the same floor. I am Jewish, therefore I left Austria 1937.

Apropos childhood: I remember, when I saw some years ago the film "Incident at Vichy" by Arthur Miller, I was reminded of my childhood. Of course, we were separated from women, but no distinction was made between men and boys, Jews and non-Jews.

Circumcision was almost exclusively practiced by Jews. In "Incident at Vichy" Jews or Jewish-looking men had been arrested by the French equivalent of the Gestapo. Their passport to either freedom, or concentration camp, was the shape of their penis. Taking a weekly shower in my youth, was an equal ordeal for me since it involved a public declaration of my ethnicity. I tried to hide what I considered my deformity with towels and body distortions. But, too often, I had to face my gentile brethren and their hostile teasing came close to hell for me.

These incidents in the "Tröpferlbad" (public showers) made me understand Miller's touching drama much better.

My brothers and I were three red-haired boys and therefore strangers didn't think we were Jewish. In this regard I have to say during the student riots staged by the Nazis at the University of Vienna before Hitler's invasion of Austria, I was usually left alone after a scrutinizing look by my brown-shirted "colleagues."

Professor Dichter, you had to leave Austria before Hitler marched in, because you were a Jew. Nevertheless you still work for Austria, why?

Okay, I am more tolerant. I have a lot of friends who wouldn't ever go back to Austria and they ask me, "why do you help these Austrians? Why do you go back? We wouldn't go back."

Well, I said to myself, "they could also be jealous of me." They have not been invited, so they couldn't go anyway. But I have been invited. . .

I still like Vienna and it is a beautiful city, I speak the dialect and feel more or less at home there. It is different with my wife, her father was imprisoned and only just escaped the concentration camps.

I always have discussions with people about this, but in the end I think we should forget it all. People get tired of it. For example, my wife Hedy has a niece in Vienna who is half-Jewish and whenever we start talking about this subject, she always interrupts, "don't talk about it! Enough! We are the grandchildren and we had nothing to do with it."

You wrote in your book *The Secret Behind Individual Motivations by the Man Who Was Not Afraid to Ask Why?* that self-confidence is not the key to later success, rather having doubts in yourself. That was your opinion ten years ago, is it still your view?

Yes. I was always dissatisfied with myself; for example, I used to wish I didn't have red hair. A good friend of mine, who was a consultant at lever Brothers, told me that I should never lose my insecurity because it would be the secret of my success. My own insecurity would make it possible for me to understand other people and find out what made them tick.

Professor Dichter, how would you judge the Political climate in Austria fifty years after the *Anschluss*? You are in touch with the Austrian Government, and with business people. What is your opinion, did the Austrians learn from history?

I hope so. I am not convinced a hundred percent, but they really have no other way. I can tell you, you have a nice chancellor, but your president has caused a lot of problems. Walter Mondale, the former Vice President, called Waldheim a criminal; I don't know what I would have done in that situation. Waldheim was a young man when he was drafted into the German Army, after that he was not really in control anymore. Probably he was indirectly involved, but I would have pity for him. Maybe he couldn't do much about it.

I know my opinion is not very popular and even my friends criticize me.

You are eighty-three years old. What do you think about the future of mankind on this earth?

I am one of the few people who uses the Holocaust as a new beginning, instead of looking backwards. I get many invitations to take part in seminars and symposia like "Die Vertriebene Vernunft" in Vienna and similar things. I always feel out of place because nothing happened to me and I feel pity for those who suffered so much. But there comes a time when we have to say: all right, it happened, but let's work on it so it doesn't happen again. We have to look forward; so many people take pleasure in crying and complaining, particularly in America.

Not only the Holocaust survivors, but also the intellectuals who say that "America has no culture," tell us we shouldn't trust the Germans. . .

I want to tell you I am particularly proud to have been asked to participate in the World's Fair Expo 95 Vienna—Budapest. I believe it should be a different kind of Worlds Fair, not just mentioning a country's achievements, which is what usually happens. I have developed two major ideas. The first is that people should be asked for their contributions, the second is that we should concentrate on how to combat traffic problems, diseases, unemployment, lack of education and other things of that nature.

". . . I'm half a Jew and pick my nose too!. . ."

Based on conversations with *Wolfgang Georg Fischer* on 2, 14, and 28 December 1987, and numerous letters.

Dr. Fischer, you were born in Vienna on October 24, 1933, so you were only a small child in 1938. Can you still recall that time in any way? Have you been told stories by your family?

Yes, something occurs to me immediately:
"Ich bin gemischte Rass'
und bohr' mir in der Nas!"
"I'm half a Jew and pick my nose too!"
With this little rhyme of my own composition on my lips I went as a five-year-old in March and April 1938 with my nanny to and fro through Wien-Pötzleinsdorf, from our flat at Wurzingergasse eight to the Pötzleinsdorfer Allee. I most probably picked up this fairy story that I was of mixed race from something I heard from nanny, or the Czech concièrge, or the woman at the milk-shop or at the grocer's, and I simply made my little verse about it.

Unfortunately it was not a fantasy, because shortly afterwards my father, who was a baptized Catholic, had to have the "generic name" Israel inserted between his first name Heinrich and his family name in what was now his German passport; and my Protestant, blonde, blue-eyed mother was suddenly living in a mixed marriage, which was a "racial violation"! But what did abstractions like the newly imported Nuremberg racial laws matter to a

five-year-old! My father told me later that for three days after
Hitler's invasion he had kept a bottle of Cognac under his bed to
deaden his fear, but I did not know anything about that then.

My "Aryan" grandparents preserved the appearance of a normal world for me for a few months more by packing me off with
my nanny on a premature summer holiday in Grundlsee in Styria.

Thus the profound changes that my fellow countryman Adolf
Hitler had willed to affect my life could proceed in Vienna without my witnessing them directly. My father's business, the bookshop Frick on the Graben, was taken over by an "Aryanizer" in
accordance with law. My parents' flat in the Wurzingergasse was
assigned as booty to a Nazi returning home "victorious," who
promised allegiance under the name Pawlikowski to the new union
of the fortunate Teutons. My parents had already gone over the
border to Yugoslavia. The nanny was given notice at the end of
summer and my grandfather took me to the barrier at the frontier
post of Greater Germany at Spielfeld-Strass, which I, as a little
chap, could easily slip under, in order to run to my mother, who
was waving to me from behind the Yugoslav barrier at the other
end of the bridge over the Drava.

It was to some extent an easy birth, the birth of this emigrant
child. Delivered by the "Aryan" grandfather to the "Aryan"
mother—what a privilege for a Jewish half-breed of the first
degree (as my correct official racial description went)!

The significance of the disappearance of these bits of scenery
from the stage of everyday bourgeois life—father's business, parents' flat, and privileged upbringing in my birthplace—were outwardly reserved for a later stage of the formation of my consciousness, but subconsciously the crossing of the Drava Bridge
between Spielfeld-Strass and Maribor in autumn 1938 must have
been the unexpected cut in the film of my life.

**Did your family suffer after the annexation in 1938? Were they
discriminated against?**

"Oh, du lieber Augustin, Alles ist hin!" Oh, dear Augustine,
Everything's gone! is all I can say. Should I catalog the suffering
and discrimination or would you prefer to start an enlightening
conversation about the deeper meaning of suffering in the sense
given to it by the sole redeeming Catholic Church. . . .?

For example, the death of my uncle, Dr. Günther Fischer, in a prison camp is actually not discrimination. The word is too civilized for that, too redolent of the nineteenth-century ethics of the Civil Code. My uncle's death was a more radical and ultimate realization of a hopeless way of thinking, feeling, and acting, for which I have found no real explanation to this day. A practicing Catholic, educated in the Schottengymnasium by Benedictines, he dies in a concentration camp—no, is killed—only because his parents are recorded in the registers of birth of the Jewish religious community in Lomnitz in Czechoslovakia (my grandfather was born there in 1866) and in Pressburg/Bratislava in present day Czechoslovakia (birthplace of my grandmother).

I regard everything else as a commonplace fate in the twentieth century which part of my family had to share with millions of others because of war or in the course of the persecution of minorities: with Armenians under the Turks, with Poles under the Russians and the Germans, with Germans under the Poles and Czechs, with Palestinians under Israelis, with Tamils in Sri Lanka. You know what the usual results are: loss of home and living, imprisonment, expulsions, problems of assimilation in the host country, and an insatiable longing for the lost paradise—at least as it is imagined.

But what about murder as a consequence of an insane medieval delusion that masqueraded as the scrupulous application of just laws? There my mind goes blank—in conscious allusion to the saying of Karl Kraus: "My mind goes blank when I think of Hitler!"—and it stays blank.

In spite of megatons of explanations, memoirs, and confessions since 1945, in spite of the clear ruling from the Second Vatican Council, in spite of films like "Shoa" or "Holocaust" and many seminars directed toward better understanding between Christians and Jews, I have to ask myself: whom do these high-frequency waves of intensive, unceasing enlightenment actually reach? Obviously they reach only me and my kind, those whose lives have actually been invaded by these problems and have been thinking about them for fifty years, but they do not reach the deputy mayor of Linz, Mr. Hödl, or the managing director of Kastner and Öhler's department store in Graz. Otherwise Mr. Hödl would not have said in his letter to Bronfman that the Jews had Christ sentenced to death, and the managing director from Graz would not have deluded himself that his decision not to lay in supplies of spirits for the store from Bronfman's family business, Seagram, established a situation for the world outside, where dialogue, meditation, conversion, facing up to the past, and discussion with the opponent were possible.

Looking about, I noticed South Africa and I ask myself how far apart are Soweto of 1987 and Nuremberg of 1935. But the Turks and Yugoslavs, the refugees from Iran and Poland, all the "foreign labor" now working for and in Austria, catch my glance too, and I hope that they and their children will not become the "Jews" and "half-castes" of the next century.

Do you know—from what your parents have told you—what the "atmosphere" of Vienna was like in 1938? Was there open anti-Semitism in the schools and universities?

My mother's and father's families were aware of anti-Semitism only in—if I may use the expression—its mildest form. Similar to the practice in other so-called enlightened Western countries, it was perceptible to my father's family in the professional sphere in that even an above-average lawyer could not reach the position of judge, public prosecutor, university teacher, or departmental head in the civil service, merely solicitor or barrister. That is why many chose the gentle, liberal way out, in order to gain entry to European culture (Heinrich Heine): they had their children baptized and let the seemingly good-natured Mayor of Vienna, Dr. Karl Lueger, decide who was a Jew.

As for mother's family, her father had been a Social Democrat member of parliament in the First Republic. For pragmatic reasons the party was at least officially philo-Semitic but was careful to restrict the Jewish share of the leadership by an unofficial quota.

The despicable gut-anti-Semitism of the Viennese, to which, for example, the orthodox Jews in Leopoldstadt were exposed, we had no experience of until 1938. We were too assimilated for that and between the sloppy, nod-and-a-wink anti-Semitism of Lueger and the liberal, philo-Semitism of cultured circles and the Social Democratic party leadership it was possible to live comfortably—or so it seemed.

**Was your family in Vienna on the day of the annexation?
What did you see or hear, what were you aware of?**

They were all in Vienna on the day. No one even thought of
making provisions abroad in Yugoslavia or Czechoslovakia, Hungary, or Switzerland for the critical hour by sending off compromising papers (my "Aryan" grandfather was a Social Democratic
party official) or by making a deposit for emergencies in a foreign
bank. Obviously people had still believed Austria might survive.
Highly educated people, politically aware and with first-hand
experience, above all, of the Civil War in 1934, must have taken
the treaty obligations of Italy and the Western Powers seriously,
otherwise I cannot explain their lack of preparation.

What were they doing on that memorable day, 12 March
1938? My father took to the cognac bottle, my grandfather perished in his party official's council flat in Favoriten, his former
constituency (the three months' imprisonment in the detention
camp Wöllersdorf after February 1934 were still in his bones).
Unfortunately, I can no longer question my uncle, who perished
later in a concentration camp. Perhaps he closed the tall windows
of his flat in the Ringstrasse to keep out the ecstatic shouts from
the direction of the Heldenplatz. . .

**Did your family realize the implications of the precarious
political situation? Did they know what dangers there were for
Jews?**

It must have been a curious masquerade, poised between fear
and hope. My mother often told me about the last New Year's
Eve in Austria in 1937. A German emigré had crept under the
table shortly before midnight. On the stroke of twelve he emerged
with a little Hitler mustache stuck on, roaring "I'll exterminate
you all!" while he hugged the Champagne bottle amongst laughter
and a rain of confetti. A carnival scene from Beckmann.

Then, when we had eventually emigrated, but were still close
to Austria on the Yugoslav side of the Drava, waiting for a favorable turn of events in a country house belonging to my godfather,
the gentlemen gathered round the fireplace for an evening's conversation were convinced that the apparition of Hitler would fade
like a brief nightmare after one or two air-raids on Vienna by the

British or French. On new Year's Eve in 1938 we would drink each other's health in our villas in Grinzing or Pötzleinsdorf or Neuwaldegg again, if possible after a good performance of *Die Fledermaus* at the opera, they thought.

At the beginning of 1939 people sat around devouring the newspapers in the emigré cafés in Zagreb, and my father hoped that the headline announcing the intervention of the Western Powers would appear at any moment like a deus ex machina. Only after the fall of Czechoslovakia did he begin to bother about a visa for England. He arrived in London two months before the outbreak of the war with a business visa for three months. Who would have guessed then that Austria and Czechoslovakia were regarded by Britain and France as poisoned bait for the rabid German sheepdog? Perhaps people knew but did not want to believe, as so often in life. Since then what has interested me above all is the status quo at the decisive moment of history and rather less the acute analyses with hindsight and from an elevated view.

At this point I hope you will allow me to make a bridge to the present. The verdict of the Waldheim Commission as to guilt or innocence is no longer of any interest to me. A new document that incriminates or exculpates does nothing for me after the outbreak of the monstrous misunderstanding, long suppressed animosities, and fears of an anti-Semitism which have obviously always been smoldering away below the thinnest surface and after the frightening oscillation between insensitivity and oversensitivity in the face of moral values. For me, Waldheim's features have been transformed to some such as are carved on the cork of a schnapps bottle—with which, however, not a schnapps bottle but a bottle of poison has been corked. The cork is out and the bottle is tipped up. For the first time, perhaps, we can really fight this poison. The poison in the bottle would be a much worse inheritance for a future generation.

Were there arrests in your circle? Did you or your relatives know about concentration camps at this time?

My father narrowly escaped arrest in March 1938, because his former business partner locked him up for safety in a backroom of his bookshop in the Kohlmarkt during a so-called round-up of Jews. Of course, people had become aware of the dangers not only through witnessing arrests but also from the music accompanying the annexation, which could no longer be drowned out. A glance at the newspaper is enough, even for people born after those times. The advertisements alone spoke volumes: "Aryan seeks business takeover. Replies to editor under 'Favorable.'"

My mother's brother, a strapping athletic teacher went everywhere with my father during the events of March 1938 as a sort of bodyguard, with a large silver swastika in his buttonhole, and in this way my father escaped the pavement washing. This is the uncle I have immortalized as the "Aryan Angel of Protection and Annunciation" in my novel *Wohnungen*.

When did you—or more particularly your family—know about the extermination camps?

That the extermination camps were by and large kept secret I regard as one of the greatest propaganda coups of Joseph Goebbels, enhanced by the cunning invention of a show camp for prominent people like Theresienstadt.

We—that is, my mother and I and the non-Jewish part of the family remaining in Vienna—had no idea of the extermination camps until 1943.

It was not until the wife of a former Austrian gendarmerie officer, who had been disciplined, made a jesting comment on an anti-Nazi remark, that my mother realized with a jolt what was happening. "Don't talk like that," said Mrs. Mandelmeir, "or you'll soon go up the chimney!" Noticing my mother's puzzled expression, the lady from Linz gave the obscure explanation: "Don't you know what happens to people like you nowadays?"

How naive one has been—or has been kept—is shown by the incident my mother experienced in Grundlsee shortly after the liberation in May 1945 (or "after the collapse," as we say with particular reference to the Austrians' state of mind), when my mother, radiant with happiness, approached the first American officer with flowers and a blessing. He rejected her greeting, angrily withdrew three paces and said: "Haven't you seen Mauthausen?" My mother actually had no idea what had been happening in Mauthausen, although the distance between Grundlsee and Mauthausen amounted to no more than fifty kilometers. I have

often told this story in the company of emigrés who would like
to have had supporting evidence for theories of collective guilt.
"You must not forget," I added, "that I was very unhappy as a
ten-year-old schoolboy in Vienna when I found out that I could
never become a member of the Hitler Youth like all the others in
the class, with a uniform belt, brown shirt, and swastika pennant."
I reject the chessboard notion of history, a primitive subdivision
into black and white fields.

You no longer live in Vienna. Why in London? Are there political reasons?

I have been living in London since 1963, but certainly not for
political reasons. My father, together with another Austrian
emigré, was able to establish one of the most successful and, at
that time, important art galleries for twentieth-century art. As a
good son, I felt obliged to follow in his footsteps and since his
death ten years ago, I have operated Fischer Fine Art myself.

In spite of that, I do believe that as an author writing in
German and an academically trained art historian I could be more
or most effective in my own country, Austria. For that reason,
since 1979, I have made efforts to return and applied several
times for a position commensurate with my education and experience. Unfortunately, in vain. I feel myself still too young for a
purely contemplative existence in Austria; that is, simply writing
in my house in Grundlsee or my flat in Vienna. I would like to
have played an active role in and for Austria, but the active cooperation of Austrians abroad is only courted when more loans
are wanted or tourism is in danger or when the image of the
motherland is so dishevelled by a figure like Waldheim that the
descent from an operetta republic to a banana republic cannot be
prevented. As you know, Austrians abroad are deprived of their
voting rights even today.

**So far you have published two novels, numerous poems and
short stories and have also written a film script (for the film
Egon Schiele). In autumn 1987 an art-historical volume *Gustav
Klimt and Emilie Flöge* appeared. How did you come to write
and why do you write?**

Ever since I was ten years old, I have gone through life as a writer. First, and still today, as a diarist. When I was seventeen and still at school my first poem was published in the newspaper *Neue Wege* (New Ways). My first novel *Wohnungen* received the 1970 Swiss Charles-Veillon-Prize. The written word and books have always had a prominent place in our family. Before his emigration, my father was a bookseller and publisher in Vienna. My maternal grandfather was a trained compositor and editor of *Vorwärts*. I have always held the symbol of his craft, the compositor's stick, in honor. I regard the living language as a barometer and a continually changing status report on a person or a nation. I can only survive life by writing about it and sometimes I regret that. I think then, how much more honorable and heroic a life like Mother Theresa's or Doctor Schweitzer's is. But I lack the physical and spiritual strength for that, the determination and also the faith.

So, Dr. Fischer, after Hitler's invasion you emigrated to Yugoslavia. As happened to so many in those days, the family split up; your father succeeded in escaping to London. Your mother returned to Vienna before the Germans invaded Yugoslavia. You went to school in Vienna, you studied art history and archaeology at the University there, and you graduated in 1961. You are a member of the Austrian and International PEN Club and have been living as an art dealer in London since 1963. How do you—who have a summer home in Austria—see the political situation today, fifty years after 1938? Have people—Austrians—learned from history?

People do not learn from history. The contrary is propagated by small-minded history teachers and people who believe you can overcome the past. People learn from other people, from people they love very much or hate very much. You can learn from a father who has lost both legs in the war and who is nevertheless not embittered, or from a sadistic noncommissioned officer, who is furious for no reason, a lump of flesh made of power-hunger and ignorance. The printed word in itself is anemic, and so-called academic enlightenment has no wider impact. But when something as stupid, crooked, deceitful, amoral, and hypocritical happens as the Waldheim affair, then I begin to hope again, because only when something gets under the skin and the unconscious agent of the undemocratic, tyrannical behavior is exposed do the effective educationalists like Erika Weinzierl and Friedrich Heer and Günther Nenning have perhaps a slight chance. I hope so, because nothing was or is to be expected from those who govern us. Up to 1955 they used the convenient lie that Austria was Hitler's first victim. Well, all right: in order to get rid of the Russians, you might accept such a transparent untruth, but after 1955 there was not even a minimum of moral responsibility displayed beyond this. No really generous material compensation for victims of Nazism and emigrés, in contrast to Adenauer's Germany, not a hint of joint responsibility for political events between 1938 and 1945. "Hitler was a German and Beethoven the greatest Austrian," was the Government's formula. In this regard, the study of Cabinet minutes from the period after 1945 by the English historian robert Knight, which is about to appear, should bring some interesting things to light. The great majority of the Austrians, who live morally slovenly lives with the greatest conviction, give hearty assent to this policy of encouraging tourism. All the emigrés were, or became, rich and, if they still like Austria as much as we do, there are first-class hotels, cheap pensions and the Salzburg Festival. Our parent's best friends were Jews and our former prime minister was one as well, and he was not afraid to take the one-time SS officer, Peter, leader of an allegedly democratic party, to Auschwitz on a Polish-Austrian friendship visit. Certainly since the closure of Glasenbach and the winning of all the less-compromised Nazi voters from Carinthia for the Socialist party everything is very peaceful! So, that was your average Austrian's government supported panorama of the past.

By virtue of the declaration of independence of 27 April 1945, STGBL (Constitutional Act) No. 1, the annexation is null and void. According to that, Austria was the first free country that fell victim to Hitler's aggression and had to be freed from German domination. In that document the annexation is defined as imposed by Germany and is therefore to be considered null and void. What do you have to say in this context about the concept of "duty" which has been mentioned in the most recent discussions on Waldheim?

As to the annexation being null and void according to STGBL No. 1, . . . naturally in April 1945 (when the war had not even ended), they had to grasp at any straw, like a drowning man, in order to be swept clear of the corpse of Germany as fast as possible. Ten years later, however, even someone in the Government could have come to see that the separation of the countries did not automatically mean dissociation from political, moral, and also material responsibility. The idea that you can dump the corpse of the past (so detrimental to tourism) in the form of Hitler, Eichmann, Seyss-Inquart, Kaltenbrunner, Stangl and other executors of the Thousand Year Empire across the German border and run quickly back to bucolic village fêtes—is naive and, fortunately, as a calculation it does not work out.

If Waldheim had talked about an imposed duty which you could not escape except on pain of death but which later by no means automatically allowed you to claim historic innocence, many people in the West, who still regard an oath and a soldier's duty as something of value, would have understood. To argue the defense of an unlimited obligation towards a criminal system once the mortal threat has passed is inexcusable and disqualifies for any office, let alone the highest.

Many people have asked me in the course of my work where the difference lies between the term "duty" and the argument "we were obedient to the law." Can you answer the question, Dr. Fischer?

Fulfilling duty and obedience to an institution which is criminal or is felt to be so, is an altogether negative thing. If, moreover, this criminal institution is endowed with great or absolute power, which can decide over your life or your family's, then that is duty under duress and as unholy obedience constitutes nothing but fear which assails the majority of humankind, the tiny majority of heroes excepted. If I feel other than deep shame about my weakness after the fall of the criminal regime, I have either been an actual supporter of the collapsed regime or an unregenerate hypocrite then and now.

According to the evidence, according to the White Paper and the judgment of the Historians' Commission that the Federal gov-

ernment set up, Dr. Kurt Waldheim was not a supporter of the
regime of that time.

**Do you think that something cannot be wrong today which was
right in the past?**

What is wrong now can never have been right at an earlier
date. It has been smuggled in under the guise of seemingly correct
laws and hallowed oaths by criminal manipulators.

The American thinker, educationalist, and author Henry David
Thoreau (1817-1862) coined the concept of a duty of being dis-
obedient to the state. That kind of individual obligation to one's
own conscience alone is unknown in Austria, a state still apparently a long way from understanding democracy. There have been
witnesses for that kind of duty but unfortunately in a dwindling
minority. I am thinking of the Pastors Niemöller und Bonhoeffer,
of the practicing Catholic Jägerstätter, of the Jesuit P. Rupert and
of the members of the Austrian resistance who gave up their lives
under Hitler.

What would you like to say in conclusion?

I would like to draw attention to two figures of Austrian postwar history, one who is a credit to us all, and another. . .

One is a writer, man of the theater and actor, Helmut Qualtinger, who proves to me that in spite of everything there are still
people in my native country worthy to shake hands with Franz
Grillparzer, Sigmund Freud, and Karl Kraus. Qualtinger will live
on not only as moral authority in his creation of "Herr Karl,"
who is the non plus ultra of Austrian opportunists, but also as a
really great writer and untiring rebel against injustice, stupidity
and self-satisfied provincialism.

The other is the incarnation of Herr Karl, the officiating
Federal President, Dr. Kurt Waldheim, whom the majority of
Austrians chose in an unimpugnable democratic election
as—unfortunately only too right—the highest representative of
their ideals.

". . . . I also saw someone shot, absolutely senseless. . ."

Based on conversations with *Walter H. Gardner* on 20, 27, and 30 October 1987 and considerable correspondence.

Dr. Gardner, formerly Walter Gartenberg, is a lawyer born in 1901. He spent 1938 in Graz and now lives in Los Angeles.

Dr. Gardner, you came from a very religious orthodox Jewish family. Your father came from Poland, later he went to Vienna and finally to Graz. You went to school in Graz, you studied in this town and practiced law here. Today you live in Los Angeles. Why do you live in the United States now?

I am a Jew and was driven out of Graz—out of Austria—in 1938.

Do you have a painful memory of the year 1938?

Yes, when Hitler came in 1938 my time was up.

Can you tell me something about the period before 1938? Did you encounter anti-Semitism?

I went to school in Graz and studied there. While I was a student I joined the Socialist Party, and I was a member of the Socialist Student Association. I got on well with the "Aryan" students. They were all German Nationalists and members of fencing associations. To my shame I have to admit that for a short time I also belonged to a Jewish fencing association, but then I got to know my good friend Hugo Tausk. He was a socialist, and so I became a member of the socialist movement.

What was the atmosphere like at Graz University?

Although generally speaking I got on well with "Aryan" students, there was a time when suddenly Jews were no longer allowed in the University. I went anyway, with two other students who were also members of the Socialist Party. I can still remember very well that a student came up to me and said that I wasn't allowed in the University anymore. I told him quietly that I was coming nevertheless. And then he told me that in that case he would have to throw me out. He grabbed me under the arms and someone else got my feet, and they laid my hat and briefcase on my stomach. In this way they carefully ejected me. So then I sat down in front of the university and they apologized to me. I can even remember the name of one of them, he was called Smorovski, and even in later years I got on with him very well. He was a nice fellow. It happened to me several times, and I can't remember that it was ever really bad.

It was the same with the professors. I was not discriminated against in the examinations through anti-Semitism. I spoke with the students a lot—above all when Hitler had given a speech. For me it was all nonsense, for them on the other hand it was "wonderful." For me it was all totally incomprehensible, but they still spoke to me.[1]

Did you read foreign newspapers?

Yes. I was a lawyer after 1932 and naturally I read foreign newspapers. My friend and I, we actually prepared ourselves for the invasion. We had no doubts that Hitler would invade Austria.

---

[1] After the First World War there was an organization at the University of Graz called the "Deutsche Studentenschaft" (German Student Body) which qualified as official representative of the students in the university. It saw its main function as pestering Jews. Foreign students were also disliked. With the return of soldiers from the front after the War, the number of students rose rapidly, and the less foreign students there were to compete with "noble Aryans" for places in the laboratory, the better. On the doors of the clinical lecture hall hung a resplendent notice of the "Deutsche Studentenschaft" saying, "The first three rows are reserved for Aryan listeners." Walter Fischer, "Kurze Geschichten aus einem langen Leben," in *Grenzfeste Deutscher Wissenschaft* (Steirische Gesellschaft für Kulturpolitik: Graz, 1985), p.107.

I thought then, I've still got plenty of time. But that was a big mistake.

Why?

Well, because then Hitler came and my time was over. My clients were too afraid to come to my office, and the Christians just ran off. Then we got the news that I would not be allowed to practice law any longer because I was a Jew. That was the end!

If you were informed by reading foreign newspapers, why didn't you leave Austria sooner?

Yes, well I saw it coming and had even made a deal with a Christian colleague to sell him my house. Not a binding contract, but I knew what I was doing. The problem was my wife's parents, who were absolutely against moving and always said, "Nothing can happen to us, we were born and bred Austrians." And my wife was very close to them, so I said to her, "Let whatever is coming to us, come."

And everything did come to us. I lost my law practice, my passport was taken away, and then I could not escape anymore. . .

What happened to you on the "Kristallnacht"?

I was taken away, first to the Paulustor,[2] then to *Dachau*. And so much has already been said about *Dachau* that I don't want to add anything more. I have tried to forget the details. It was terrible enough, and I have to tell you that I was fortunate enough to spend only two months there. But these two months showed me how terrible it all was. My wife was very brave and got tickets to Shanghai—that was the only way to get out of the country.

How did you get out of the concentration camp?

---

[2] A prison in Graz.

My wife went to a policemen—or was it an SS-man? In any case this man could remember me and that I had once represented him without charge. He promised my wife to help her get me out of prison. Whatever it was, I got out of the concentration camp and we traveled immediately to Italy.

What were the Italians like?

The Italians were tremendously nice. We had a residence permit for only three months, and when the time was up I went to the police president in Genoa—I could speak good Italian in those days— and told him quite honestly of my situation: that I did not intend to go to Shanghai but had obtained this Shanghai visa simply in order to get out of Italy and travel to England or America.

He was very decent. He called his secretary immediately and dictated to her that my wife was "very sick," not capable of traveling and that for this reason he was granting me an extension to my permit. He then shook my hand and said that if I needed a further three months, I should come straight to him. That was the police chief of Genoa, and I found that really very decent.

You then traveled to England?

Yes, then I went to England. I had actually only a visitor's permit and could not work. I was there for barely a year and then my wife and I traveled on to America. At first I was in New York, then in New Orleans and finally in Los Angeles. And I stayed in Los Angeles for twenty or twenty-five years until I retired from the bank.

May I return to 1938: what happened to your family?

After my period in the concentration camp I couldn't return to my apartment. It was occupied by the *Gestapo*. My mother had already died. My father simply stayed in Graz, and after a long time he went to Vienna. Later we succeeded in getting him out to Cuba. From Cuba he traveled to New York, and there he stayed until he passed away.

My wife's parents were sent then to the concentration camp at *Theresienstadt.* From there the trains went to *Auschwitz. . .* and one knew what these trains were for, one knew that in *Auschwitz* people were gassed. . . at the last moment it was possible for us to negotiate to protect her parents from the worst. A Jewish organization negotiated with the Gestapo and for a certain sum of money they let a number of Jews go free, including my wife's parents. They came to Switzerland. We read in those days the journal *Aufbau,* which concerned itself with important problems of the Jews. And one day we learned that her parents had made it to Switzerland. We immediately got in touch and made the necessary money available to bring them to us. Then they lived with us. My wife's father died soon afterwards, her mother died eighteen years ago.

How was all that financially possible? Did you have enough money?

I already had a job. Later in America I took out a loan. And good friends helped me. I think I had only ten Schillings in my pocket. Then I remembered a good friend in Holland. He was the head of a pharmaceutical factory and I asked him if he could help us. He cabled back immediately that he was making his Italian bank account available to me. And this bank was instructed to honor every check with my signature on it. So for the time being our financial problems were solved. In England I was a guest, and my host took care of my living costs. They were astounded when I started to think about leaving England. But I could not continue to live on the charity of others, and in England I had no work permit.

How did you pay for the Shanghai visa?

You could still withdraw money if you wanted to leave the country. Since we never traveled to Shanghai, we got the money back from the Italian steamship line.

Dr. Gardner, how do you see it all today, looking back?

Well, for a long time I was embittered over everything to do with Austria or Germany. But that did not last forever, because I told myself that not everybody was involved in what happened there. Even if there were hundreds or thousands who can be called culprits, they were still only a small percentage of the whole. You can't make everyone responsible. That would be the greatest sin! The first of the Ten Commandments should be: one must not generalize! Then I also think that there were many who knew what was going on, but what could they do? The real culprits, they were these hundreds or thousands: well, some of them were caught and punished. And it is praiseworthy that they try to show the people today what really happened then. But I think it's essentially in vain.

How do you mean?

These atrocities were committed by thousands of people. How can you reach them? If you publish these atrocities you show the symptoms, but you don't fight the disease itself.

I always ask myself: where is this poison? And I can't find an answer! Perhaps it's utopian, but one of these culprits should be questioned in order to find out what he really thinks. Of course one has to analyze exactly what they did, and many of them of course are already dead. Many would refuse, but perhaps they could be moved to tell the world where the poison is!

Do you think that such a thing could happen again?

Those atrocities have not deterred people, so my opinion is: yes, it could happen again any time. I think one has to question the culprits anonymously, to find out what motivated them to commit these crimes.

There are already written statements. These people don't often change their minds.

It should be analyzed. Just to describe to people the facts of the atrocities doesn't help much.

In your opinion, isn't a "mass psychosis" always possible?

I fear, yes. These crimes were committed by young people, and they looked on as people were burned and beaten; they murdered without a care. It didn't stop them at all. . . there must be a key to where this "poison" lies.

If it is not too painful for you, could you say something about your experience in Dachau?

You were transported there, at first in railroad cars. . . then in trucks, it was like a "cattle truck": you were cooped up so you could hardly breathe, the doors were locked and in this way you went to *Dachau*. When you arrived, there were SS people standing around with weapons pointed at you, they chased us out of the trucks, then we stood around for hours. . . marched and then stood around for some more hours, and then in the evening we were cooped up again in barracks, only then we were allowed to take our clothes off. Finally we received a prisoner's uniform, not even underwear, just light clothing and it was November and already bitterly cold!

Then there was the much-loved "play": we were awakened very early and given a black liquid that was called "coffee," then we had to run for long stretches and when we were sweating, we had to stand at attention. . . in the cold! A lot of people collapsed. Then people were kicked, and I also saw someone shot, absolutely senselessly shot! I suddenly heard a cry—I inquired about it—a man had apparently said, "shoot me, that's what you want!" It was a non-Jew, and I heard two shots. . . the next day a commission arrived and investigated. I'm convinced that it appeared in the newspapers as, "shot while trying to escape." That was the usual news!

I am trying very hard—as you know—to retrieve these things from my memory. It was terrible!

And I had only two months of it. Of course it got much worse later, and then the transports to *Auschwitz* began. That I didn't experience.

Over and over again I ask myself: what is the meaning of it all, how could such atrocities take place? What's the answer? I don't know.

"... We just sat there in despair. .."

Conversation with *Edith Gebell* on 2 September and 26 October 1987.

Mrs. Gebell was born in 1906. In 1938 she was in Aflenz and today lives in Graz.

Mrs. Gebell, you spent your youth in Abbazzia and only came to Graz later. Can you tell me anything about 1938?

I attended a German elite school in Abbazzia. In 1919 I came with my parents to Graz. My mother was from Vienna and my grandparents had a printing works. They were prosperous people by the standards of the day. They had their own house and servants, and my mother grew up in a very middle-class background.

In 1930 I got to know my husband. He came from a Jewish family but was himself a Catholic, and we got married in 1933 in a Roman Catholic ceremony. We had two children from the marriage: Peter Heinz (born in 1935) and Hans Josef (born in 1942).

Immediately after my marriage I went with my husband to Aflenz. He had bought a book shop there, and we tried to make a living.

You say that your husband came from a Jewish family. Did you experience any anti-Semitism in Aflenz?

In 1933 one couldn't detect any anti-Semitism. But by 1935 it was different. Moreover, my husband was a very good businessman and was certainly an important competitor for some people. One could see it, people started to discriminate against him. For example we were no longer invited out by friends or acquaintances. Gradually even people who had always greeted us in a friendly way now refused to acknowledge us on the street. They looked across to the other side of the road instead.

What was it like at the time of Hitler's invasion? Did it change your life?

Fundamentally! The moment that Hitler appeared on the scene, our life changed! Anti-Semitism in Aflenz became a duty. They were all terrific Nazis. Everybody, I would say! From now on nobody took the risk of contacting us.

Why do you think the situation changed so drastically? Do you have any specific, decisive memories from that time?

I can tell you about some episodes that were very painful and wounding for me, and in my opinion completely unnecessary. It was Easter, and I had gone with an acquaintance to the Church for Communion. There we met the daughter of a general, and this woman remarked quite openly, "now the Jews are coming to Church!"

I shall not forget this woman. God rest her soul, she's since died.

I remember something else. It was also in 1938 or 1939 and I went to the cinema. "Die Wiener Madln" was playing. Then just after the lights were dimmed, I heard a loud voice saying: "Jews Out!"

I still remember the name of the man who shouted that. I would like to keep it to myself. I had to stand up, leave my seat and get out of the cinema as quickly as possible. The feeling of humiliation was indescribable. I suddenly didn't know what had happened to me! This new life, this new situation was so awful, so dreadful for me, I felt simply destroyed. I thought it was the Day of Judgment. . . I lost hope. I couldn't even cry. It was completely incomprehensible for me. I can still remember exactly how shattered my husband and I were after this trip to the cinema, we just sat there in despair.

Did the situation reach a climax?

It certainly did. The Nazis put a guard on the door of the bookshop and tried to deter customers from coming in to buy anything. The district Nazi leader later ordered that our business be closed. We also had a radio store. We had to bring all the goods from these two businesses into our apartment and store them all there. We lived in pretty chaotic conditions! In the dining room we had to push all the furniture to one side and keep the stuff there.

What did you live on then?

Since we had a radio business my husband was able to repair radios. He did that later as well.

What happened to your husband after that? Did you have financial problems?

Money was not the greatest problem. We didn't need too much. No toilet, nothing. . . you were happy if you got something to eat. My husband was then called up for military service. That could have been after 1943. He worked in a glass factory then.

When you look back on these years—the years after Hitler's invasion of Austria—what occurs to you? What do you think of fifty years later?

I think of the fear! A life of running the gauntlet, filled with fear. I hardly ever dared to go out of the house, I just wanted to crawl away.

Did you know about the concentration camps?

Of course we knew that there were concentration camps. I don't believe anyone who says he didn't know about the camps.

How did you know about the existence of the concentration camps?

A cousin of my husband had a textile business in Vienna. On the day after the *Anschluss* an employee of his came in and said "Heil Hitler!," to which my husband's cousin replied that a normal "Good Morning" would suffice.

That was enough. He was sent to *Buchenwald*. He was released from there after a year and a half. It was about 1940 when we—my husband and I—sat with him in the Café Heinrichshof after his release. Two SS men went by, and one of them had lost a leg and walked with crutches. "This SS man with the crutches," said the cousin, "he'll never be able to hold the head of a concentration camp prisoner in a puddle of water with his foot till the man drowns, because for that he needs two legs. . ."

That was the reaction of my husband's cousin at the sight of those two SS men.

What did your husband's cousin tell you about the concentration camp?

He got out of the camp only on condition that he never speak to anyone about what it was like and what had happened to him. I don't think he even spoke to his wife about it.

Was your husband in a concentration camp?

According to the Nuremberg Decrees, he was a "half-Jew." So he didn't go to the front, he wasn't "worthy of fighting" for the Fatherland. Instead he worked in a glass factory in Vienna, where it never leaked out that he was a "half-Jew." This is the only explanation for the fact that he managed to escape being sent to a concentration camp.

At the end of the war my husband returned on foot from Vienna to Aflenz. He was very sick with typhus. The hospitals were all closed at this time, in May 1945, so I had to look after him at home.

The man who had forced me out of the cinema also suddenly appeared at this time, and with outstretched hands asked me to accept his apologies. I remembered the inhuman, incomprehensible scene when he shouted in the dark cinema auditorium, "Jews Out! Jews Out! . . ." and how I had to slip out, humiliated and scared. We just said that we would like him to leave our house.

Soon after the end of the War my husband was made Mayor of Aflenz. He surpassed himself in efficiency, generosity, and humanity. I can tell you that in his office as Mayor he helped many former fellow travelers, who nonetheless had remained loyal to us. And he also helped many imprisoned Nazis, who had not been fanatical National Socialists, and got them out of prison. My husband never had any feelings of revenge.

Back to 1938: you happened to be in Graz on the day of the Anschluss. Can you remember this day? What happened in this town on 13 March 1938?

I was visiting my parents in Graz, when the *Anschluss* to the Thousand Year Reich was proclaimed. It's indescribable what took place in Graz then: torchlight processions, waves of flags, shouting and howling. People simply went crazy.

I can see it as if it were yesterday. I stood in the Hauptplatz squeezed by the masses, pushed here and there, and had the feeling that something terrible and unstoppable was coming upon us!

I met my parents in a restaurant for dinner. After the torchlight parade people were pouring in with little swastika flags. They had beaming faces and seemed certain of victory. Only a few of them survived that victory however. They didn't die; they drowned in the sea, they crashed in airplanes, they were hit by bombs, they starved, they froze or died some other wretched death on the front!

How do you explain these celebrations—now, fifty years later?

People wanted to believe in a beautiful, rose-tinted future. The economic situation of the little Austrian republic was bad. There was a lot of unemployment. Those people who were affected hoped that through the *Anschluss* to the much bigger

Germany the economy would get going and there would be prosperity.

Unemployed shoemakers, journeymen tailors, civil servants, and academics who had made secret contributions to the Nazi party when it was an underground organization. These people now appeared in uniform and had authority to give orders—they felt like pseudo-generals!

Incidentally, everybody in the country started urgently to find out about the origins of their grandmother. Without proof of "Aryan" ancestry you were lost, you weren't a human being anymore!

Do you have any memories from this time of other towns? And what is your impression of the world today?

I went to Vienna at this time with my parents to visit relatives. I saw hundreds of people with the Star of David on their lapel, it was compulsory for "non-Aryans." These people were not allowed in any bar or restaurant, they weren't allowed on the street-cars, or in most of the stores. I saw tragedies of which I prefer not to be reminded. A time of "celebration" had begun. One had to have flags hanging out all the time for God knows what reason. They wanted to keep the people in a sort of frenzy.

Suddenly there was the German haircut, the German boot, the German stew (Eintopf) and the German greeting (Heil Hitler!) In other words, before we knew it, we were all in uniform! It wasn't possible to go into a bar, meet an acquaintance, or enter an office without first raising your arm and blurting out, with a stupid grin, Heil Hitler!

And we had no idea that this endlessly repeated Heil Hitler! would bring only disaster on us. How many families there were, where at least one person never came back from that murderous war, and how many apartments, houses, and ways of life were destroyed in the next seven terrible years?

You were never personally enthusiastic about Hitler? Not for a single moment?

I was already a pacifist when I was a little girl. I am even more so today now that I understand life better. I'll never understand why whole nations want to destroy themselves. What's the use of all the religions of this world, all the lessons on peace, all the equal rights between people, and the recognition of human rights if at certain times nobody takes any notice?

". . . It's not a question of 'mea culpa,' but of knowledge. . ."

Conversation with *Paul Grosz* on 2 November 1987.

Mr. Grosz was born in 1925 and spent 1938 in Vienna, where he still lives and is president of the Vienna Jewish Community (Kultusgemeinde).

You were born in Vienna, in 1925 as the son of a furrier. You went to high school in Vienna and in 1938 you were expelled. You were still a child then—what do you remember from this time?

I only have a few impressions from 1938.

The only experience that I had then which really sticks in my memory and with which I have never come to terms, is the fact that my parents, my brother—who was later killed—and I lived in a small apartment in Ottakring with a "drop toilet" and water in the corridor. We were completely integrated, my friends were the children of the household, and my mother was friends with the neighbors.

Everything appeared to be in order with the world, and then suddenly, after Hitler's invasion, everything was different. There was a list with signatures, and within a month we had to move out to make the house "Jew-free" (*judenrein*).

That was an experience I've never got over to this day. It has stuck in my mind although it has no relationship to my later life, yet then. . .

Did you personally experience Hitler's entry into Vienna?

Yes. I saw the "Führer." I was going to school and had to cross the Mariahilferstrasse and Hitler was arriving at the Westbahnhof. I climbed on a street car and could see him, he was standing up, with his arm raised.

Were there many people?

There was an enthusiastic crowd on the streets. . . I can remember it like a series of photographs. It culminated, in a negative sense, on 10 November.

So you had to leave the apartment with your family quite suddenly. What was that like? Where did you live then?

I have never lived so badly as I did then in that apartment that I had to leave. But that's another story.

What happened to your family?

My brother was killed two years later—I wasn't there. . . none of my family was there. . . we found him in the apartment with a head injury. We were told that SA men had come to search the apartment. We found him lying on the floor with his skull smashed.

How old was your brother then? Did he recover from this trauma?

My brother was eighteen years old. A few days later he died in the hospital.

Did you leave Vienna then?

No. I stayed in the city with my parents and survived.

How was that possible?

My mother qualified as a so-called "Aryan." Then I was conscripted into an Army service unit. That was more or less a privileged position which I owed to my "Aryan" mother.

What was the *Kristallnacht* like for you and your family?

We all hid ourselves. We went to an uncle and I think my father went to a Christian family and slept there. Two cousins of mine were arrested on the street and sent to a concentration camp.

Incidentally, my father worked at the synagogue. That night it was burned down. It was terrible, absolutely terrible. There was a mob loose, plundering—that was their specialty. I experienced that once again after 1945, probably the same people. Of course nobody wants to know about that today.

What is necessary for today?

This "mea culpa" was always missing and will never be recovered, neither in tracking down nor in condemning war criminals—what's important today is to make people realize how false it all was. But apparently even that is being avoided. The only thing that can protect us from raw emotions, for which no one can be condemned, is real knowledge. Knowledge will stop us slipping into the same situation again.

Could such a thing happen in your opinion?

It sounds unlikely, but under certain conditions it seems to me to be absolutely possible that something similar could happen again. Because it didn't really get into the consciousness. And knowledge and consciousness go together, and not just regarding the root of the word. Nothing has really happened to fix in the consciousness of the people the fact that what is called the Holocaust was really a series of crimes. And such crimes can't be prevented by concerns about the level of unemployment or the social climate. We can't guarantee that there won't be any more unemployment or other crises! It seems we can't get it anchored in the consciousness of the people that everything then was false. The people don't seem to have been made sufficiently receptive to this idea.

What do you think that we can do to make the people more thoughtful, more sensitive?

I have no recipe. Perhaps it would make the most sense to start where people are most responsive: at the emotional level. I really became aware of that when I saw Peter Sichrovsky's *Schuldig geboren* (Born Guilty). It is about the feelings of the children and grandchildren of the war criminals. It is easier in my opinion to effect change when the knowledge of the crimes is set not against the suffering of the Jews but against the emotions of the criminals.

Is it always a question of lack of knowledge?

Yes, absolutely. The knowledge is suppressed. There are certain defense mechanisms, and without them we couldn't live.

Look, I'll give you an example: if I knock over that glass of red wine on our table and wine flows everywhere, my first reaction would be, who put that glass in such a stupid place that it could be knocked over. Although of course I'm guilty. . . but it's not a question of "mea culpa," but of knowledge. One of the best known tricks is to shift the blame for serious transgressions by exaggerating everything.

You know the story where Mayor Zilk of Vienna got me into an argument in a press conference by saying "Vienna is not the capital of anti-Semitism." Of course it's not. Nobody believes that anyway. But at the moment when something like that is said, then a subject that has not yet been resolved is cleared from the agenda. And this type of getting over the thing is practiced all the time! One of the most interesting aspects is that all these words like *Vergangenheitsbewältigung* (coming to terms with the past) are losing their meaning. They have become slogans . . . it is more important that we overcome our present. But to do that it is important that we know our *Heilsgeschichte* (an interpretation of history stressing God's grace). If we don't know our conduct in the past, if we don't accept our past, then we will not be able to go on living, so to speak, as we have. What is going on in Austria at the moment is an instance of the self-defense mechanism at work. This is what happens when one cannot cope with one's past.

Back to 1938. As I said, this dark, damp, backyard apartment of just one room and a kitchen—nobody begrudged us that. We lived in peace with people for years before.

How do you explain this phenomenon?

People no longer feel the full extent of what they do. People who gave their signatures didn't think any further: "What do I cause for him now?"

When you imagine what happened, how it developed later, how many murders and ransacked apartments—it's relatively few. But it was the beginning of a process that dehumanized the victims and also of course the perpetrators.

They were both dehumanized: in so far as the victims became mere numbers for the perpetrators, and the perpetrators became real murderers. Unscrupulous murderers because they were no longer able to develop a conscience. This dehumanization of the victims, this stripping of their citizenship, this de-individualization was a gradual process, a sort of policy of small steps, which made it impossible for the victims to defend themselves.

To what extent do you think that Nazi crimes were unique?

Well, there had been genocide before. The special nature of the Nazi crimes doesn't lie there, and I take into account the fact that this time it was carried out in semi-industrial fashion.

No, its uniqueness lies, as I said before, in the step-by-step way in which the victim was dehumanized to the point where he became just a number or a thing, and the perpetrator no longer had any scruples or conscience because he wasn't murdering or killing, but merely exterminating.

It wasn't sadists who made the Holocaust possible. It was respectable, guilt-free, socially-accepted people. It was certainly possible for anyone to see the injustice, it was "visible" to everyone—it is just that people were given the opportunity not to have to see it. And people grasped that opportunity: the guilt lies there! There is the obvious, immediate guilt. To judge what is right and wrong one needs only to follow the inner, not the outer voice, and those who have developed no conscience thereby had the opportunity during the course of the Holocaust, to imagine that they were, so to speak, guilt-free.

If we could sum up, what would be your conclusion?

If I had to bring it all together and say where the fault lay, I'd say it was in a lack of the knowledge that is needed for conscience to develop. And I have to repeat, it's not a question of somebody crying "mea culpa," but a question of understanding how false everything was then, and of accepting it as a part of one's own past and not as a piece of history that doesn't concern one.

What should happen now? What positive things remain to be done in this direction?

The discussion which has now broken out in our land speaks for itself. And unfortunately in a negative fashion! It would be wrong not to look reality in the face. It is reality of course that there are intellectuals and others who have gladly adopted a sophisticated attitude, but they constitute a thin veneer. The great majority of people are not political, and so they are easy to manipulate.

Do you think the media are always correct in its approach?

The media are to a large extent guilty in this mess. The government is certainly making a real effort but without much success.

What is the opinion of people generally? What do you think?

They just think that it is "talked about too much."
"Let's stop talking about it for God's sake. . ." is typical of the emotion that is generally felt.
Unfortunately it is an emotion based on an incorrect view of history.

". . . those men and women who had enough insight and, above all, courage to offer resistance. . ."

Numerous conversations with *Franz Gschiel* in December 1987.

Colonel Gschiel was born in 1934. He lives in Graz and is presently Press Officer of the Military Command in the Austrian province of Styria. In 1938 he lived in Birkfeld.

Colonel Gschiel, you were a small child in 1938, so you would probably have hardly any memories of that time. However, perhaps you can tell me from today's viewpoint, what is understood by the concept of "fulfillment of duty," if the soldiers of that period operated with it today?

Naturally it is difficult to interpret what the soldiers of that time understood by the term "fulfillment of duty." In my experience of talking to former soldiers they believed that through their action they fulfilled a duty that they had towards their country and their comrades. Research has revealed that soldiers in combat feel a primary duty towards their comrades and that ideological convictions play little or no role at all.

According to the Austrian Declaration of Independence, Article 2, the *Anschluss* is null and void. The Moscow Declaration (Article 5) of 1943 called for a contribution from us towards the destruction of National Socialism: for the restoration of a free Austria. Who, in your opinion, made this contribution?

This contribution was undoubtedly made by those men and women who had enough insight and, above all, courage, to offer resistance to injustice. Amongst them were many soldiers who laid down their lives. Today we have garrisons of the Austrian Army named after them—Major Biedermann, Captain Ruth, Lieutenant Raschke, Field-Marshal Jansa, Major Heckenast, just to mention a few.[1]

To them you must add all those people that took other action, from the rescue of persecuted people to offering passive resistance.

I am going to ask you quite consciously the provocative question: didn't those people who "fulfilled their duty" under Hitler also make this contribution?

I oppose the attempt to discriminate against those people who risked their lives, their health, their youth, and their futures in an unfortunate war. They believed they were doing the right thing then. That should not be made the object of reproach today. Corporal Meier did not serve under Hitler but under the commanding officer whom he had to obey. That's how I would answer that suggestive question.

What about young people? What do you mean when you say it should be talked about in the schools?

Of course it should be talked about in the schools. But I also think that the young should be given a rounded and objective picture, taking into account the historical research. Subjective representations of the past, based on personal experiences, can

---

[1]Cf. Friedrich Vogl, "Widerstand im Waffenrock," in *Materialien zur Arbeiterbewegung* (Nr.7), Hrsg. Ludwig-Boltzmann-Institut, (Wien, 1977).

only serve the truth when they are set in context. *Audiatur et altera pars* (the other side should also be heard).

Is it possible to be a "fulfiller of duty" and a "victim" at the same time—on the one hand a victim, as we want to be according to the Moscow Declaration, on the other hand a "fulfiller of duty"?

Yes, it's possible. I think that most of our parents were victims of hopes that can only be understood in the context of the time. Most of them were bitterly disappointed because they had embraced a false ideal. However, only a few of them are ready to admit that openly.

Was Hitler's war a war of aggression?

Yes, absolutely.

The League of Nations resolution of 1927 and the Kellogg-Briand Pact of 1928 declared the war of aggression to be a crime. So Hitler's war was a crime. . . how can one therefore justify the term "fulfillment of duty"?

Nobody can ask a soldier to make decisions which, by virtue of his knowledge of the circumstances, he cannot make. I repeat, in my opinion fulfillment of duty is based not on political or ideological factors but on the obligation to one's immediate environment—to one's comrades.

In the summer of 1987 there was a solidarity action by the ÖKB (the Austrian Veterans Association) in support of President Waldheim. Some of its officials like former Minister Piffl-Percevic, State Councillor Heidinger, State Parliament President Wegart, and many others wanted to be placed on the American "Watch List" with Waldheim. What do you think of this solidarity action?

I can only try and explain it again: you can't make soldiers into war criminals simply because they were soldiers. The entry ban on Waldheim was felt by many to be an example of condemnation of all soldiers. So they protested against that with their solidarity action. Such reactions cannot be explained rationally, but only understood in terms of the emotion felt by someone who feels himself unjustly accused.

We know today that Hitler's war was a crime. The solidarity action we've spoken of spread throughout Austria and was even reported in the foreign press. Do you think that this action has contributed to Austria's standing in the world?

We must accept that feelings are an important part of our lives. Emotions cannot be rationalized away. We know that demagogues throughout history have been able to awaken the emotions of the masses and use them for their own ends. Woe betide us if we don't find out in time where a demagogue is leading us, because we can't see straight for one reason or another. You can't condemn people in general because they show emotions.

Probably my attempt at interpretation is completely unsatisfactory, in fact it must be insufficient. Who can correctly interpret from a distance the motives of people whom he knows hardly or not at all? Who knows what feelings played a part in individual actions? Everybody had personal grounds for behaving in a certain manner. What is certain is that many people who participated in the solidarity action felt themselves, as former soldiers, to have been unjustly attacked and condemned by the discrimination against a former officer, the Austrian head of state and the commander-in-chief of the Austrian armed forces. They feel that with the charge against Dr. Waldheim every soldier who served in that Army is charged.

There are many examples from the last war that show that soldiership has nothing to do with hatred against other peoples, where a soldier has saved the life of another, even though that other wore the uniform of the enemy.

Hitler's war was a crime, but the criminals were those who pulled the strings, not the soldiers who remained human beings even in times of life-threatening danger and who carry no personal guilt.

Those things that everybody knows today only a few knew about then. The overwhelming majority of soldiers believed they were doing right when they carried out orders correctly. Who can hold it against them, if they defend themselves against generalized condemnation? Who can blame them if they haven't forgotten the terrible time during the War? We know that it is exactly in times of great crisis and danger that people move closer together. I have seen many old soldiers who have shed a tear over the "Lied vom guten Kameraden." They are certainly not mourning the passing of the Nazi regime, but lost comrades. Perhaps one can understand the reactions of soldiers better from this point of view.

How far Austria's reputation has been affected by the solidarity action, I wouldn't care to judge.

Colonel, it is not necessary to have been a commander to be entered on the "Watch List." Translators, administrators, and guards are also included in the Holtzman amendment, if the people concerned served in units that were involved in persecution. The American State Department follows the "Watch List" principle, but not because the Jewish World Congress wants it. How do you see this decision? How do you talk about it with young soldiers?

I don't doubt that the placing of Dr. Waldheim's name on the "Watch List" was in accordance with U.S. law. But the fact that our head of state is barred from entry into the United States, has affected me deeply as it did many Austrians. And it would be worthwhile if the American authorities made public the evidence that supports their step.

Within the Army, as far as I know, the subject is hardly ever discussed. I don't think having such a discussion with conscripts would make much sense, because according to the law, the presiding President is the commander-in-chief of the Army. The pledge of allegiance obliges the soldier ". . . to be loyal and obedient to the legally-appointed authorities, and to follow exactly and punctually all the orders of my superior. . ."

So there is no doubt about the legal situation. Opinions, demands, or prognoses about the head of state have only speculative value, from whatever side they come, and no influence whatsoever on the constitutional assignment of the Army and the individual soldier. In my view, such discussions could only lead to uncertainty among the soldiers.

Karl Schiffer, one of my interview partners who died last September, asked me shortly before his death to ask people in public life the following question: is it reconcilable that on the one hand the government sends out special envoys to show other countries that we are not a fascist state, and on the other hand solidarity actions for the President are created which contradict that notion. Piffl-Percevic said, after all, "The home is where the front is!"

I don't see a contradiction here. If people subscribe to a solidarity action, that is their private affair, born out of reasons which I have already described. The dispatch of special envoys was, I think, very important because Austria does not have the image abroad that Austrians have so far talked themselves into believing. The world of violinists and *Heurigenseligkeiten*[2] can be swept away in the meantime. The reality, I'm afraid, is that we are looked upon as a crafty Balkan people.

What can we do, Colonel Gschiel, to improve our image?

We must learn first of all to recognize and accept the truth! We should entertain no doubts that we have contractual agreements to observe. I am referring to our obligation to neutrality, up to the purchase of weapon systems. Who is going to believe that this time we are ready to withstand a threat from beyond our borders if we keep giving the impression that Austrians would really prefer to wriggle out of their responsibilities?!

If we can return to the solidarity action. What is your personal verdict on this ÖKB action? Is it reconcilable with our constitution? How do you explain the action to young soldiers when they ask about it?

---

[2]The general jovial atmosphere of celebration accompanying the introduction the year's new vintage in the wine gardens around Vienna.

I can't say whether there are constitutional provisions that forbid such an action. When asked by soldiers, I reply as I have indicated above. We can't spend all our time laying blame, seeking the guilty ones, and attributing evil intent. It's more important to work on understanding the motives and background.

How do you think President Waldheim should have reacted?

If I were President, I would resign in the interest of Austria. However I would not give up trying to prove my innocence. In any case it is clear the President takes a very different perspective from myself.

What do you understand by the term "authority" in connection with your trainees? Are the eighteen-year-olds being brought up to think critically or to blindly obey?

Blind obedience is to be rejected, moreover it is not required in the Army. Orders that are illegal have to be refused in any case according to the law. The six-month draft period is obviously not long enough to produce a critical person, moreover they are already too old for that.

I think that authority is a function of democratic society. When it is used to strengthen one's own position at the cost of subordinates, then it's dictatorial and to be rejected. Properly administered authority leads to higher achievement and to increased satisfaction among all the members of the group. In the democratic sense, "to lead" means to set goals and agree on them, as well as creating the preconditions under which those goals can be achieved.

You have said that the sense of history among twenty-five to thirty-year olds is more lethargic than anything else. What can you do in your job to improve the sense of history among people?

The relevance of history for the present must be made clearer to the young, the eternally human qualities of people must be demonstrated. That doesn't mean trivializing past crimes, but rather explaining the circumstances that led to that behavior.

Then history will become something of substance. In this way I attempt, within my range of possibilities, to create those conditions that will ensure that such terrible things are not repeated.

What does "fulfillment of duty" mean to you?

The concept of "fulfillment of duty" has acquired such a negative character that I'm afraid it will soon be despised. However no society can dispense with functions that carry certain obligations, that means tasks to be carried out for the good of the whole community. It applies to the doctor as much as to the soldier. You can't have a situation where consciousness of obligation, loyalty, discipline, and similar values suddenly are turned into negative characteristics.

What is being done in the Austrian Army in 1988 to get rid of old prejudices?

We offer all soldiers sessions on contemporary history (seminars, lectures, discussions, visits to exhibitions), and we will increase our coverage of this period in political and military education.

How do you explain that there was a revival of anti-Semitism in Austria last summer?

Anti-Semitism is an ancient problem and not just in Austria —that needs no proof. It seems to increase and subside in waves throughout the course of history and loses its importance. Political and economic conditions always tend to bring out anti-Semitism. In other words, it's always there in latent fashion, although after the war it was perhaps somewhat less visible. In cases like the last Presidential election campaign, which was fought with strong emotions, the latent prejudices resurfaced again.

What can you in your position do to correct it?

Within the realm of officer training in the Army (leadership, rhetoric, political education), and at the pedagogical academies, I can try to make clear how strong prejudices are among us. Anti-Semitism is, along with racism, the most detestable form of prejudice.

Would you serve in the Army under any government?

Yes, so long as they had come to power democratically under the constitution.

In the 1930s there was civil strife between the Heimwehr and the Schutzbund.[3] How would the Austrian Army react in the event of a civil war? Would it shoot its own people?

The Army is made up of people and one has to ask, how would they behave? And are foreigners any worse than one's own people?

The Army has a constitutional assignment that includes, "beyond the realm of national defense also the protection of institutions and their freedom of action, as well as the democratic freedoms of the population and the maintenance of general order and internal security."

This assignment is the responsibility of the legislator. If, however, the political leadership ordered the Army, for example, to suppress a "Putsch" that threatened the established government, then the Army would fulfill that mission.

The responsibility for the order to action would be carried solely by the political leadership—that was the same in 1934. The Army would never act on its own. They like to hide the fact

---

[3]The *Heimwehr* was the Austrian fascist militia, which grew up in the 1920s with Mussolini's support and the tacit agreement of Seipel's government. In 1931 it attempted a *Putsch*, which failed everywhere except Styria, where the capital, Graz, was surrounded for a while. In 1934 the *Heimwehr* leader, Prince Starhemberg, joined Dollfuss's Fatherland Front, but after the Chancellor's assassination the *Heimwehr* disintegrated with many members joining the still-illegal Austrian Nazis.

The *Schutzbund* was the paramilitary formation of the Austrian Social Democrats.

that the Army was also used against the Nazi Putsch in 1934—but why?

How do you explain to young people about Auschwitz and Dresden? Do you address both issues together? Is it possible to bring them together?

There is no connection between Auschwitz and Dresden. Auschwitz is the very embodiment of criminal genocide and can't be compared with the bombing of a large city. Of course that is also atrocious if it is carried out with the aim and in the sure knowledge (which I do not know) of killing defenseless wounded people and civilians.

In conclusion, one thing is clear: one should not make the mistake of accusing each other of crimes. It is much more worthwhile to ensure that the conditions that gave rise to such horrors never occur again.

". . . Schuschnigg carries some responsibility for the outbreak of the Second World War. . . !?"

Interview with *Karl H. Heinz* on 11 November 1987.

Mr. Heinz, a businessman, was born in 1907 and was a close colleague of Dr. Ernst Winter, the Third Deputy Mayor of Vienna until 1936. He headed the publishers GSUR & Co, which produced a large number of anti-fascist books.

What did you do in 1938 and the years before?

In 1938 I was a free-lance journalist. I spent my youth in Vienna. I attended the Technical High School and the School of Economics. Because of the unemployment I made my living after I had finished my studies as a ship's musician on a Dutch ship. That was between 1930 and 1933. Through this work I visited several countries (eg., in Central America) and began to write about them. In this way I got into journalism. From 1933 to 1934 I wrote for the *Arbeiterzeitung* and also for the weekly *Tagblatt.*

I came from a Social Democratic worker's family, my father was a railroad man. Although he came from a middle-class family, he had already joined the Social Democratic party by 1906.

98   *Karl H. Heinz*

What memories do you have of 1938? Did you see any anti-Semitism?

I came from Floridsdorf and that was a wholly working-class neighborhood. In this district there were many Jewish stores. They weren't rich Jews. The only difference we noticed as kids was that the Jewish children all went to the High School. That was practically impossible for workers' children—I was an exception. As a worker's son I passed the examination and went to the Technical Vocational College. After this I was able to go to the School of Economics because I graduated with very high grades.

Was there a separation between Jews and non-Jews at this time?

There was a definite contrast between "Aryans" and Jews. Even the children did not mix. I can remember the rhyme that my friends used to recite over and over: "Jud, Jud, spuck in Hut, sag der Mutter, das ist gut!" ("Jew, Jew, spit in your hat, Tell your mother how good is that!") Personally I did not do that, and I actually had a good friend who was Jewish.

In this district there were, interestingly enough, also Jewish artisans, for example, a decorator, with whose son I was close friends. I played with him on a handball team. But generally there was no contact with Jews. Many of the Jewish business people were in the Social Democratic Party. There was even an official who was Jewish. I have to tell you that there was anti-Semitism even within the Social Democratic movement. Even among workers people said "the Jew" in a derisory fashion.

But there was no boycott because people bought quite simply where it was cheapest. It was pure opportunism. Inside people had a contradictory position.

I couldn't be an anti-Semite on account of my upbringing. The leader of the Social Democratic Party and main representative of Austrian Marxism, Otto Bauer, was Jewish and was always accepted by the workers.[1] Anti-Semitism among workers was most evident at the lowest level. There was a strong aversion in journalism. I made a good salary as a free-lance journalist, and the newspaper's editors were mainly Jews.

The economic crisis did not hit us too badly, since my father received a good monthly income as a retired employee of the railroad and had earned a good salary well before that. But I knew about the depression from my work as a lecturer in the education section of the Socialist Party.

1938 was no surprise for me. I have to go back here to 15 July 1927 and the Schattendorfer trial. This had consequences. The events are known well enough. It led to the beginning of the decline of the Social Democratic Party.

If we come to 1933, the dissolution of parliament on 4 March caused terrific domestic unrest. On 16 April the first edition of the *Wiener Politische Blätter* appeared. It was published by the thirty-eight-year-old sociologist and historian Dr. Ernst Karl Winter, in fact largely written by him. He called it "an organ for the scientific clarification of political questions." The *Wiener Politische Blätter* documented the path of an upright Catholic between the different fronts in Austria between 1933 and 1938. I got to know this man and was his closest colleague. The motive for his work was a deep belief in the Catholic Church and a deep belief in Austria. His main goal was to protect Austria, before the Anschluss, from dissolution by the National Socialists.

He was unattached to any political party but he felt compelled to get involved in the constitutional battles of his country after the practical overthrow of democracy in 1933/34. He sent two open letters to the Austrian President Wilhelm Miklas, extracts of which appeared as leading articles in the *Arbeiterzeitung* on 12 March and 2 April 1933, and which showed his political involvement. The full text of the letters appeared in the *Wiener Politische Blätter* on 14 April 1933. This first number was confiscated, but he had already sent a certain number of copies to people, so the confiscation of 15 April had little effect.

---

[1]Otto Bauer (1881-1938) was the Marxist Leader of Austrian Social Democracy and a champion of the *Anschluss* movement after 1918.

Winter, as a conservative and devout Catholic, appealed at first to Miklas' Catholic conscience, but he also brought the family into it and presented a solution to the constitutional crisis as being in the general interest. He criticized Seipel's domestic policies after 1920 and supported the claims of the Social Democratic Party.

What was your relationship with Winter?

As early as 1929 he had sought a professorial chair, and it is striking that he was rejected then by the Senate. And not on academic grounds! He was callously told he should write a leading article for the *DÖTZ* (*Deutschösterreichische Tageszeitung*, the organ of the Greater Germany Party), then he could get his professorship. But this appeared as treason to a man who wanted to build up a new and self-confident Austria.

In the "corporate state" (1934-1938) Winter tried again to get a professorship. But the Senate and the Ministry of Education also stopped this attempt. Winter would have given anything, even risked his family, before he made the slightest ideological concession. After these two failed attempts, he was also unsuccessful in the Second Republic, although by this time he was already a university professor in New York. I will tell you more about that later.

Was Winter in personal danger through this steadfastness?

He had seven children then, and I knew his apartment before he became deputy Mayor. They were extremely poor. This man has plumbed the depths of life.

How can Winter's views and activity be understood from the Left?

He was very critical of Marxism. But he saw in an understanding between the constitutional conservative state and Marxism a real possibility of building a front against dictatorship and tyranny. He tirelessly sought to expose the destructive role of Seipel, whom he saw as responsible for the whole rightward slide of political Catholicism in Austria to the right.

What was Winter's relationship to Dollfuss?[2]

It was through Dollfuss that Winter came from academia to politics. Nonetheless he didn't shy away from seeing Dollfuss' tragic death (in July 1934) as an atonement for the events of 7 March 1933 to February 1934.

In October 1936 Winter was thrown out of the City Hall. There was an agreement between Schuschnigg and Hitler on 11 July 1936. We published a special brochure about it with the title "Monarchy and the Workers," which was a deliberate thematic sequel to his February 1934 "The Workers and the State." Winter attacked Schuschnigg sharply, and I can remember that he portrayed him indirectly as a traitor and accused him of capitulation. On 23 October 1936 a leading article appeared in the *Reichspost* (organ of the former Christian-Social Party), with the title "Volksfront Slogans in Austria Too" and written by his friend Professor August M. Knoll. In the article Winter was accused of doing a "dance with the Kremlin," which could not be tolerated. Winter's publications were confiscated, and it was insinuated that he sought an open attack on the government. Winter was fired from City Hall in humiliating fashion by Mayor Schmitz. He wasn't even allowed to clear out the desk in his office. In the twinkling of an eye Winter's idea for a strategy against the Nazis was reinterpreted as a criminal act, and a decent Austrian patriot was publicly stigmatized as a traitor. He was back where he had started. Overnight he lost the basis of his livelihood.

How did he live then?

In comparison with his Deputy Mayor's salary he made a pretty wretched living from publicity work.

---

[2]Engelbert Dollfuss (1892-1934) was Austrian Chancellor and leader of the Christian Social Party from 1932 to 1934. Closely allied to Mussolini, he instituted a "clerical fascist" regime in Austria. He ordered shelling of the workers' quarters in Vienna during the bitter five-day civil war of February 1934. He was assassinated by Austrian Nazis in an abortive coup attempt in July 1934.

Winter was not only an idealist, he was also a seer. He was completely right, but he couldn't bring his ideas to fruition. Already in 1936 he was planning to emigrate. So I was surprised to learn in 1937 that Winter was still here and was on holiday in Faaker See in Carinthia.

Schuschnigg and Winter were still working silently together. Winter told me later that he had tried with all his strength to prevent Schuschnigg from meeting Hitler on the Obersalzberg. But they met anyway. After his return, Schuschnigg spoke of the "wild animal" with which he had had to deal (he meant Hitler). But Winter had the impression that Schuschnigg was now ready, after this humiliating meeting with Hitler, to defend Austria. Winter would not have been Winter if he had not offered his services again to Schuschnigg instead of turning his back on Austria, that is, emigrating. He was against the plebiscite and advised Schuschnigg to take the path of military resistance. Winter was convinced that Austria was the key to decisive developments in Europe that could lead to a world catastrophe.

I am sure that any hold-up in Hitler's plans of conquest would not only have strengthened the resolve of Czechoslovakia and Poland to resist, but also given a breathing space to France and England. It would have been possible for them to rearm much more.

Are you saying by this that Schuschnigg carries some responsibility for the outbreak of the Second World War?

Yes. Most definitely, in fact. If Schuschnigg had followed Winter's plans, the Second World War—if it had happened at all—would have run a different course.[3]

Did your life change in March 1938?

Yes, totally! The biggest surprise was in the editor's office. People who had been in the Social Democratic Party, for example, the final editor of the *Arbeiterzeitung* and the chief

---

[3]For further details on Winter's life, see Karl Hans Heinz, *E.K.Winter, Ein Katholik zwischen Österreichs Fronten 1933-1938* (Wien, Köln, Graz, 1984).

editor of the *Arbeiterwoche* and also other colleagues, so long as they weren't Jews, suddenly on 12 March came out of their offices with Nazi Party insignia on their lapels. The insignia had been illegal for a long time.

I was able to warn many Jewish colleagues in time. One person who wasn't Jewish but who was a convinced Austrian patriot, Dr. Bernhard Birk, was immediately arrested. I said goodbye, went underground and was expecting to be arrested. A girlfriend of mine got me a job in the Finance Ministry. So I was a civil servant, but not a Party member. Such things happened. . .

Did you have Jewish relatives? Were you in the resistance?

There were no Jews in my family. I was active in three resistance groups. So far as the resistance is concerned, I have to say that the Austrians would have certainly defended themselves against Hitler if Schuschnigg had carried out just the minimum program of the revolutionary Socialists. Then the whole working class would have been behind the resistance.

Did you personally see discrimination against the Jews in 1938?

I saw how Jews, equipped with buckets, had to clean the streets under the supervision of the Hitler Youth. I also saw how one of those rascals took a bucket and struck an old man on the head!!

What did the people standing around do when this was going on?

Some of them laughed, or looked on indifferently, never uttering a word and showing no concern at all.

Another experience I had: I was on a street-car and the Jews had to wear a yellow star. There was an old Jew standing, and I got up and offered him my place, at which practically every passenger on the street-car turned on me in unison.

I can also remember how Jews in Floridsdorf were discriminated against. I warned many of them before. Immediately after the invasion their shops were smashed up and those Jews who had not escaped were led away. I also heard that patients who had just been operated on in the Jewish hospital in Währing were carried down in stretchers and thrown in the back of a truck.

Serious cases from the operating theater? Thrown from stretchers into trucks?

Yes, acute cases, and that meant of course certain death.

I experienced at this time a terrible emotional shock. I have to tell you that what affected me most deeply was that I, a February (1934) Fighter, suddenly saw convinced Socialists marching in SA uniforms. Of course there are explanations. They were people who had steered away from trouble for years. They viewed the economic crisis with alarm. In my resistance group there were people of course who were not seduced by Hitler. But it was very dangerous in the resistance. You had to live every moment with the possibility of arrest and execution. A schoolfriend of mine who had just given a few marks a month for the "U-Boats" (the term for Jews who were hiding) was executed for it, just because of his contribution!

My friends in the resistance helped the Jews by collecting ration cards in order to be able to buy some food for them.

Why did you risk your life to help the Jews?

For us in the resistance, the Jews were just as much people as you and I. We didn't pay any attention to that racial nonsense. How many people belonged to the resistance I don't know, since one only knew one's contact man.

How do you see it all looking back?

I have to say this: after the war I discovered a moving correspondence between Winter and Schuschnigg. In it some of the central political events and possibilities of their pasts were interpreted and judged. Some passages of a letter from Schuschnigg to Winter of 13 June 1947 occur to me when I think about the "afterwards." In regard to the missed opportunity to resist Hitler, Schuschnigg's opinion to Winter was that in March 1938 there was never a chance of resistance in this infected Nazi country, above all in Styria with persons such as Ottokar Kernstock or, for example, Paula Grogger. Winter replied, deeply hurt, that he had not received an appointment to Graz University, despite his academic qualifications, because of the passionate resistance of Messrs. Gorbach, Funder and Knoll.

In 1955 Winter optimistically returned to Vienna, but besides the Venia Legendi—a mere authorization to accept a professorial chair, if one was offered—the University of Vienna, the city of which he had been Deputy Mayor at a very difficult time, had nothing to offer him.

Schuschnigg came back to Austria in 1964 and got a Chancellor's pension.

You mean one should give that some thought?

Yes.

And what happened to Winter?

He died four years later in Vienna—he was just 63. And official Austria took about as much notice of his death as it had of his work.

He wasn't the greatest Austrian who was treated in this fashion, and he won't be the last.

"... I wanted to return to my old homeland. .."

Conversation with *Paul Heller* on 29 September 1987.

Mr. Heller was born in 1912. In 1938 he was in Graz where he still lives today.

As a Jew, how do you remember 1938?

Well, it wasn't good even in the years before 1938. Newspapers like the *Tagespost* had already become very anti-Semitic. And certain customers made remarks like, "I'm not buying from Jews." My father had a store in the Annenstrasse, and a lot of people came in, and one often heard anti-Semitic remarks. "When Jewish blood flows. . .", songs like that I can still remember well.

Of course that was after the *Anschluss*.

Do you still have memories of the time before 1938? Of your schooldays?

The gymnastics and mathematics teachers both made anti-Semitic remarks in the school. In the elementary school I didn't hear any of that because I went to a Jewish school. On the way home, however, kids from other schools would make remarks and rhymes like "Jud, Jud, spuck in Hut, sag der Mutter, das ist gut."

It was the sort of daily occurrence that a child gets used to.

Did the situation reach a climax in February and March 1938?

It wasn't really fear that I felt at this time, rather a strange feeling.

Do you remember the days of the *Anschluss*?

I still have the feeling that there were only Nazis in Graz then. Everybody seemed enthusiastic!

I noticed also that there were Hitler supporters among the socialists, who assured me: "You know what I really think, but all my colleagues are wearing these (swastika) badges so I have to wear one. . . ." Then a colleague with whom I traveled on business suddenly appeared after the *Anschluss* in SA uniform. At this moment I realized that this man must have always been a Nazi.

What was it like meeting him?

We glanced at each other, with hardly a greeting. After that I lost touch with him. He didn't survive the war.

What happened then in 1938?

It got progressively more difficult.

My sister had married a Czech and thought she would be safe. But this safety didn't last long. At the end of October 1938 she visited us once more. . .

In the course of 1938 I—and many other Graz Jews—started to think about emigrating. We trained "for work in the fields," as we were already thinking about going to Israel. At the same time we took Hebrew lessons. I can remember the course met on 9 November and on this evening there were various reports of riots in the town. We went home and on 10 November, at about 4 o'clock in the morning (I was already asleep) there was a shout:

"The police are here, the SA are here."

They were civilians, about four or five of them. They broke in the doors to the cupboard, threw the china on the floor. I had to get dressed quickly, and as I was putting on my coat, one of them said to me: "You won't need that, it'll be hot enough where you're going."

My father was also forced to get dressed, and we were led out of the apartment. I remember my father was shoved and almost fell over the staircase. We went down the stairs and had to line up outside the house with our hands up. People passed by and of course looked at us. We remained there for about two to three minutes and then a car came, and we were thrown in it. There were four men in the car and we had to squeeze in. One of these men gave me his revolver and said:

"If you want you can shoot your father with it."

I gave him the revolver back and said, "No thanks, that I won't do."

These men were already wearing SS uniforms, and the one that had handed me the revolver actually went to school with me.

Where were you taken in the car?

We were driven along the Bahnhofgürtel. In those days there were still wooden fences and lawns. We were pushed out of the car and, in the middle of November, told to strip naked. They put guns to our necks, and we had to repeat phrases like,

"I am a Jew sow" or "I am a pig."

I had only one thought: "We are going to be shot but what will happen to our poor mother? . . . she's all alone."

This thought tortured me—it was terrible.

Suddenly a newspaper delivery girl came by and that seemed to save us. Apparently they didn't want any witnesses, and they took off with the words, "Stay there till we come back." My father told me immediately that we should get dressed, and we took to our heels. Dawn began to break as we walked home. I can't describe the feeling that we had then.

What these men actually intended to do with us has never been clear to me till this day. Did they want to kill us? Or just humiliate us? I don't know. Whatever it was, we felt that we were going to die.

On the way home we saw lots of cars, full of people. . . a lot of people were arrested that night. It was what is known in history as the *Kristallnacht.*

About ten in the morning I had a call from a former girl-friend. She was very upset and told me that her husband had been arrested and also her father, and she wanted me to come over. I went immediately. As I went over the bridge I saw the synagogue burning. While I was at my friend's, the police came to my house and arrested my father. They made a house search and once again everything was thrown about. They took my father away with them. By not being at home at that time I escaped being sent to *Dachau.*

Did your father go to Dachau?

Yes. My father was sent to *Dachau.* I can show you the card that he wrote to my mother from there. After a month he came back.

But I have to tell you something else.

There was a man who had a delicatessen on Annenstrasse. A little while later he came to us and said completely openly:

"I'm taking your apartment, it's confiscated."

He was a good acquaintance of ours and we had always bought from him. Very generously he declared that he only claimed "one room at the moment." So we continued to live in our "confiscated" apartment. . . that was what it was like in the weeks and months after the *Anschluss.* . .

Your father was sent to Dachau. What happened to you in the end?

I found out that a transport was going to Palestine in a few days. I decided without further ado to emigrate to Palestine. My mother remained behind, and I never saw my father again after 10 November 1938.

It was an adventure, this trip to Palestine. We went by ship down the Danube. . . we waded through the last few yards of water to Tel Aviv. I began a new life in a new country—Palestine—as a field worker on the orange harvest.

How long were you in Palestine?

From the end of 1938 to August 1947.

You didn't want to stay in Palestine, present-day Israel?

I had the opportunity to return to Austria. I wanted to return to my old homeland.

What happened to your parents?

As I told you, my father was sent to *Dachau* after the *Kristallnacht,* and he stayed there about four weeks. After that I had only written correspondence with him. My parents had the intention to come on to Israel, but they never made it. They even sent furniture to Israel, but somehow or other they never came.

Who organized everything for the Jews, so that they could get out at all?

Isidor Preminger organized it. This man did a great deal for the Jews of Graz. Many people were able to get out at the last minute thanks to him.

Tell me more about your parents. What happened to them?

I lost track of my parents. I only know that they were killed. I got that information from Dr. Biro, a lawyer in Graz. The last letters I got were in 1941/42. I got a card from my sister—I can show you—and this was the last sign of life from her. I never learned anymore about her either from this time onwards.

In 1938 my family life ceased to exist. I lost them all.

What professional opportunities did you have in Israel?

I had lots of jobs. I worked in an orange grove, then later I was a fitter, and some time later I set up a pickled gherkin factory with a friend. But this business took some time to get going, and in the meantime I got a job in a brick factory. I worked for about two years as a crane driver. Of course I also had to go into the Army. As a soldier I went to Cyprus around 1942. I stayed in the Army until 1946. In 1947 I returned to Austria.

When you got back to Graz, did you still have relatives in the town?

No, my relatives were killed in concentration camps. I stayed with old friends and acquaintances. From 1947 to 1959 I was alone and had to start a new job from the beginning. . . I opened a textile firm with a cousin, and later I had a shop in the Annenstrasse. I was married and started a family only in 1959.

Today I am seventy-five years old and I look back with a lot of nostalgia. . . it was a thorny path.

". . . rarely has so much trust been so badly abused. . ."

Conversation with *Kurt Jungwirth* on 8 December 1987.

Professor Jungwirth, who was born in 1929, is the deputy head of the Styrian provincial government. He was in Graz in 1938 and lives there today.

Professor Jungwirth, you were a child in 1938, so what do you remember from this time? Were you aware of what was going on?

I was eight and half years old when Hitler invaded Austria and fifteen and a half when the terror of the war ended in 1945. So I can only speak from the viewpoint of a child and young person.

I was already interested in politics then. I can remember that in the 1930s as an elementary school pupil, I took an interest in the political pages of the newspaper. I have to admit it was a schoolboy fascination with reports of wars from around the world, for example, the war between the Chinese and the Japanese. Later I followed the Spanish Civil War avidly—still at elementary school.

Do you have special memories of 1938 or the years before?

I was brought up in Graz, in a poor neighborhood, and what I remember of 1938 is the dreadful depression and social need.

It was always knocking at the door. Beggars came in hordes to ask for money or bread. The usual expression was "A non-tax-payer is there!," in other words, someone who no longer had to pay taxes, because he no longer earned anything.

That's my basic memory.

Yes, and the rag-and-bone men and the street singers who hung around. Or an old man, who came with an ancient gramophone and a few bad, scratched records and played them in the front courtyard in the hope that someone would throw a few pennies out of the window. So it was an economically hopeless time that I remember, with many people unemployed.

And that for me is the main explanation for the success of National Socialism, because it gave people hope. The hope that they could survive. That they would find work and have something to eat and something to wear. It was simply the urge for survival that's in every human being.

And then there was news from Germany, where Hitler had seized power in 1933 and where people had jobs again. I don't think anybody knew then that these jobs consisted of preparing for a terrible war.

That's the one strong memory I have from my childhood. From my point of view, therefore, it's impossible for the present generation to simply pass judgment on those people who cheered Hitler in 1938. They saw in him a hope for survival, to live as they had before the depression. Not many of them were the kind of people who wanted to march off to war, to provoke war, to beat other people and to shoot them. No, they just wanted someone to give them hope for the future, that was all.

Do you think Professor, that the hopelessness and the enthusiasm on the part of many people for the *Anschluss* was connected with the collapse of the Austro-Hungarian Empire in 1918?

Yes, that is a second reason. The whole thing took place in an Austria that was very young, that was really an amputated Austria. In 1918 the old monarchy ended. Then there was the Versailles Peace Treaty and the old empire was broken up and the new states became independent: Czechoslovakia, Hungary, Yugoslavia, etc.

Austria became what was left. Clemenceau said that literally at St. Germain, "L'Autriche, c'est le reste!." And this rest had to see how it could survive. People didn't think that this Austria was capable of survival, and at first it was called German-Austria. There was a clear wish after 1918 to unite this German-Austria with the German Reich. The political will was there, but the Allies opposed it because they were afraid of Germany getting too big. So Austria became a republic against itself. And the people grieved, consciously or subconsciously, for the nation's lost greatness. And they longed for a new greatness! And that was achieved with the Austrian *Anschluss* to Germany.

I think that these two roots were essential: firstly, the desire to be part of a greater Empire, in which one "was in good hands," the desire for a greater *Heimat* (homeland), and secondly, the very practical consequences of the economic depression and social need.

Can one say that Hitler recognized this situation and exploited it? That he built up a propaganda to suit it and seduced the people?

Of course. One can certainly say that at the beginning there was an enormous hope and trust in Germany and Austria together. It was a blind faith that the leadership would make everything better. And one can say that seldom has so much trust been so abused. Because the people were seduced. They were eager to be seduced, and it was a terrible awakening for them to find out along what an evil road they had been led.

But the machinery was huge. A young person brought up in a democracy today simply can't imagine how the machinery of a dictatorship works, how control through spying neighbors is exercised. There were block leaders, and then cell leaders on the estate, in the back alley, in the district, in the factories—everywhere the Party had its agents. And how dangerous it was to say anything, to criticize the regime, apart from the fact that there was no information anyway. There was no television, nothing.

Don't you think, Professor, that the Austrians had plenty of time to see what Hitler really wanted, after his seizure of power in 1933 in Germany—if they really wanted to see?

I don't think so. Look, a lot of what happened there seemed very positive to the Austrians then.

For example?

The *Autobahns* (freeways) were built, industry was booming, there was plenty of work. The arrests and the persecutions weren't talked about in Austria in public. Moreover, there was no TV, there were no foreign radio stations. It was a luxury to even have a radio set that could receive foreign broadcasts.

In fact there were these People's Radios specifically to bring the voice of the "political boss" into every home. The newspapers were trimmed to a single political line. There were no opposition newspapers, no critical press. Censors everywhere. The people knew nothing at all. It was an atmosphere that you just can't imagine today.

Did you know anything about the concentration camps when you were growing up?

As a young and very alert person I only heard one name in connection with the concentration camps before 1945, and that was *Dachau*. That was because many Austrians went there. For us it meant a camp for political prisoners, and when we spoke of concentration camps we meant political offenders, so-called "enemies of the people," as they were called then, people who damaged the state—and homosexuals. That's what one heard.

But nothing else—nothing about *Auschwitz*, or *Buchenwald*, or *Bergen-Belsen*—nothing, absolutely nothing.

When did you first hear of other concentration camps like Auschwitz, Bergen-Belsen, and Buchenwald?

I can remember the first newspaper after 8 May 1945, it must have been on 10 May. This newspaper was composed of a single sheet of paper, and I remember it had an article on the atrocities and mass killings in the camps. That was the first time I had heard about it. It was a shock for me! It was a terrible shock for me to read about it and hear about it. We started talking about it immediately, and it was like scales falling from our eyes, that we suddenly realized that they'd been systematically gassing Jews there.

You didn't know about the extermination camps during the war?

Absolutely not. I knew that the Jews weren't wanted and that the Jews disappeared. But we all—that is, myself and the people I knew—thought that they'd emigrated.

Did your family have any Jewish friends at this time?

No, we never had any.

Do you think that people who had contact with Jews knew about Hitler's atrocities earlier?

Yes, it could be that they got information sooner. They were the ones who were affected. But that didn't happen to me.

What is necessary to make young people treasure the democracy that we now have in Austria? That they should be alert and ready to defend democracy? Especially looking back on this dictatorship that we got rid of?

In reality one has to experience a dictatorship. If you grow up with democratic freedoms, you can't imagine what it's like to live in a dictatorship. You can't imagine that there can be anything else but freedom. The people who don't know how to appreciate the freedom that we have in Austria should go abroad to find out what it's like to live in a dictatorship. There are plenty of dictatorships in the world. Young people must understand that a democratic system is a tremendous achievement. Only a minority of countries have democratic governments. Of the 170 countries in the United Nations only thirty or forty, or fewer, are democratically governed—that means that there are several parties and the possibility for a change of power through elections.

Sometimes people say cynically, "Okay, every five years I'm allowed to drop my voting slip in the box, so what?"

But that's nonsense, because everyone can do more if he or she wants—and in any case it's a great deal to be able to bring about a change of political power with a voting slip. You can't do that in a dictatorship, where the regime gets steadily stronger and more inhumane, repressive, and barbarian.

You are talking about the concept of tolerance?

Yes, the spirit of tolerance is very important in this connection. People find that generally pretty difficult. Tolerance means that your neighbor can express a different opinion to you. It reminds me of Voltaire, who said "I disagree entirely with what you say, but I'll fight to the end of my life for your right to say it." That's tolerance! And that's a tremendous achievement! And we have to strive to protect that achievement.

To come back to the year 1938. How do you understand the *Anschluss*? Was it what the majority of Austrians wanted, namely, the reunion of Austria with the German Reich or were we occupied?

It's clear that for many Austrians, the *Anschluss* was grounds for celebration—for the reasons that I've already outlined.

But it's also a fact that the Austrian government up until 1938, under Dollfuss and Schuschnigg, was absolutely against the *Anschluss* and had done everything possible to preserve Austria's independence. For a while they followed Italy, but then Mussolini became closer to Hitler. There was a joke then:

"What's the Rome-Berlin Axis?" (the Hitler-Mussolini Pact), and the answer was, "The Rome-Berlin Axis is the spit on which Austria will be roasted brown."

So we lost this support. And domestically there was too little stability, because the ruling right wing tragically excluded the left from government. This division opened the way for the Nazis.

It has to be understood against the background of economic crisis and the civil war years of 1927 and 1934, when the people were shooting at each other and it wasn't possible to find a policy of broad consensus. If the workers and the middle classes had found one, then Austria would have been in a very different situation. It was tragic. The Austrian government fought till the end for Austrian independence, but Austria was deserted by the world and that's why Schuschnigg said at the end: "I had to give way in the face of violence."

In your opinion, did Austrian soldiers fight for a legitimate ruler? Or was Hitler an illegitimate ruler?

Illegitimate is not the correct term, because Hitler came legally to power in Germany in 1933. Only later when he excluded the democratic opposition did it become a permanent *coup d'état*.

From a foreign policy perspective, all his wars were wars of aggression. Naturally he told the German people, "We are threatened! Versailles left us defenseless—we must protect ourselves!" The people were poor and they thought they were fighting for the homeland, not realizing that they were engaged in straightforward wars of aggression. They thought they were conducting preventive wars that would guarantee the German people's right to live. They really believed that. It was seduction, an enormous, a total seduction.

The Moscow Declaration made clear that the outcome of the war for Austria would depend on the extent to which it contributed to its own liberation. Accordingly, we should have tried to keep our participation in Hitler's war to a minimum. How can we reconcile this with our great pride in having "fulfilled our duty"? Was that "fulfillment of duty" in this sense?

The Moscow Declaration was important. I heard of it for the first time at the end of 1943 and also heard the name "Austria" for the first time since 1938—a name which had been completely wiped out. And suddenly I realized that from the Allies' point of view we were a problem and that it concerned what would happen to us after the war that now appeared to be lost. The Allies were saying we were a victim of Hitler's aggression and we should make our own contribution and that it would be weighed in the balance. That was completely new! That started new thoughts in our heads, but also fears: what would happen to us? The war was lost—it was after Stalingrad and El Alamein. We were retreating and victory was a thing of the past. . . what would happen now? That was a great question mark.

May I repeat the question? Today, fifty years after, what is "fulfillment of duty"? Was it the same as that understood by Waldheim?

Waldheim made an unfortunate statement, because he should have added what he thinks today—his opinions must have changed, and some commentary was necessary. From the point of view of a young man living then, he spoke correctly. Those trusting young people had taken an oath of allegiance. It was a sacred promise, despite the mistaken conviction it involved.

Behind it stood this belief in a good future and a "just world order." People felt ill-used by 1918, by (the Treaties of) Versailles and St. Germain. Now there was a chance for a "new justice," the restoration of rights that had been abused by the victors of the First World War. That was the basic position.

In the declaration of independence of 27 April 1945 (StGBl No.1) the *Anschluss* is ruled null and void. If the *Anschluss* is null and void, then Hitler was not entitled to introduce new laws and our President should have expressed himself differently. Shouldn't he have explained the term "fulfillment of duty" so that there were no misunderstandings? Isn't it possible that the whole discussion about this term "fulfillment of duty" could have been avoided?

Yes, it is certainly necessary to bring both halves together. Both halves are right, but they must be explained together. Waldheim did that on other occasions. It is right to span the whole range of problems—as people felt them. Only in this way was it possible to begin Austrian politics anew in April 1945.

I must say that I have the greatest admiration for those Austrian politicians who started again in 1945. Really started anew with conviction. These men achieved a lot, right up to the *Staatsvertrag*.[1] One time enemies like the Christian Socials and the Socialists have found themselves again. The common suppression which they suffered after the *Anschluss* has led to the creation of a new Austria, which in 1938 people thought of as so weak as to be unfit to live anymore. They found new faith in Austria through Hitler's reign of terror. People said: "We want this Austria! And we want to help rebuild it together!"

Has the Waldheim discussion caused a new anti-Semitism that could create an atmosphere like that between 1933 and 1938? Do you believe that "the Jews are to blame"—as one hears here and there—if our President does not enjoy the respect abroad that we would all like? And do you think, Professor, that the Holocaust, after everything that we now know about it, could ever be repeated?

No, I don't think the Holocaust could ever happen again. And I don't see it in such a simplistic way. You can't compare the situation today with that of 1938. Maybe there are people who think what you say, but we all know that this campaign against Waldheim began at home and didn't have its origins with Jews. That's well known. It's a completely domestic problem, and one can say with safety that the whole discussion in 1987 is not comparable to that in 1938. In other words, our situation cannot be equated with that of fifty years ago!

What would you like to say about the future, Professor, now, fifty years after?

There are many truths, or better, there are many facets to the truth. And perhaps we can't always appreciate all these facets. However, one should try. One has to put oneself back in that time, to understand the *Zeitgeist*, to get the feeling of what was happening, to understand the social basis on which it all took place. It's not always easy to differentiate between ordinary demagogues and deadly demagogues.

---

[1]The 1955 Treaty that ended the military occupation of Austria and gave her independence under neutral auspices.

In my opinion it is important for the future to have an unconditional faith in freedom and the desire to cultivate and protect democratic rule. Democracy has to be prized and loved, and we must strive to be tolerant. We all know that intolerance leads to inhumanity, self-righteousness, and indifference to suffering. And this indifference to suffering, that is perhaps what we were guilty of then. Is it possible that a lot of things happened fifty years ago that could have been prevented? With one person or another.

". . . If Hitler comes, we march. . ."

Conversations with *Josef Keckeis* on 19 and 30 November 1987.

Dr. Keckeis, born in 1915, is a former high court councillor. He lives today in Frastanz in the Vorarlberg region of Austria.

Can you remember 1938? What memories do you have in particular?

In the winter of 1937/38 I was a law student in my last year at the University of Innsbruck. As a twenty-two-year old I was liable for the military conscription that the Schuschnigg government had introduced in the summer of 1938, I was a soldier in the so-called Dollfuss Regiment in the Tyrolean town of Hall.

We recruits were told during training by the platoon leader, F. Posch, that "if Hitler comes, we march." I followed developments from 12 February to 11 March (my birthday) exactly and I was surprised when on the evening of March 11 Dr. Schuschnigg declared in his farewell speech that there would be no military resistance. I was also astounded at the failure to carry out the plebiscite planned for March 13, because as a patriotic Austrian student I had reckoned that at least two thirds of the Austrian population would vote to retain their country's independence.

After Schuschnigg's March 9 speech in Innsbruck, when he announced the March 13 plebiscite, I and others with similar views were asked to help campaign. When "Hitler & Co." invaded our country I went home (March 12) and prepared for my final examinations.

What did you feel about the declaration of the Austrian bishops on 18 March, 1938?

I was amazed by the Austrian bishops' declaration and that of Dr. Karl Renner on April 3, regarding the *Anschluss*. I am still amazed today.

Did you already know in 1938 that, for example, there were concentration camps?

We knew in Austria in March 1938 that at the time of the "Röhm Putsch" in 1934 (in Germany) Hitler had ordered several hundred people killed and that *Dachau* concentration camp already existed.

What did you do after your studies were completed?

After I'd finished my studies I started as a law trainee at the state court at Feldkirch, although I had to work from October 1938 to April 1939 without payment, because I wasn't an "illegal."[1] Having been brought up after the death of my father in the First World War as a war orphan, I was taken on as an articled barrister after 1 April 1939.

Did you serve in the German Army under Hitler?

When I was called up to the *Wehrmacht* in July 1940, I understood my legal situation as follows: outwardly I swore a new oath to Adolf Hitler, but I considered the one that I had sworn to the Austrian Army in January 1937 in Hall as still valid, and I felt obligated by it.

---

[1] "illegal" = The term used for underground Nazis, before the *Anschluss*. As of 12 March they openly wore a distinctive swastika badge, which was a sign of their special status and privileges.

I made contact immediately with the resistance inside the *Wehrmacht,* I rejected every offer of special training, and had no interest in a military career. I was very lucky to return home as a corporal to Frastanz in April 1945 without having being wounded.

Did you have difficulties on account of your resistance activities?

The worst time was in 1941 in Salzburg, where I was accused by the *Gestapo* of "subverting morale." I had to appear before a court martial, but was lucky enough to be acquitted.

After the war, were you honored as a resistance fighter?

As a recognized resistance fighter I received a decoration in 1978 for services to the liberation of Austria. I am also the state leader of the Union of Politically Persecuted Comrades.

How do you see those events now, fifty years later?

In my opinion we Austrians haven't yet come to terms objectively with those terrible events, and in particular we haven't paid attention to the legal situation of Austrians between 1938 and 1945.

What do you say about "fulfillment of duty" or "obedience to the law" in this time? From the perspective of a jurist?

Because the *Anschluss* has been declared null and void, Adolf Hitler was never our legal ruler. The oath that Austrians took to Hitler is meaningless. From a purely legal point of view, all Austrians were obliged to resist him, and there was never "a duty to fulfill" or "laws to obey" for the Austrians.

The words, "I was in the *Wehrmacht* like many others and did my duty there," which the President uttered during the campaign in Spring 1986, have been heard and read about ever since under the rubric "fulfillment of duty." Here and there people also think that with these words the episode of Waldheim's "brown past" can be closed.

Dr. Soswinski, head of the Concentration Camp Association, said during a meeting of the Association at *Mauthausen* in April 1987, which took place under the motto "Duty to Austria meant Resistance," that for Austrian resistance fighters fulfillment of duty in the Nazi state meant treason to Austria.

Then in October the *Wiener Zeitung* published former President Kirchschläger's views on fulfillment of duty. He said about duty in the *Wehrmacht*: "we were, I would say, obedient to the laws." He explained further that resistance seemed pointless to him, but that he had great respect for the courage of those who from their convictions were unable to obey the law "the way we did" and chose instead the path of resistance.

"Fulfillment of duty" and "obeying the law" are the same. Because Waldheim has admitted that he wasn't in the resistance, his view of the legal aspects of resistance is the same as Kirchschläger's. They were both officers in the Second World War and they were both lawyers.

In the spring of 1986 it became known that Kirchschläger, as a *Wehrmacht* captain in the area around Wiener Neustadt at the end of March 1945, had fought with the SS against the advancing Russians and that he had ordered 1,200 cadets from the military academy there into the battle, in the course of which 200 of these youngsters were killed. At the same time, in Wien-Floridsdorf, three Austrian officers were hanged by the SS for joining the resistance.

It strikes me as odd that certain circles seek to draw doubtful conclusions from Waldheim's notion of "fulfillment of duty" about his attitude to the Nazis, while Kirchschläger's words, "we obeyed the laws," and his military activity in Wiener Neustadt apparently warrant no criticism.

Thinking people, who are in a position to judge the Nazi years in Austria, find that difficult to comprehend.

From the "White Book" on Kurt Waldheim that appeared on November 28 in the *Vorarlberger Nachrichten*, it's obvious that today—fifty years after the Nazi occupation of our country—the legal situation of Austrians between 1938 and 1945 is still not clarified.

People apparently don't want to understand what is meant by "null and void"!

How do you mean?

It said in this publication that Waldheim, on the basis of the available evidence, did not break any laws; in other words, he'd "fulfilled his duty." I'll repeat: legally the laws introduced by Hitler were meaningless for Austrians, since Hitler was never our legitimate ruler. "Fulfillment of duty" is treason to Austria, as Dr. Soswinski put it.

What do you think will happen in this case?

In the case of Waldheim, I'm very curious to see how it works out.

Do you want to say anything else?

Yes. There are Austrians who served loyally during the Second World War and rose to high office after 1945. Also within the law! That's my statement after living through fifty years of history.

". . . I never expressed an opinion about what my successor should or should not do. . ."

Conversation with former President of Austria *Rudolf Kirchschläger* on 13 November 1987.

Dr. Kirchschläger was born in Upper Austria in 1915. He was a judge before taking a position in the Federal Chancellor's Office. From 1970 he was Austria's Foreign Minister, and from 1974 until 1986 her Federal President.

Mr. President, in your book "Der Friede beginnt im eigenen Haus" ("Peace Begins in One's Own House") you devote a chapter to the years before 1938. You point out that it was not an overnight decision that moved Austria to an "authoritarian regime" in which parliamentary democracy was excluded and party ideology replaced by state ideology, but that it was rather a long process culminating in the events of 1933 and 1934. In this chapter you analyze the causes of the *Anschluss*.[1]

---

[1]Rudolf Kirchschläger, *Der Friede beginnt im eigenen Haus: Gedanken über Österreich* (Wien, 1980).

Can you tell me what you felt then in 1938? Were you for resistance?[2]

As I have said recently, I was uncertain! I wanted the government to resist and at the same time hoped that there wouldn't be any resistance.

My personal situation was that I was found unfit for military service in 1936 because of anemia. So the question of reporting back for duty did not occur in my case, because I had never served in the first place.

However, there was the question of war or peace, and there I was uncertain. And I've remained uncertain ever since. Even today I cannot say with absolute certainty that under the conditions that prevailed then we should have resisted. From the hindsight of 1945 it's easy to say: yes, resistance, then we'd have held South Tirol, etc. That's easy to say with the knowledge of 1945, but from our position in 1938 I have to tell you: I said to myself, hopefully we won't put up with that and hopefully there isn't a war.

Today, fifty years later it's easy to be clever. I have already told you that by 1945 we were cleverer and have said that we should have resisted, but then it was already easier than in 1938.

Mr. President, you know of the action of the Austrian Veterans Association last summer. Also the statements of the former Education Minister Piffl-Percevic as well as, among others, that of State Councilor Heidinger, who declared solidarity with President Waldheim by asking to be put on the US "watch list" themselves. Karl Schiffer, a witness whom I interviewed shortly before his death, felt deeply insulted as a patriotic Austrian. He asked me especially to ascertain your

---

[2]Rudolf Kirchschläger refused to join any arm of the National Socialist Party. At this time he was a young socialist student in Vienna. After the *Anschluss* an order appeared to join the Nazi *Studentenbund* or another Nazi organization. With his clear refusal to do so he forfeited for himself all the benefits available to needy students. He wasn't afraid to break off his law studies in April 1938 after seven semesters at the alma mater Rudolfina. He worked as a bank clerk in Linz before being called up in December 1938. He did two years military service. See Marco Schenz, *Bundespräsident Rudolf Kirchschläger* (Wien/Köln/Graz, 1984).

views. Therefore my question is: what do you think of this solidarity action?

I was approached to support this solidarity action. I refused to do so for the following reasons:

Firstly, I think that a solidarity action by former members of the German *Wehrmacht* is hardly what we need at the moment to restore our somewhat battered reputation abroad.

Secondly, I believe it is an oversimplification to see the attack on Herr Waldheim purely in terms of his military service. If that was the case then many former officers of the *Wehrmacht* would have run into trouble. I was such an officer myself and never had difficulties, although my career during the War has been fully known since the moment I became a public prosecutor.[3]

Shouldn't Waldheim have spoken out immediately against this solidarity action? Many Austrians expected that.

I never expressed an opinion as to what my successor should or should not do. That would have been unfair because I am in a much more fortunate position than he and in any case I would not have done that to any successor. My principle from the outset was not to stand in the shadows as an "adviser"—I mean "adviser" in quotation marks.

Don't you think that such a solidarity action works against the Austrian resistance, in other words, against those Austrians who fought for a free Austria and against Nazism—often at the cost of their lives? And don't we want, now more than ever, to emphasize that we fought against National Socialism and to show that we are an anti-fascist country?

I did not perceive this solidarity action to be against the Austrian resistance, rather as a well-intentioned but misunder-

---

[3] "A new vision of Austria also arose in the thoughts of those Austrians who, regardless of their convictions, had been obliged to participate as soldiers in a war of aggression which they never wanted. . . ." Kirchschläger, *Der Friede beginnt*, p. 61.

stood attempt to help the President. The resistance as such will not be harmed by a number of Austrians wanting to be put on the "watch list."

Piffl-Percevic—who, after all was a former Education Minister—has said, "The border of the homeland was where the front was. . .," and that Austrian soldiers in the Wehrmacht "defended the homeland from evil."
Surely this is in contradiction to the fact that we were occupied!? Doesn't it mean that we weren't victims?

I am not the censor of former Minister Piffl-Percevic, whom I personally admire.

I also believe that the declarations of individuals do not alter the constitutional situation.[4] The constitutional situation in Austria does not depend on the opinion of one person or another, even if he is in a responsible position. Rather it depends on the facts, and the facts are that Austria defended itself against the *Anschluss*, that Austria wanted to have a plebiscite on the question of such an *Anschluss*, or to put it another way, Austria's independence, and that Nazi Germany wanted to stop this plebiscite at any price, up to and including the risk of military invasion. If Hitler had not believed that he would lose this plebiscite on Austria's independence, then he certainly would not have chosen this hasty and poorly prepared ultimatum and invasion, but would have awaited the result of the plebiscite with confidence. Then there would have been a maximum of 25% popular support for the *Anschluss*.

It is on this fact and the ultimatum that "if the government does not resign by tonight, then German troops will invade," that the Occupation rests, and that has determined Austria's constitutional position, and not the later opinion of an individual as to the meaning of his service in the German Army.

---

[4]"If the exhortation 'nip in the bud' applies anywhere, then it should be where there is a threat to the cornerstone of our constitution. The task before every elected representative and before every citizen is to see that the basic principles upon which our Republic is founded are sustained in both great and small; yes, even in the small things!. . ." Kirchschläger, *Der Friede beginnt*, p. 56.

I think we are missing the basic point here.

That's the Occupation theory.[5] But doesn't what Piffl-Percevic said—his personal opinion—contradict this theory? According to his view, that was surely Annexation and not Occupation theory, wasn't it?

What's theoretical about it? That was no theory, that was awful reality; the ultimatum, the invasion, and the breach of the constitution were facts. Whether one later sees these three things as Annexation or Occupation is only of importance in relation to the continued validity of agreements after Austria's reconstruction, otherwise not at all. It had no political relevance for the time when Austria was forced into the German Reich. Occupation or Annexation was decisive only for the continued validity of those treaties that Austria had signed up to 1938.

In the Occupation theory, the state remains, even if it is occupied, and the treaties continue in force.

With Annexation, the state becomes—even under force—a part of the state that has assimilated it, and the treaties are invalidated.

The difference between Occupation and Annexation has absolutely no political relevance for the year 1938![6]

[5]Occupation Theory is the thesis that Austria's sovereignty was merely suspended by the German occupation, while the state itself remained. Accordingly, "Austria's international agreements would be 'revived' after the discontinuation of the German occupation, and moreover there would be significant consequences for Austria's claims against the German Reich and the regulation of the peace treaties." See Hermann Baltl, *Österreichische Rechtsgeschichte: Von den Anfängen bis zur Gegenwart* (Graz, 1987), p. 306-307.

[6] "After the reconstruction of Austria in 1945 a legal controversy arose over the international condemnation of the *Anschluss*: was it an annexation which led to the end of Austria's national sovereignty and to the creation of a new national sovereignty in 1945, or was it only an occupation, which between 1938 and 1945 removed the occupied state's power to act, but which did not affect its existence as a separate international body." Ludwig K. Adamovich & Bernd Christian Funk, "Österreichisches Verfassungsrecht. Verfassungslehre unter Berücksichtigung von Staatslehre und Politikwissenschaft," in *Springers Kurzlehrbuch für Rechtswissenschaft* (Wien, 1985), p. 83.

You have said in an interview in connection with this over-worked concept "fulfillment of duty," that you fulfilled your duty in respect to the laws of the time. What do you mean by that?

No. I did not speak about fulfillment of duty. I said, I obeyed the laws of the time!

Were these laws legitimate for you?

The military law was certainly legitimate, because the invasion of Austria and its assimilation into the German Reich was accepted without a murmur by the whole international community with the exception of Mexico and a short speech from Moscow. And through this extension of the law the citizen was automatically obligated. The individual citizen could not then say I am only obliged to obey Austrian law; but he had to obey all the laws, even if they were imposed by force.

However, Austrians were not obliged, any more than Germans, to obey those laws—such as the racial decrees—that were obviously a breach of natural law. Here there was no justification for obedience, in my opinion. The military law did not have anything particularly Nazi about it.

A basic question: if these laws were legitimate, then do you think, Mr. President, that what was right then, could not be wrong today?

There was the military law which did not breach international standards by requiring men of a certain age to serve in the Armed Forces, but then it was used to wage a war of aggression. That was the illegitimate decision. That was established at the Nuremberg Tribunal.

What do you say to the letter of the Deputy Mayor of Linz to the President of the World Jewish Congress, in which he writes that the latter's opinions are of the same value "as those of his co-religionists who allowed Jesus Christ to be condemned to death in a show trial two thousand years ago, because he did not fit in with the concepts of the gentlemen of Jerusalem."?

This letter was a confirmation of everything that we Austrians have been accused of—it draws on the theological views of the 1920s and 1930s.

I pointed out in an evening discussion in Vienna—I think the title was "Schalom for Austria"—that we Christians bear a certain responsibility for this development.[7] The Church has concerned itself with the Jewish problem since Pope John XXIII.

---

[7]On the occasion of the Christian meeting, "Shalom for Austria," on 26 October 1986 in Vienna, former Federal President Rudolf Kirchschläger said the following: "I have at home the Catholic Mass book that appeared first in this German translation in 1884. There you can find as the eighth, or if you drop the prayer for the Emperor, the seventh Good Friday intercession, the prayer for the Jews: 'Let us pray for the faithless faithless Jews, God, our Lord, take the veil from their hearts, so that they. . . Almighty, eternal God, You exclude not even the faithless Jews from your Mercy: hear the prayer that we offer to bring the Light of Your Truth, which is Jesus Christ, into their darkness. . .'

This Intercession and Prayer was altered by Pope John XXIII in 1960. When you think about this, then you'll understand why (Christians and Jews) can really rejoice over becoming brothers. . . however terrible the Holocaust was, it has produced a change for the better. It has allowed a new spirit to germinate between Christians and Jews which would scarcely have been thought possible without Popes John XXIII, Paul VI, and John Paul II preparing the way. It also led the Second Vatican Council, after a standstill in the theological view of Judaism since the classical epoch. . . to a great new reappraisal that allows us to view the Jewish faith and therefore the Jews in the spirit of brotherhood.   The Council documentation to 'Nostra Aetate' shows with great clarity that the new conception of the Jews does not spring from political opportunism and pity, but from the religious finding of the Council.

It is a great good fortune, or more correctly, an act of divine providence, that the Jews also see it in this light. . .

Of course two decades will not suffice to wipe out the experiences of one thousand years of Jewish history, and we will have to get used to that, despite all our haste. The more so as in some places amongst us Catholics, the new spirit of the Council is still not blowing very strongly. In any case we must be aware that it is not up to us to determine when it is no longer necessary to speak of *Auschwitz*—that rests with the tortured and the survivors of the Holocaust. And it can only be in our common interest that this point occurs neither in our time nor in that of the next generation. . . ."

We have a lot to learn from one another in order to correct this lack of understanding that has built up through the centuries.

I gave the example in this speech of the Easter Friday accusation of "perfidious Jews" ("Let us also pray for faithless Jews. . ."), which was only abolished at the time of the Second Vatican Council.

I described the following experience: I had a visit from a rabbi, and as he was accustomed to do, he spoke a blessing, but in Hebrew not in English. I asked him what he had said. So he repeated the prayer in English, at which I mentioned that I knew it, it was a Psalm that I also used in prayer and I fetched my little prayer book. We established that it was the same Psalm that the Jews had used from time immemorial as a thanksgiving prayer on the Sabbath. I told the rabbi that we Catholics used this Psalm as part of our Sunday evening prayer, the so-called Compline. And we rejoiced over this common prayer, which had survived down through the ages. It is unbelievable how something in common like that can survive over the centuries, and yet we sit next to one another and don't know anything about each other, and it isn't noticed because we don't talk about it.

It has to be said, in order not to carry out a whitewash exercise for the Deputy Mayor of Linz, that what he wrote came from the type of teaching that still emanated from the Church when he was going to school.

But don't you think that on the basis of this letter the Deputy Mayor had to resign? What is your personal opinion?

It would have been wise if he had gone on his own. I should like to point out that with regard to dismissals, as much between states as in political life, there is not only something tremendously positive there, but also something tremendously dangerous. And that is solidarity! Out of a personal or contractual obligation to someone or to a state, people exercise solidarity and refrain from making the accusations that might be made. We have already experienced that at the international level. . . that is a solidarity that is tremendously valuable for human life but also a tremendous danger at the same time, and that's what happened in the case of Hödl.

Are you saying, Mr.President, that the solidarity for Hödl was bad?

Yes, this solidarity was bad.

"...Go to Palestine..."

Conversation with *Otto G. Klein* on 28 September 1987.

Mr. Klein is a teacher in Graz.

What memories do you have from 1938?

It's well known that the anti-Semitic rioting of the March days in 1938 had their roots in the basic anti-Semitism that had existed in the population for a long time. This can be seen from an occurrence in the period before 1938:

For years we Jewish kids of the Second Graz-Överseegasse High School had had few problems with the non-Jewish children. However, some professors descended to making anti-Semitic joke, at which most of the non-Jewish children laughed obediently.

Our mathematics professor went further. He didn't make jokes, but indulged instead in verbal attacks and nasty, hateful remarks. The Communists were included in these attacks, and he wanted to send them to Moscow. The Jews, in a somewhat more friendly manner, he just wanted to send to Palestine—obviously an indirect sympathizer with the Zionist movement!

Most of the non-Jewish kids laughed, as I mentioned; but his tirades of hate didn't have much success with them—much to the satisfaction of us Jews.

On 13 March 1938 Professor Franz Kabelka left us, or more correctly, he had to leave us. He was an ardent supporter of the Christian Socials and a member of the ultra-Catholic "Vogelsang" organization. He was arrested by the Nazis and sent to Dachau, from which he returned to Graz in 1945.

In his place we had Professor Franz Fauland. He was what we called then an "illegal," but he was a good teacher to us five Jewish kids until the end of the school year in 1938 and never permitted any anti-Semitic remarks. We Jews have a good memory of him.

Incidentally, Professor Kabelka even wanted to send the Austrian Nazis "to Berlin." His whole attitude was "go to Moscow (the Communists), go to Berlin (the Nazis) or go to Palestine (the Jews), we don't need such people here!"

You have told me of your memories of 1938. Certainly more has happened in your life. How do you see the present time, after fifty years?

I don't want to say any more. . . if you honestly want to know what I want: it's to be left in peace.

". . . Tulips are more important than our Ambassador. . ."

Interview with *Teddy Kollek* in April 1989.

From 1965 Teddy Kollek has been Mayor of Jerusalem, the city which is holy to the three monotheistic religions, Judaism, Islam, and Christianity. Kollek was raised in Vienna and is named after Theodor Herzl. Called Teddy by his parents, he now is universally called "Teddy of Jerusalem." Arriving in Palestine in 1935 he helped found a Kibbutz on the eastern shore of the Sea of Galilee. Later he was mobilized to assist in the effort to rescue Jews from the Nazi regime and care for the refugees of World War II. In 1947 he found himself on a secret mission—in the USA and in 1949 he had senior positions in the Israeli Foreign Service, including the Israeli Embassy in Washington. Later he became Director General of Prime Minister Ben-Gurion's office.

Mr. Mayor, how do you view Austria today, after fifty years, reflecting on it as Mayor of the world-famous city of Jerusalem?

To this question you will get a rude reply. I think the Austrians have behaved abominably, and continue to do so. Nothing has improved.

How am I to understand that?

I'll be happy to explain. We have had Youth Delegations here for twenty or thirty years. Many of them come from Germany and they say, "We were not part of what happened then, before and during World War II, yet we feel our responsibility for all those horrible crimes, because we are Germans. We come to Israel and work as volunteers, thus demonstrating that we feel responsible, though many of us were not even born then." We have not yet found such Austrians! They say: "We were conquered by the Germans, and therefore this is none of our business!" The Austrians continue to consider themselves as victims!

Listening to you it sounds as if there is no common ground with Austria?

It depends on what you mean by "common." We have visitors from Austria, we talk to them and find them very agreeable. This is quite normal. It is only when I am asked about Austria, and Vienna specifically, that this reply occurs to me spontaneously.

Did you ever have any connection with Graz?

Yes, there was a professor from Graz who was responsible for the reconstruction of the Austrian Hospice on the Via Dolorosa. This Prof. Sauer of Graz University was unique and did his job very well; we understood each other and naturally I assisted him. But he was one of a sort!! Here one such Youth Group about which I spoke previously could have been of help to all concerned; then we too could send our youngsters to Austria, if they were invited. That would be nice!!

Mrs. Rothschild showed me the Nittel Park. So you must have some good contacts too? I heard of the groups of Israelis which the Israel-Austria society, under Prof. Weissbrot, brought to Austria.

Yes, I know we have had some good cooperation with the Viennese, and I would gladly see it enlarged to the extent of the exchanges with Germany.

Mr. Kollek, it's so long since you were in Vienna last! If you think of Austria now, do you associate it with a special kind of anti-Semitism?

I grew up on Landstrasse-Hauptstrasse, which ends at the statue of Lueger! While it was unpleasant, it never reached the terrible depths of German anti-Semitism.

What is you special wish if you think of Austria?

I wish for Jerusalem to receive many visitors from Austria, so that they could see for themselves how we live, under what conditions, under what dynamism. We often hear that Austrians have absolutely wrong conceptions. . . .

Mr. Mayor, I know you are fascinated by the conception of a peaceful, united, and happy Jerusalem, as a model for co-existence between Jews and Arabs. We have had the Intifada since December 1987. The entire world watches daily the revolt led by women and children in the occupied territories of Judea, Samaria and Gaza. How will all this continue?

It will continue!! But it certainly is not a matter of a few days. We have been waiting for our return for 2000 years, so what significance can 20 years have? In June 1967 the wall that divided Jerusalem into two separate, inimical parts was pulled down and the barbed wire with embrasures disappeared; yet parts of another, invisible wall remained. It too will dissolve, after a certain period of time.

Mr. Kollek, you once compared the city of Jerusalem to an anthill, saying: We the ants, have built the most beautiful anthill that ever existed and hope that no one will ever destroy it with a stick. Should this happen however then there are more ants, who will build it up again.

Has the Intifada seriously interfered with your endeavors?

Jerusalem will remain united, but it will have to overcome many serious difficulties; this is a matter of two hundred, perhaps five hundred years. . . .

The Palestinian revolt started in December 1987 and the occurrences on the Jordan River, in Gaza, in the refugee camps and in the villages have had their impact on the Holy City of David, Christ, and Mohammed. Here too stones were thrown, streets blocked off and shops closed. . .

Look, Jews and Arabs have lived together for hundreds of years; there were always people from different religious groups, from conflicting political and ideological camps. Sometimes things were quite smooth, at other times less so, it is the eternal zigzag.

In your book[1] you describe your romantic meeting with your future wife, Tamar. Also that neighbors had complained that the daughter of a venerable Rabbi had nightly meetings with a young man who looked rather "goy" (gentile). Mr. Mayor, when you think of that time, do you not long for Vienna?

Yes! But I also remember that at the same time I met Tamar, I became aware of anti-Semitism in Vienna. There was that large department store which announced it would not sell to Jews. The position of Jews in Austria grew worse from day to day.

When you think of the years prior to 1938, of the time of your youth in Austria, what do you recall?

I joined the Zionist youth movement when I was eleven years old. I cannot tell now, when I became a convinced Zionist. This was at a time that the Viennese Jewish community had more than 200,000 members, i.e., 10% of the entire population. These were Jews from all parts of the k.u.k. Empire, from Hungary, Poland,

---

[1]Teddy Kollek, *Amos Kollek*, Ein Leben für Jerusalem (Hamburg, 1980-1985).

Moravia, Serbia, Croatia etc. I had left Vienna in 1933 and on my journey to Berlin—Hitler had just assumed power—I felt that the local Zionists feared the worst. . . .

Yet, even without the threat of the Nazis, I felt the desire to go to a country which we could call ours: Palestine. For me, the feeling of being a Jew and part of the Jewish people and its history was something natural, based on deep roots!

Let us return to the present: would you not think it important to reappoint an Israeli ambassador to Austria? Would it not be of mutual benefit to our two countries?

In this connection I must tell you a story, which is perhaps related. When Holland transferred its ambassador away from Tel-Aviv, some Dutch people got together in protest and sent us 100,000 tulip bulbs. They now do it every year! A short while ago, I met the Dutch Foreign Minister here and remarked to him: "Look, naturally we would like to have your ambassador in Jerusalem again, but if you ask me, I have to tell you frankly that people see the flowers much more than they see the ambassador and for the people the tulips are of greater importance than the ambassador!"

". . . We discovered a spy. . ."

Conversation with *Cardinal König* on 24 September 1987.

Franz König, a Cardinal since 1958, was Archbishop of Vienna. A participant in the Second Vatican Council, since 1965 he has been head of the "Secretariat for Non-Believers." He was born in Rabenstein in Lower Austria in 1905. In 1938 he was in Scheibbs am Ötscher (in Lower Austria); he lives today in Vienna.

Cardinal König, where were you in 1938?

In 1938, even in the critical days of the invasion by Hitler and the German *Wehrmacht*, I was curate in a small Lower Austrian town called Scheibbs am Ötscher.

After half a year I went to the cathedral parish of St. Pölten. I experienced those terrible days when Austria was taken over by the Nazis as a simple chaplain in Scheibbs. The parish priest had previously been very close to the Fatherland Front.

What do you think of, looking back to 1938?

In my experience history can be misunderstood and misused. When one looks back to 1938 and 1939, when the synagogues were being burned to the ground, when neighbors were arrested and led off somewhere. . . then people say to me, you kept quiet, you didn't protest, you didn't defend yourself. I can understand these questions very well from the perspective of today. Because today one would protest and appeal. Then it was different. There was the complete terror of the police and the fear of the unknown, which crippled people. Moreover, people were scared that their whole family would be liable if they did anything wrong.

We didn't know that at the time, only later, but relatives and acquaintances—the whole family—could be imprisoned. In my case I was worried that people would be arrested by the *Gestapo* because they had had contact with me—I was responsible for the young people's spiritual problems then. It was no simple matter!

So I repeat, history can be misunderstood.

But my second observation was that history can also be misused. That means using the events of those times as a political weapon with which to defeat others in the present time. And that misuse of history is not right. To misunderstand history is one thing, that's always been with us, but to misuse history for present purposes, that I don't like. That should not be done!

But back to me. I was a simple chaplain much like many other people in this little town of Scheibbs. Before the *Anschluss* I was catechist in the school, and pastor in the hospital; I had to look after people who needed me. I was pastor for the scouts and for old people—yes, I even had to look after the old people's home.

Can you remember the days of the *Anschluss* exactly?

I can remember that on the day of the *Anschluss*, I awoke in the night and saw from my window that the whole side of the street was covered with Hitler flags. . . that was no small shock for me.

I met the priest before Communion and saw how shocked he was. He wasn't certain what would happen.

One had heard many rumors, and at first we didn't believe them. There were reports, but we knew hardly anything at this stage about foreign radio stations. Only much later, in St. Pölten, did we find out that there were regular bulletins from the English BBC. We heard about Hitler's triumphant entry into Vienna, although I neither saw nor experienced it. Hundreds of thousands cheered him. Those are the facts which can't be denied! But there were more—I believe—who stayed at home and cried.

There were about 600,000 unemployed in Austria then, at least according to my information. The situation was sad, I knew, and people hoped: now there'll be a change! Now there'll be something new! Now we'll get work.

And the enthusiasm in the Heldenplatz? What do you think of that now?

Well, my personal view is that thousands of those in the Heldenplatz were really afraid. They didn't really want it, yet they concealed their doubts and thought, "something'll get done with this new guy." They had a bad conscience though.

That's my personal opinion. But I know a few cases where there were people, even those that I saw in Scheibbs, who appeared enthusiastic, who cooperated, so as not to lose their jobs. People who just kept quiet, didn't say anything. . . just waited for it all to be over.

Can you remember autumn 1938 more exactly. Where were you?

When I came as chaplain to St. Pölten, the Bishop told me I should take over parish duties and also scripture lessons at the High School. I did it five or six times, then came an order that religion would no longer be taught in schools—simply forbidden.

But I had made real contact with the pupils and some of them came to me and said: "We must do something! Perhaps we can meet outside of school?" I said yes, and suggested the Cathedral Sacristy.

In this way I had regular classes for the young—my pastoral work, whatever you want to call it. We even took excursions and talked about everything, but the basic theme was the religious instruction that had been banned.

Do you still see people from this time?

Well, last Sunday I did some pastoral work near St. Pölten, and I met a school inspector who was one of the young people who had come to my classes all those years ago. I hadn't seen him for twenty years and he had gray hair, but he still remembered and said, "Those were interesting times and the classes had an influence on me."

I thought to myself, if you'll forgive me, "See, perhaps you did more good back then, than you thought."

Were your students later called up for military service?

Yes, many were drafted.

There was an unspoken agreement that every letter should be written so that anybody could read it, i.e., the *Gestapo*. I had whole sack-loads of mail from the field mail service, and I replied regularly to all of them. After the end of the war, the St. Pölten postwoman came to me and said, "Now everything's over at last, I have something to tell you—I have to unburden myself. I was asked by the *Gestapo* to show them your mail before I handed it to you. So all the mail you received went through the *Gestapo's* censors." I never knew that and I wondered how it could have been possible.

What was your situation?

It was already critical for me in St. Pölten. I was asked periodically to come to the *Gestapo* there for interrogation. They asked me about all kinds of things. I realized immediately that they knew about my meetings with the students and the people who came to me. After the fourth interrogation, they fined me a thousand marks. I didn't have the money and had to borrow it from the bishop. I returned it to him after the war. That was a lot of money in those days.

How did you behave after that?

I didn't let myself be put off. The young people themselves were brave, and they gave me courage.

They said, "Let's have a rally of young people".

I can't remember the exact month, I should think it was in the early summer of 1939. We had a youth vesper in the St. Pölten Cathedral—the cathedral was full! There was terrific enthusiasm, and at the same time we were all scared: my God, what was going to happen? Who would be arrested?

We waited. The *Gestapo* must have been watching everything carefully, as I found out at the next interrogation.

Were there informers?

We discovered a spy among our group. There were about eighty youngsters who met from time to time in small groups but who felt themselves to be part of one great community. It was sort of romantic for them to have to trust one another, run risks, to be different from others, and to have courage!

And it was the first time that the Church found itself in the resistance.

Were you conscripted in the Army?

It was always touch and go whether I'd be called up or not. There were two categories of chaplains, and those at the Cathedral were not usually conscripted. But later I was summoned to the military command, because they found out in Vienna that I could be conscripted after all. I told them that I organized my meetings with the young people in my spare time. "That doesn't interest us," they said, "if you've got time for that, then you've got time for the military."

So then you were conscripted?

No, remarkably I wasn't, but then shortly afterwards I had another summons to the *Gestapo*, this time in Vienna in the Morzinplatz, the *Gestapo* headquarters!

I sat there from seven or eight in the morning to eight at night. Before going into the building I had to fill out a form, and I said to myself, this means a concentration camp!

After that I was interrogated and threatened by several different people at different times, and it was made clear to me that what "I had been doing" would have serious consequences. I was asked for names. . . and I remember how one official suddenly said to me, "You know I'm amazed how cleverly you keep talking your way out of it."

I think that the Holy Ghost must have helped me.

Then I had to wait in a room alone for an hour and then suddenly someone said to me, "You can go home."

Why were you allowed to go home?

Why, I don't know. I think that in 1943 and 1944 resistance among the people was growing and they knew that arresting a priest would not increase public support but would only cause damage.

What was it like in your town then?

Yes, I've gone off the track in the story; to return to the town.

Many people were scared, but few knew anything about the concentration camps. We only found out later when close friends were arrested and reports started to go around describing what it was like in the camps.

Didn't you know about the concentration camps in 1938?

No. In 1938 I hardly believed that anything such as a concentration camp could exist. I knew about arrests and prisons, and that people were being interrogated and beaten. But I didn't know anything about concentration camps in this terrible form. One had heard amazing reports from Germany, of course, but then one heard lots of things in those days.

I would like to show you a passage from a letter signed by Cardinal Innitzer on 18 March 1938, from which it is clear that he voted "yes" to the plebiscite in April 1938. What is your reaction to that?

I had to address this issue in another connection, and I was informed by Dr. Hildegard Holzer, the founder of the Seminar for Women's Religious Careers, that Cardinal Innitzer only signed his name with "Heil Hitler!" because pressure was put on him by a number of Catholic laymen. They wanted him to show that it was necessary to work together at that moment to prevent the worst happening to the Austrian Church. I remember the names of two of the men, although they are no longer alive today.

It wasn't so simple, you know. Cardinal Innitzer was certainly naive, but he genuinely believed at the beginning that an attempt should be made to work with the Nazis. Yes, he was certainly naive, but I don't feel able to judge him. It all changed very fast, as you know. In October of the same year he realized his mistake—Dr. Holzer told me that also, she was there at the time—and he gave a sermon that provoked tremendous enthusiasm in the Cathedral and encouraged the young people to such an extent that it led to one of the greatest manifestations of resistance that ever took place between 1938 and 1945.

What was Cardinal Innitzer's attitude towards Jews?

He was the only one in the interwar period who helped Jewish students defend their rights. As one of the few bishops in the so-called Greater German Reich, he founded the Archbishop's Aid for "non-Aryan" Christians in his own house and thus tried to help Jewish people. For many Jewish citizens this assistance was the last chance to save their lives.

How did they get help?

They got food, medical attention, medicines, and the possibility of emigrating.

It is also well known that Cardinal Innitzer had to hide himself in an attic later, because they wanted to get hold of him. I was told that as he came down from the attic, the first thing he said was, "Thank God, now I'm justified."

Looking back, Cardinal, was 1938 a decisive year for you?

Yes, certainly. I didn't know then what would happen to me, or to Austria. My pastoral work was very difficult. I was very worried about the young people with whom I was in contact and who could get into trouble through that contact.

Were you in Austria before 1938?

I had a scholarship to study in Rome until 1935. So I experienced the Dollfuss years only in the holidays, so to speak. Of course I knew about Hitler's seizure of power in Germany on the basis of very conflicting reports.

Even at this time, of course, there was anti-Semitism in Austria. Later it broke out with a vengeance in the persecution of the Jews. . .

How do you see it all today?

Of course one could have resisted—with the obvious risk to one's own life. But one could not offer an *organized* resistance. From today's perspective, you could accuse me of having done too little, and how could I answer you? I can only keep quiet.

But then I could ask you, would you have had the courage to do more?

What did you feel at this time?

I was shocked by the fear that I felt all around me. I was afraid for my family, for my brother, who had been a professional soldier in the Austrian Army and was then commandeered into the German *Wehrmacht.*

It was a time of insecurity, full of rumors—one didn't know what was true and what wasn't. I remember, above all, that morning when I got up and saw the Hitler flags. . . that's an image I'll never forget.[1]

---

[1]On Sunday, 27 September 1987, Cardinal König spoke on radio and TV with concern about developments in Austria. He said he was ashamed, as an Austrian and a Catholic, to hear arguments employed that after the Holocaust he thought he would never hear again.

He pointed out that fifty years ago, Church circles also shared a portion of guilt for the Holocaust: "Many were guilty. Talk of collective guilt has led to a lot of discussion. Well, there is no collective guilt, but there is a common need to carry the burden and show solidarity in the question of compensation for Holocaust victims. The notion of collective guilt leads to the doubtful argument that a whole people should be condemned, because some—perhaps many—people were personally guilty. There should also be a positive moral dimension: the desire to help others and to offer atonement. The mistake is to say, I excuse myself. Then the relationship is back to front, because one can't excuse oneself—only others can forgive one's guilt.

How are we Christians to behave? We know that the simple forgiving of what has happened doesn't solve the problem. We know that reference to the circumstances of the times doesn't explain everything and doesn't whitewash everything. We know that guilt can only be overcome when it is recognized and when repentance is made for it. We know that it's easy to see enemies everywhere and hard to achieve reconciliation with all its consequences."

Cardinal Franz König, *Autumn Conference of the Austrian Catholic Action in St. Pölten*, 27 September 1987.

"... My hope lies with the young people. .."

Interview with former Chancellor *Bruno Kreisky* on 9 November 1987.

Dr. Kreisky was born in Vienna in 1911. A lawyer, he was imprisoned after the rising by the Social Democrats in February 1934. After the Anschluss, he fled to Sweden. He entered the government after the War and was Foreign Minister from 1959 to 1966, becoming Chairman of the Austrian Social Democratic Party in 1967. After his party's electoral victory in 1970, he became Federal Chancellor and held that office until 1983.

Dr. Kreisky, your memoirs have appeared recently.[1] You speak there of the "warmth of the family," of your mother and your aunt Rosa, whom you saw before that Tuesday after the *Anschluss* when she was arrested.

I have here another book that you'll recognize—the *Totenbuch Theresienstadt: Damit sie nicht vergessen werden.*

You have signed it for me on the page on which there is a photograph of the five Kreisky brothers. Your contribution to the book is very moving.

How many of your family were murdered by the Nazis?

---

[1]Bruno Kreisky, *Zwischen den Zeiten. Erinnerungen aus fünf Jahrzehnten* (Vienna, 1987).

Yes, here on this card you can see my uncles Oskar, Ludwig, Otto, and Rudolf, as well as my father Max.

Otto was deported to Auschwitz on 28 October 1944. He was a noble man whom I liked very much. On 30 October he was sent with Friederike Kreisky and another 1,689 people, after the selection process by the SS doctor, to the gas chamber.

But already two years before that, a cousin of mine, Karl, was transported to the east from Theresienstadt. Not only Karl, but also his entire family were killed along by the Nazis. My Aunt Julie, who was married to Wilhelm Schnürmacher—he's called "Schniermacher" on page 122 of the book—was also killed with her husband. I should tell you that Wilhelm Schnürmacher had been a soldier at the front (in the First World War) and was an invalid, and yet he wasn't spared deportation.

In addition all my mother's brothers were killed, as well as some sisters and cousins. I know that one cousin, Elfi Felix, escaped, but she was driven mad.

What happened to her?

They killed her only child before her eyes. And if you read further in the *Totenbuch Theresienstadt*, you'll see the cruelty with which the Nazis dealt with my family. A list from the *Auschwitz* commandant contains the names of many of my family.

There's my cousin, Dr. Wilhelm Felix, who was only a "half-Jew" and was actually a strict Catholic, but he refused to leave his parents when they were deported to *Theresienstadt*.

Also on the list was my Aunt Grete Felix, who was married to my uncle (a brother of my mother). I remember her as a good and beautiful woman.

And then there were the Fischers, Berta Fischer, the sister of my mother, with her children, and then the Kreiskys I mentioned before, Otto and Friederike, and many more Kreiskys whom I didn't even know about.

Once again I would like to ask you, Dr. Kreisky, how many relatives did you lose through the Nazis?

I know that a report from the small Moravian town of Tre-
bitsch mentions 650. A rough estimate would be over twenty of
my closest family, murdered by the Nazis. But the longer I look
at the names, the more I realize it must have been greater than
that. . . and I have to tell you, I don't really have the strength
any more to complete these statistics of horror.

**There are witnesses for terrible events. Today, in 1988, we all
know what happened fifty years ago—the machinery of extermination. What do you think, Dr. Kreisky, one can do to prevent such a thing from ever happening again?**

There are, of course, thousands of books, some impressive
films and sensitive plays, and yet sometimes I wonder whether
that's enough—I don't think it is. Mass murder still goes on, and
in the last few years it has increased. I ask myself whether the
struggle isn't in vain.

Is there a lack of sympathy on the part of people?

The plain fact is you can only get sympathy and understanding from people when you touch a chord in their own
personal destiny. I've often said that what began in 1938 for the
Austrian Jews very quickly stretched beyond those bounds.

First there were Jews from other European nations, but
eventually not even "Aryans" like the Dutch or the Norwegians
were spared—no one was spared.

The balance at the end was millions of dead, hundred of
thousands missing, armies of homeless refugees moving across
the face of Europe.

**In her book, *Kreiskys grosse Liebe*, Irene Etzendorfer de-
scribes you as a man who has attached less importance to the
Austria of traditional Catholic anti-Semitism and anti-
socialism than to the Austria of international solidarity. And
your strength lies in the ability "to see what you want to see."**

**It is said that you were never revengeful but always con-
vinced of Austria's potential for good. Your commitment and
dedication to this positive Austria is well known.**

However, I would like to ask you how, as a human being who suffered so terribly during the Nazi regime, you could protect somebody in your government like Friedrich Peter?[2] Here is a man who irrefutably served in an SS brigade, responsible for massacring thousands of Russians and Gypsies behind the front in the Soviet Union.

Look, I've known Friedrich Peter for decades. I also know his thoughts.

I can still remember how the whole story began with Simon Wiesenthal, how they said they would soon have all the evidence against him assembled. In the meantime many years have gone by and nothing that was promised has happened. None of the evidence which was talked about then has been presented. And there were many informers among these groups even then. If there was something, they were denounced.

I know Peter from hundreds of conversations. And if anybody has repented the sins he committed as an eighteen-year-old and since become a convinced democrat, then Friedrich Peter has.

Would that be your view even if he had committed those acts?

Look, it would have come out long ago.

Let us assume he did commit them.

Then he was a relatively young man. . . and it's over forty years ago. . . and he has lived the whole time since then as a decent man.

What do you say to the fact that the Austrian head of state —elected by a majority of the Austrian people—has been put on the American "watch list"?

---

[2]Friedrich Peter, an ex-Nazi, former member of the SS, and now a deputy of the Nationalistic Freedom Party was chosen by Kresky to join his government out of sheer design to govern Austria *without* the Conservative People's Party (ÖVP).

When you speak of a majority, I would point out that 70% of the Viennese did not vote for Waldheim. And approximately a quarter of the population lives in Vienna. And 54% of the electorate in the whole of Austria did not vote for him.

I would also add that I supported his application for the United Nations job. It didn't occur to me to check his credentials, although now I admit it would have been useful then to have had a commission go very carefully into Waldheim's past.

All right, Dr. Kreisky, you didn't check his past, but why wasn't this done by the major powers when he was seeking the UN General Secretaryship?

Yes, they are at least partly guilty. After all, they had the documents on Waldheim. I never saw them.

Returning to the "watch list" question, what is your opinion?

Well, to have the Austrian head of state on the American "watch list" is, of course, an intolerable situation.

But whoever believes that the whole thing has been engineered by a few Jews in America is making a serious mistake!!

It is well-known that the Reagan Administration is very pro-ÖVP (the Austrian People's Party). I am of the opinion that this "watch list" decision must be fought, but in America.[3] Someone should invite Waldheim to America to fight against the entry ban. Then it would involve the brightest of the US legal profession and it would be sorted out, although I accept that going to trial would involve considerable risks. . .

Dr. Kreisky, you know about the action of the Austrian Veterans Association. What do you think of this solidarity action in support of Waldheim?

It's anti-democratic! Waldheim should have said immediately, I forbid it! He should really have said something immediately.

---

[3]Kreisky expressed this idea in an address in Vienna on 11 November 1987.

How would you judge the climate in Austria in 1988—fifty years after Hitler's invasion? What is your opinion of Hödl's letter?[4] And what do you think of the latest reawakened anti-Semitism?

I don't think you should do Mr. Hödl the favor of making him into a personality just because of this utterance. First of all it should be pointed out that the man who was crucified was also a Jew. Of course I can see that intellectuals and others demand that he resign. But when you have a certain experience in these things, you know that his resignation would only immortalize his action.

As regards the climate in Austria—it's not good, and I am sad, very sad.

And so far as anti-Semitism in Austria is concerned, there's a photograph of a young man in my book *Zwischen den Zeiten* —for me he's a symbol of the new generation. This is the generation in which I believe.

Anti-Semitism will die out with the older generation, and my hope lies with the young people.

---

[4]See Appendix III

"... I've never come to terms with this loss. .."

Conversations with *Herta Maria von Kubinzky* on 26 August, 21 September, and 29 November 1987.

You come from an anti-Nazi, but nonetheless absolutely conservative family. What do you remember of 1938?

My life changed completely in this year.

My parents and their friends were mainly monarchists. This circle really ceased to exist—through emigration, arrests, and death.

I was just a little girl then, and we were already involved in politics—in anti-Nazi circles and also with Jewish families.

Was this before 1938?

Yes, before 1938 we were involved with monarchists and the Fatherland Front but never with Nazis. So far as the Fatherland Front was concerned, we were for Austrians, whether on the left or the right, but Austrians first and foremost.

I grew up in a time of political unrest and was already concerned about the danger that threatened us. I always presented my views which sometimes led to fierce arguments in the last few years before the *Anschluss*.

I remember particularly the events of July 1934. We were in the Aussee-Ennstal and in Graz. The situation reached crisis proportions—there were demonstrations and riots, which had to be broken up by mounted police with rubber truncheons. I remember the use of the military with cannons and bombs, bayonets and the Spanish Cavalry in the city center—I remember the burning swastikas.

We were very worried as more and more concessions were made to the other side, and I remember the hopes we had for the promised elections, which we assumed would unite all the forces against Nazism. I remember the disappointment when the election was called off, the awful minutes listening to Schuschnigg's last speech, and I remember the tears we shed.

Can you remember the end of Austria?

I have an awful memory of Schuschnigg's departing words. In youthful exuberance I sent him the same evening a registered letter, in which I said that I envied everyone older than myself because he'd had a Fatherland longer. This had repercussions. In April 1938 I was summoned to the Gestapo, where they showed me the letter and tried to force me to admit that I had written it at my father's behest. It was obvious that they wanted to further incriminate my father, who was already under suspicion. However, I kept my father out of it because it really had been my idea. Then there were further interrogations at the Gestapo and they told my parents that a letter like that, from such a young person, deserved a place in the Gestapo museum—secretly I was very proud of that.

What happened to you then?

Then we were persecuted. My father was arrested and so were my uncles Rittmeister Herbert von Hoffinger and Colonel Karl Grebenz. The first one was sent to Buchenwald, and the second was tried for high treason in Vienna. Simply because he was an opponent of the regime. He was the first from this group, as far as I know, who voted against the *Anschluss*. Everyone else was too scared, because we knew that it wasn't a secret ballot.

Do you have any particular memory of Hitler coming to Graz?

Looking back it appears like an almost cheerful event.

We were the only ones in our neighborhood who didn't put flags out when Hitler came to Graz in March 1938. Early the next morning the local block leader woke us up and told us that if we didn't get some flags up right away, we'd be prosecuted. My parents wanted to spend as little as possible on such flags, so we took the Austrian red-white-red flags, which we had in abundance, and cut out the white section. Of course then the flags were so pathetically narrow that the swastikas which were stuck on them didn't suit at all—the hooks on the swastika had to be bent, and in the end we had the most miserable flags in town.

But to return to more serious matters. Our circle of friends changed immediately: some were arrested, our Jewish friends vanished without trace or emigrated—we simply lost sight of them. Our passports were withdrawn, I had difficulty in school, and my father had even more at work.

At least we were fortunate that our servants held the same political views as we, and therefore there was no fear of betrayal at home within our four walls—for example, when we listened to foreign radio broadcasts.

Our bank deposit box was opened by the Gestapo and my parents' gold coins were confiscated.

Who was your father?

My father was a pilot in the First World War: Flying Officer Eugen von Steinner-Goeltl.

Were there Jews in your family?

No. My family was completely "Aryan"—to use that "beautiful" word.

But you still had difficulties?

Yes, we had the greatest difficulties. Our house was searched several times, and in the autumn of 1939 my father was arrested.

Can one say that for you and your family 1938 was the beginning of a sad time?

Sad's not the word—it was an absolutely tragic time!
After the *Anschluss* we were all in danger.
Even our maid's later husband was sent to *Mauthausen* and died there. He was a Social Democrat called Hans Massl.

How did it come to that?

Well, we had to have servants who were completely in agreement with us politically—in other words people who were against the Nazis. Otherwise we would have been betrayed.

What happened then?

In the summer of 1938 I got to know a landowner from Czechoslovakia, and we were married in the autumn of 1939. He was Rudolf Ritter von Kubinzky and half-Jewish on his father's side. His mother was "Aryan" and a Streer von Streeruwitz— actually she was the niece of the Austrian Chancellor Ernst Streer von Streeruwitz.

My husband was "advised" to sell his property for an absolutely ridiculous price. He was actually "insufficiently Jewish" to justify a legal confiscation—in so far as one can speak of legality in this context. Anyway he naturally refused to sell his property. But the SS wanted to settle farmers there because it lay on the border between the Czech and German languages. So they began to persecute him.

He was twice arrested by the Gestapo and the property was administered by a trustee.

What happened to your husband then?

He was arrested for the third time in July 1941 at Ossiacher See and was taken to Karlsbad, to the *Gestapo* there. Then after a few months in the Karlsbad prison he was sent to the concentration camp at *Oranienburg-Sachsenhausen* near Berlin.

But there's something else I should tell you. Before my husband's last arrest, in November 1939, we were expelled from the Sudentenland Gau (district) and neither of us was allowed to return there.

Which date from this time is most painful for you?

25 February 1942, when I received notice that my husband had died. The telegram read: "Dr. Rudolf v. Kubinzky died of broncho-pneumonia. Further details follow. The Commandant."

Does anything else occur to you from this time that you can't forget? Anything that touched you deeply?

Yes, I mustn't forget the tragic story of the Jewish Dicker family. The old Mr. Michael Dicker and his wife Mary and his sister Anna lived in our house. When they left it was very sad indeed—they were very dear friends and neighbors.

But I was much closer to the Latzer family, which was also Jewish. Gerti Latzer, the daughter, was my best friend. Thank God the Latzers were able to leave Graz at the last minute after paying the Reichsfluchtsteuer (Reich Exit Tax). The parents and the son emigrated to Palestine. The daughter spent the war in England. Our friendship has lasted until this day, I'm glad to say.

Can you tell me how your life continued after the arrest?

When my husband was arrested, my son was eleven months old. I wandered about the Great German Reich with a baby on a Traveler's Pass, forbidden to enter either Graz or the Sudetenland.

What was this Traveler's Pass?

It was an identity card for people without fixed address, like actors or even Gypsies.

Actually it was an advantage to have it, because I was obliged to report to the *Gestapo* wherever I went. When I arrived at a new place and reported in, nobody there knew me, and by the time the *Gestapo* got the file on me I was over the hills and far away. It was important for me to protect my anonymity.

How long were you married?

It wasn't even two years. And I can tell you, I had a "dream man" for a husband. He was clever, educated, elegant, prosperous, and very good to me. It was a very happy relationship, but it lasted only two years.

Did you marry again?

No, I never married again.

What happened to your husband's property?

My husband's property was declared to be that of an enemy of the people and the state and was confiscated for the benefit of the German Reich. There were over two thousand hectares of land, a baroque castle, a brewery, a distillery, a brickworks, twelve guesthouses and pubs, a postoffice, a barracks for the gendarmerie, and quarries for basalt and kaolin.

Have you come to terms with your fate?

I must say that in the last forty-seven years I have not been very healthy. There was always something missing. I've never really coped with this tragedy, this loss in my life. And I know that I will never come to terms with it until the day I die.

We had many acquaintances who were in concentration camps, but they survived. The Gorbach family were our friends, and the Stepan family and Colonel Zelburg. All the men were in concentration camps. We kept in touch with the families while they were away.

". . . My encounter has been with assassins of the spirit. . ."

Interview with *Herbert Kuhner*[*] on 11 November, 1987.

In 1938 you were three years old. Do you remember anything that happened at the time?

There was an incident that has remained fresh in my memory. It happened at my grandmother's apartment. The doorbell rang and I ran to the door and opened it. My mother swept me away as two men in street-clothes entered. One of them, I remember clearly, wore a brown suit and limped. They searched the apartment. The brown-suited man pushed my grandmother, who was eighty-three, away from the sideboard in order to ransack it. And indeed it contained her shopping money.

In 1939, when I was four, my parents left Austria with me before the juggernaut could crush us. Other members of my

---

[*]As editor of this book I want to state the following: There are differences of opinion between Harry Kuhner and me. But I want to quote Feliks J. Bister in *Das Menschenrecht*, No. 1, (March 1991), Vienna: "It is often events that may seen 'insignificant' to some which often cause careers and lives to be ruined. It is our obligation to provide a forum for the injured party."

The publication of this interview with Harry Kuhner takes place in this spirit.

family weren't that lucky. They stayed and were crushed. My grandmother had the good fortune to die of a broken heart before a worse fate could befall her.

My family first went to England. We were in London during the Blitz, which I remember very vividly. We left for the United States on one of the last passenger ships. I grew up in New York and New Jersey and received my B.A. at Columbia University.

When did you return to Austria?

I came back to Austria in 1963. Surely I can't be blamed for having been born in Austria, but I must take the blame for returning. Going from New York to Vienna was like going from the frying pan into the fire. When I lived in New York, I thought I'd been uprooted. After I moved to Vienna, I knew I'd been uprooted. When I returned to my birthplace, I was made to feel as if I had never left.

What do you mean by that? It sounds as if not much has changed as far as you're concerned. You're an internationally published writer and translator whose work and papers are archived at Boston University Library. You've translated such prominent authors as Bachmann, Bernhard, Celan and Handke. Since you've been active as a translator for over two decades and have made a major cultural contribution, you must be welcome in Austria.

The welcome mat was a bed of nails and the spikes haven't been dulled by time. They're still as sharp as ever. Although I have translated about 180 Austrian authors and published a dozen collections of Austrian poetry, the doors have remained sealed. In spite of my achievements on behalf of Austrian literature, I have never received a red cent or a grey groschen of support from an Austrian office. I have invariably ended up having to foot the bill myself. As far as my own literary work is concerned, opportunities for exposure have been less than minimal. Apparently the Nuremberg Laws have not been invalidated since the constant pretext for my exclusion is that I am "not Austrian!"

My citizenship is merely a pretext since there is a clause on every application for a stipend or prize in Austria that states that anyone who was a citizen before the *Anschluss* is eligible.

In 1946 my parents abjured their Austrian citizenship and became American citizens. I received my American citizenship through them. According to American and Austrian law, I could maintain dual citizenship, however, I see no reason to apply for something I never gave up.

Since I had spent my early years in boarding schools and had not been tutored in German, English became my primary language. I began to relearn German at the age of fourteen. I have used my bilingual abilities to promulgate Austrian literature internationally, but the rewards have been nothing but punishment. I have been exploited, defrauded and plagiarized as an author and translator and constantly had my name expunged from my literary work, translations, articles, and even from my books.

Things came to a head in 1976 when an invitation to attend a literary festival in Australia to read translations and my own texts was intercepted by an Austrian public official who termed me "an exceedingly weak author who could not represent Austria in any way." After I had published an article on the interception in *Index on Censorship*, I was described by the official in written and oral statements as being mentally unbalanced. Subsequently, I was called into an office where two interrogators attempted to extract a signature from me. Of course I refused, and after two and a half hours, I managed to leave the premises. A file was kept on me, and when I tried to exercise my right to examine it according to Austrian law, I was cynically rebuffed. When I filed suit for libel against the official, the case was barred from court. I then attempted to provoke a suit from the other party by sending an open letter to the senior interrogator. Ten days later, I received an anonymous call threatening me with commitment to a mental institution if I did not drop the case.

But this isn't 1938. I cannot understand you. Austria is now a functioning democracy. Listening to you, one could conclude that there is a certain continuity.

The fact is that since the war neither the Austrian government nor Austrian universities have invited or encouraged emigrés to return. I came back of my own accord. At this juncture, I can only term my return as an act of madness. In a nutshell: I've run the gauntlet up a dead-end street. As far as other emigrés are concerned, let me get up on a soapbox to proclaim: "Fellow emigrés, if my experiences can be used as a gauge, you better stay right where you are!" In contrast there's the case of Major Walter Reder who was the last Nazi war criminal serving a sentence in Italy. When Reder was released in 1985 at the behest of Austrian political luminaries and Church dignitaries, the Austrian Minister of Defence flew to Graz to welcome the "old soldier" back personally. Reder discarded his Austrian citizenship in the thirties before Austria became "Ostmark" in order to embark on an SS career in Nazi Germany. He did not have to apply to regain it. It was handed back to him on a silver platter along with a pension and other benefits. No Jewish emigré can boast of such red carpet treatment.

It there anything else you would like to say in closing?

If they asked me I could write a book. They didn't ask me, but I did anyway. *Der Ausschluss (Memoirs of a 39er)*. One Austrian publisher agreed to take it on with the stipulation that I use my own imprint and canvass for support. Of course I ended up paying the tab—and worse. After I had the audacity to inform him that the translator's name did not appear on the cover of a book of poetry he had published as had been agreed upon, I was told over the phone: "Your behavior is revolting and uncouth. You have a persecution complex." On March 19, 1990, the senior editor wrote: "We hereby cancel *Der Ausschluss* by Herbert Kuhner from our publishing program. All copies are to be returned to the author." And they were.

My encounter has been with assassins of the spirit.

". . . many of our so-called comrades suddenly appeared in the ranks of our enemy. . ."

Conversations with *Heinz Mayer* on 12 November and 1 December 1987.

Heinz Mayer was born in 1917 in Innsbruck and has lived in the city ever since with the exception of a period in prison and in exile. He is President of the Association for Victims of the Struggle for Political Freedom in the Tyrol and Vice President of the Association of Austrian Freedom Fighters.

Did you notice Nazi propaganda in Austria before 1938?

Yes, of course. As early as 1933, when in high school I belonged to the "Young Fatherland" organization, there was Nazi propaganda in our school, and we had to protect ourselves against it. Unfortunately Nazi influence grew steadily, and its tactics became more and more outrageous.

After Kurt Schuschnigg's memorable speech we hoped that there would be a clear decision for Austria. But that was not to be the case, as we soon found out.

What did you do at this time?

It was ever more incomprehensible to me that the Nazis' influence was growing.

I was an official at the time for the Fatherland Front and its defense league, the "Frontmiliz." My Austrian friends and I had to be increasingly careful about the Nazis.

Did you and your friends accept everything?

No. We planned an action against the illegal SA. Then suddenly a large police formation appeared, and we were told to abandon the action on the specific instructions of the Chancellor —or else we'd be arrested. So it was no surprise to us when SS units tried to intimidate the population and strove to prevent the plebiscite being held.

Could you see what was coming?

Yes. I knew how weak the Austrian patriots had become.

There were still students and workers who called for struggle for Austria. And there was still hope that help might come from abroad against the brown aggression. But it didn't.

Our section got smaller and smaller, and we were amazed at how many of our so-called comrades suddenly appeared in the ranks of our enemy. I quickly realized that the brutality that had followed Hitler's seizure of power in Germany would now hit our dear Austria.

What did you do after the invasion of Hitler's troops?

After the invasion I immediately joined the First Tyrol Resistance Group "Freies Österreich," and worked with it against the Nazi occupation.

These resistance fighters were betrayed and arrested. I was imprisoned from October 1938 to April 1939 and then required to work as a construction laborer. Then I had to work in an armaments factory.

But I was still politically active and I was arrested again and put in the *Gestapo* camp in Innsbruck-Reichenau. From there I was sent to *Buchenwald* concentration camp, where I remained until the camp was finally liberated by the inmates. I came home as a complete invalid.

What would have been the result of the plebiscite planned for 13 March, in your opinion?

There is a completely mistaken idea today among the Austrian people that the German invasion was simply a political confirmation of an existing preference in Austria. That is not true! If the plebiscite called by Schuschnigg on Austria's future had been held, the result would definitely have been in favor of continued Austrian independence.

Why didn't the plebiscite take place?

This plebiscite wasn't allowed to take place, because it would have made Hitler's invasion of 17 March look like an act of aggression to the rest of the world.

How was it possible then that a few weeks later Austrians voted as if to indicate that they were happy to be part of Germany?

Mass suggestion—the work of dictators.

Later the economic situation improved and Hitler appeared like a miracle worker.

And then of course the same powers who presided over Austria's creation as a separate state in 1919 now stood by and didn't lift a finger to help defend its independence.

Where were the Austrian patriots?

Austrian patriotism remained amongst individuals, and it manifested itself particularly amongst young people who because of their age had been denied participation in the plebiscite and who were not ready to accept the new situation as some kind of historical inevitability.

For schoolkids and members of the clubs it was incomprehensible that their love for Austria was suddenly wrong, that the idealism of Austrian culture was suddenly worth less than stupid songs about the German heath; about stiff-necked Prussian discipline and bootleather! At the same time these young people were aware of those colleagues and acquaintances who had prepared the way for Hitler with their pamphleteering, bomb-throwing, and machinations, and had now suddenly achieved their goal. Because without the German invasion these people would have remained political criminals.

Did you have further plans?

We realized that it would remain possible through little things to remind people of the fact that even in the Nazi "Ostmark" the love of Austria had not died out.

Pretty soon after the invasion, people started listening to foreign radio broadcasts, believing that there must be powers out there that had not forgotten Austria. The voice of Otto von Habsburg was heard quite soon. There was a station in Strassburg to which we listened.

Young people were just not prepared to accept the *Anschluss* as the final verdict of history. Of course the romantically inclined also saw illegal political activity as a sort of romantic thrill, but it was a thrill that served Austria.

How did you accomplish this political work?

It began with meetings of four or five in someone's apartment. News was exchanged, and there were reports about new "cells" that had been established. There were big arguments about how much people should know about the existence of sabotage groups. I remember I had set up three personal groups in the Tyrol, all of which were ready to do whatever was asked of them, but whose names were known to no one except me. This was an advantage under *Gestapo* interrogation because nobody knew who else was involved.

Bigger meetings took place only outside the city. We had one disguised as a picnic at Maria Waldrest or at Matrei am Brenner. This was a pilgrimage spot about 1,400 meters up in the mountains. It was looked after by the Servite monks and it was a very suitable meeting place. Of course you must remember that most of the young people who belonged to "Freies Österreich" came from Catholic families. They hadn't accepted the appeal of the Austrian bishops to support Hitler. For them a pilgrimage place up in the mountains felt right. We were able to talk about a lot, even if it did not make much sense for us young and inexperienced people to fight a state which was bristling with arms.

Thanks to these discussions it became clear that our goal should be to make underground preparations for the right moment, to be simply armed and ready for when this moment came. We in the first Tyroleon circle of resistance fighters hoped, of course, that we'd get help from abroad, but also we thought something might topple the Nazis from inside. For example, a rebellion by the Prussian General Staff or perhaps a conflict between the SA and the SS.

You were all young lads. Did you have any connections to established politicians, who continued to support Austria?

Yes, there were contacts to older, more experienced politicians who had remained true to Austria and were ready to give us advice.

There was a feeling among us of a "historical calling," which on the one hand gave us strength but on the other hand threatened to give us away as an underground organization. We stuck up posters at night. We had a printing apprentice in our ranks who organized the printing of red-white-red stickers and "Krukenkreuze." We did it in several places around the Tyrol, in Innsbruck, and once even in the Bavarian capital, Munich.

After such nights, red-white-red stickers could be seen all over—on the walls of houses, on trees, and on the doors of certain buildings. The "Krukenkreuze" were strewn around and reminded people hurrying to work the next morning that not everybody had been asleep the previous night.

What sort of people were in the resistance groups?

The "Freiheit Österreich" organization had both arch-conservative boys and girls, and people from the extreme left. I shouldn't forget that it was a Young Communist who tried to uncover a *Gestapo* informer whose job it was to trace the organization's whereabouts. His name was Viktor Karnitschnigg, and he was in seventh grade at the high school. His efforts allowed us to get rid of incriminating material and hide weapons.

You had weapons? How did you get them?

Certainly stockpiling weapons was an important part of our task. We knew enough people from the Austrian organizations who were connected with weapons. And we were able to get some from them. We had a proper weapons store near the city in a barn by a farmhouse—the farmer was a member of our organization. It was a good choice for a weapons cache because there was a pub on the estate which acted as a cover. The estate is still called "Waldhüttl," at that time it was a most extraordinary arsenal of youthful weapons, all protected by Hans Maier, the farmer and publican.

Thanks to the work of Viktor Karnitschnigg, the leading member of the organization, Franz Ortler, was not uncovered as a *Gestapo* spy, and Maier was able to dispose of most the weapons before they were discovered. I personally threw three good rifles into the River Sill, one the day before we were arrested. All the *Gestapo* found were some old rusted bayonets and rifles. Maier tried to explain their existence to the *Gestapo* by the fact that the "Waldhüttl" was very near to Castle Mentlberg, which had been a military hospital during the First World War.

How did you feel about this resistance activity?

Nobody felt they were doing anything illegal. Everybody thought the presence of German troops was illegal!

How did you get arrested?

On 14 October 1938 the *Gestapo* swung into action and there were arrests all over the Tyrol. Then we saw just how wide the organization "Freiheit Österreich" had spread.

Then there was another resistance organization?

Yes, it was called "Vergissmeinnicht" (Forget-Me-Not).

When was this formed?

When the "Freiheit Österreich" members were released by the *Gestapo* after numerous interrogations and five months' imprisonment. Some people escaped and started again immediately.

Using the experience of the *Gestapo* interrogations, we rebuilt a network of intermediaries through the Tyrol, so that nobody knew about anybody else and messages were passed only through "forget-me-not" holders. Whoever had these little natural-looking "forget-me-nots" built up his own local membership. Then in a headquarters known to only a few, every "forget-me-not" was registered with a number according to how many members he had. By having numbers we avoided using names.

Was "Freiheit Österreich" comparable to "Vergissmeinnicht"?

The "Vergissmeinnicht" differed from the "Freiheit Österreich" in that it was non-party and monarchist. This resulted from the fact that Hitler had placed 50,000 marks on the head of Otto von Habsburg. For many loyal Austrians that was a clear indication of the kind of Austria which Hitler feared most.

Because of this sharper image the people in the "Vergissmeinnicht" were not the same as in the "Freiheit Österreich," although it must be said that the latter organization came first.

How long did this organization survive?

Only for three months. In fact one had the impression that the *Gestapo* only released people in March 1939 so that they could watch them and gather more exact information on their activities and possible foreign connections.

"Vergissmeinnicht" sought foreign ties, and actually it brought about the death through betrayal of the son of a well-known Seefeld citizen and former mayor. He fell under a hail of bullets on the Swiss frontier, after having been lured there by henchmen.

In July 1939 the *Gestapo* arrested everyone on the "Vergissmeinnicht" list—or at least everyone they could get hold of—and
for them began the misery of long-term incarceration.

What was your goal?

The re-establishment of a free, democratic Austria with Otto
von Habsburg.

**How do you see the phenonomen of anti-Semitism in the
Tyrol, fifty years after 1938—that fateful year for Austrian
Jews?**

Unfortunately it's an incontestable fact that anti-Semitism
has been very widespread in the Tyrol. And it's still around today although at a more subliminal level. And this is despite the
fact that there were never many Jews here, and today hardly any
at all.

How many Jewish businesses are there in the Tyrol?

There are no more Jewish businesses in the Tyrol and unfortunately almost no young Jews.

What can you tell me about the "Kristallnacht" in 1938?

The Nazis found very fertile soil in the Tyrol. They were
fanatical here and that showed in the pogrom in November 1938.
There were three murders and many people injured, so, considering their numbers in relation to the population at large, the
Jews in the Tyrol had the most to complain about. The *Gauleiter*
of the Tyrol, Franz Hofer, was a particular Jew-hater and he was
able to report to his *Führer* the first *judenrein* (Jew-free) district
in the Reich.

**How do you explain the pronounced anti-Semitism in the
Tyrol?**

I attribute it and the corresponding support for the Nazis to
the fact that the Tyrol bordered on Germany and was used to re-

ceiving a large number of German tourists. When Hitler introduced the 1,000 mark restriction, tourism came practically to a
standstill, with the result that there was a lot of unemployment
and people were driven, so to speak, into the arms of the Nazis.

They thought that only Hitler could save them. The fact that
the Jews were blamed for the situation, only increased anti-
Semitism.

**Did this have anything to do with the case of "Anderl of
Rinn"?**

Certainly. Without doubt the legend of (Jewish) ritual murder
at Judenstein (a village near Innsbruck) contributed to the general
anti-Semitic atmosphere. Before 1938 whole school classes made
pilgrimages to Rinn-Judenstein, where they were told this blood-
thirsty fairy tale by teachers, etc. There was even a play about
"Anderl of Rinn," which always had a good audience.

Unfortunately, it has to be said that the Catholic Church was
not blameless in this affair, and after 1945 it took a lot of effort
to stop these pilgrimages and theater performances. Even the ban
was often ignored without any significant sanctions being taken.
The League of Victims and the Action against Anti-Semitism
needed decades until eventually a Papal Bull stopped the whole
business.

The offending figures were removed from the church, and
the Church's seal no longer appeared on the brochure about the
ritual murder. But the ceiling fresco, which is actually the most
offensive to Jews, could not be removed because there was a
preservation order on it. It's not the Church, but the Department
for the Preservation of Historical Monuments which is responsible for that, and it considers the painting (by Giner) to be
irreplaceable.

Nonetheless the Church hasn't really made a great effort to
forbid the ritual murder legend.

**The Bishop of Innsbruck strongly opposed the worship of
Anderl, did he not?**

Yes, it definitely got better when Reinhold Stecher became
Bishop of Innsbruck. He opposed the Anderl cult without com-

promise, and, of course, in the process made a lot of enemies. But fortunately he stuck to his principles, and it is to be hoped now that we have heard the last of that legend.

How did people react in Judenstein and Rinn?

They rebelled. But that was mainly because they didn't want to lose a "good business," particularly with all those German tourists coming to make a pilgrimage to "St. Anderl."

Of course there was a great fuss about the ban and all the anti-Semites came out of the woodwork, so to speak. For them, nothing is too stupid if it serves to make them more noticeable. All those German *völkisch* sport and singing clubs, which were anti-Semitic and Nazi before 1938, now find modern-day supporters.

We know today that there was a Holocaust, and yet we see no progress—why is that?

Well, the opponents of anti-Semitism in the Tyrol can point to some notable successes, but we are still a long way from getting rid of it entirely.

Do you think there is still a long process of enlightenment necessary before people reject anti-Semitism completely?

Yes, the Tyrol is proud of its great freedom fighter Andreas Hofer, but nobody mentions that the only lawyer who was prepared to defend him—and to do so without payment—was the Jew Basevi.

It would be worthwhile for school classes to visit the Jewish cemetery in Innsbruck. There they would see how many Jews gave their lives for Austria in the First World War! To die for the Fatherland was good enough for the Jews, but the Fatherland still hasn't thanked them. Hitler had Jewish heroes and invalids from the First World War put in concentration camps. Apparently Hitler, who only got the Iron Cross, couldn't stand the thought that Jews, whom he always referred to as cowards and shirkers at the rear, had received higher decorations in the War than he himself.

What should happen in the future?

It's high time that the Austrian people, particularly the politicians, recognized what the Jews have given Austria as artists, scientists, composers, and musicians.

We can only hope that young people have learned from the terrible past. We want to help as witnesses, even if our numbers are getting steadily smaller. But the millions of victims must remind us that anti-Semitism led to the crimes of the Nazis.

When you look back on your life, what stands out?

Well, I lost my entire youth.

My father was a Tyrolean Cavalry officer in the Imperial Guard in the First World War and was wounded and decorated several times, but nonetheless he was gassed in *Auschwitz* in October 1944.

When I returned from the concentration camp I was a complete invalid, I had nowhere to live, I had no relatives, and I had to build myself a new life from scratch. I started a family and now I live happily with my wife and children.

My wife also lost many of her family to the Nazis, because she was just as stupid as I, not to have the right grandparents! What clever people the Nazis must have been, that they looked for "Aryan" grandparents.

I'm just a retired tobacconist and don't have much money, but I'll do anything to ensure that our descendants don't have to endure what we went through.

And I'm optimistic.

If I'm not boring you I'll tell you a story. A few years ago I had a call one evening and was asked, "Do you remember the former SS-Führer so-and-so? I'm the daughter of that man—he was involved in murdering Jews."

She wanted to know if I thought her father was a murderer, to which I had to reply in the affirmative. However I explained to her that we anti-fascists, in contrast to the Nazis, did not make the rest of a person's family liable for his crimes. I agreed to discuss the matter with her and was able to show her documents on her father which were in my possession. I noticed that the daughter did not share her father's political views and had studied the crimes of the Nazis intensively. She works in West Germany as an educator and is very active in the area of Christian-Jewish reconciliation. Today I count her as one of my friends. I think she's exactly the sort of person to explain our terrible past to young people.

You were persecuted. My question to you is: should one talk about these things even with an incurable Nazi? Should one even let him speak?

Yes, absolutely. We mustn't adopt Nazi methods. Even their practice of making the whole family culpable. We must let the "other side" have their say, but not without a commentary. Therefore I think that in your book you should let even incorrigible former Nazis speak, so long as you have suitable qualification accompanying their words.[1]

I was recently asked, "do you believe in six million murdered Jews?" What is your response to such questions?

It should be remembered here that it was not six million people who practiced the Jewish religion, so much as six million people who were arbitrarily categorized as Jews under the Nuremberg Decrees (e.g., Sister Edith Stein).

Of course there is sufficient evidence in the Austrian Resistance Documentation Center to establish the number of Hitler's victims.

What can a good Austrian do in the future to improve respect and credibility for our country abroad? Are we concerned about our image?

I always emphasize that we were liberated in 1945 not in 1955, since the Nazis occupied our country illegally, (albeit without opposition from the powers). Austria's name was stricken

---

[1]*Author's note:* to include such people in this anthology would, in my opinion, counter the intended purpose of the book, which is to make a contribution towards better understanding between Christians and Jews.

from the atlas, and only victory over the Nazi barbarians brought it back. And Austria would do well to make clear—particularly to young people—what the years 1938 to 1945 meant.

And of course it alerts us all when someone like Jörg Haider goes searching for votes with cheap, banal slogans. However, he won't succeed in putting the clock back.

". . . I never got an answer to this agonizing question. . ."

Conversation with *Freda Meissner-Blau* on 23 January 1988.

Freda Meissner-Blau, born in 1927, is a publicist and a leader of the Green Alternative Movement in the Austrian Parliament.

In 1938 you were a little girl. Could it be that you nonetheless recall an impressive experience from that time?

Yes, I remember well what for me was a shattering story from this time. An experience that expresses the whole tragedy of the epoch. But I must explain. I come from a liberal middle-class family. My parents both studied in Prague before the First World War. My mother was actually one of the first women to attend the university then. They studied in the atmosphere of the "Prague Circle" and knew intellectuals and writers like Max Brod, Oskar Baum, Franz Kafka, Franz Werfel, Johannes Urzidil, and others. The writer Urzidil studied with my mother; she and her colleagues called him dear Ouistiti.

In 1931 we moved to Linz, and I spent 1938 in this town too. I remember a day in the spring of 1939, when I returned from school and found my mother in her room, terribly pale and holding a letter.

"The Adlers have killed themselves!"

The Adlers were Jewish friends of my parents from Prague.

They had two daughters who were friends of my sister and me. I was completely shocked: "Eva and Ilse too?" I asked. "Yes, Eva and Ilse too."

"But why!?" was my urgent question. "Because they were Jews" was the incomprehensible answer.

"But why then, why? Why must one kill oneself because one is a Jew?"

I never got an answer to this painful question, which I've carried around with me ever since—as a taboo.

By 1943 I had grasped that "to be a Jew" in the country in which I was growing up meant death.

Ever since then pain and rebellion against what some people do to other people has been part of my life.

". . . it's better that I die because of him, than for him. . . ."

Conversation with *Franziska Motschnik* on 11 December 1987.

Mrs. Motschnik was born in 1902 and is now a pensioner. She has lived all her life in Graz.

What does 1938 mean for you? Has your life changed since this time?

Absolutely!

Why?

At the beginning of 1938 we were unemployed. My husband and I had had no work for years, like many of our friends and neighbors. The years before were politically very difficult for us, because we could see Nazism coming with all its terrible consequences. My husband felt certain that war was coming, and in 1938 the catastrophe hit us. . .

How do you mean?

My husband was already convinced in 1934 that Hitler would overrun Austria and other states too. We were socialists, democrats and real Austrian patriots, and we rejected Nazism completely.

On 13 March I remember we stayed at home in order not to get into any trouble. To be honest I'd talked my husband into staying at home, because it would be clear from our behavior what our political views were, if we went on the streets. We found out from neighbors and newspaper reports how a huge enthusiastic crowd had stormed into the town.

Why do you think the crowds were so excited Mrs. Motschnik?

Most of the people to whom we spoke and who were excited, explained that they saw Hitler's seizure of power as a sign that unemployment would end. That was the only important thing for most people.

You didn't see it in this way? You saw the situation differently?

Yes, indeed. We saw the danger of war from the outset. We knew Hitler would end the unemployment,[1] but we also knew he'd end the peace.

Did you find work then?

Yes. My husband was hired as a welder at the firm of Simmering-Graz Pauker AG, and I was taken on at the Puch works as an employee. Both firms were in armaments and were strictly controlled. This fact forced us to be cautious. Nevertheless, my husband didn't stop his political activities. He was a total opponent of the Hitler regime and wasn't prepared to make the slightest concession towards it.

What did your husband actually do as of 1938?

---

[1]The number of unemployed in Styria who received government support in 1929 was 20,000; in 1933 it was 40,000 and in January 1938 it was exactly 32,887 which amounted to approximately 72% of all unemployed in Austria.

He collected money for the dependents of political prisoners. He did this until 1942, when he and many of his colleagues were arrested. He was arrested on 21 August in our apartment. He never came out of prison and was sentenced to death on 29 June 1943.

On 7 October 1943 he was beheaded.

Did you have a good marriage?

We had an excellent marriage. We had known each other since childhood. I lost my partner in life through this fateful blow, and since then I've lived only for my daughter.

But still I really hope that young people today understand that there were people who out of deep humanitarianism rejected Hitler's criminal regime and even sacrificed their lives in doing so.

How could you carry on living after this tragic event?

My husband spent thirteen months in prison. During this time I was allowed to visited him once every month. On one such visit he told me, "Perhaps I should have been forced to join up, then I would have died on the front for Hitler. Thus, it's better that I die because of him than for him!"

These words have helped to overcome my desperation through the long years since he died, although I'll never get over it completely.

". . . now 'another wind was blowing'. . ."

Conversation with *Gerda Ortens* on 22 April, 2 May, 30 October, 13 and 26 November 1987.

Gerda Ortens was born in Graz in 1908. She is a writer, actress, and musician, and holds the Silver Medal of Honor of the City of Graz for special services to culture.

Was the year of 1938 decisive in your life?

Indeed! From this point onwards my life was turned upside down!

Why?

You must understand, I had a very harmonious upbringing as an only child in a Catholic family. My parents were both artistically gifted. My mother taught the zither and guitar, while my father was for many years the stage decorator at the Graz Theater. After he retired he worked as an usher in the cinema.

Were your parents very religious?

Yes, certainly. I have to tell you about my father and his family so that you'll understand what came after 1938.

My father was an outsider in a good Jewish family.

As a little boy he had a beautiful singing voice and sang in the Leopoldskirchner Boys' Choir. And it was there that the spark of Catholicism took hold in him. Even when he was still learning his trade as a decorator, he no longer lived within the family tradition. In 1901 he was posted to the Deutschmeister in Bosnia (a prestigious regiment), and when he was twenty-one he converted to Catholicism, although he couldn't reveal the fact until he returned to Austria in 1903. He distanced himself from his family, and when in 1906 he married a Christian—from a cloister no less—the break with his family was practically complete.

You can hardly imagine a greater difference. My mother was a country girl, brought up in a convent, but an early victim to burning musical ambition. She joined a traveling troupe, the Luigi Family, when she was barely sixteen years old. They had her as a singing "boy" and zither player. She was on tour when my father saw her in Graz and said to himself, "It's either her or nobody!"

Of course, there were difficulties. The young child was under the protection of a "watch dog," Father Luigi, and he only got to know her through her parents (her father was a smith). My father even made a pilgrimage to Mariazell to prove his credibility. But only the mother's ultimatum to the girl, "Either you get married or you go into service!" brought her to the altar.

There followed thirty wonderful years of marriage—the golden years of my childhood and youth—finally broken with rude abruptness in 1938.

Why, what happened then?

My parents' marriage was declared "void." Despite his baptism, my devoted father was still a Jew, according to the Nuremberg Decrees, and to save my mother, he sacrificed himself and separated from her.

It was thereby possible for her to continue her life without fear or difficulty. She was a music teacher and part owner of a house, and she would have lost everything if they'd carried on together, and she would not have been able to stand that. She took her maiden name Selko, while I changed my name and that of my child to Ortens.

My parents continued to meet in secret at Semmering and also in Vienna, where I lived with my father. Through the organization Gildemeester, I got a "Mischlingwohnung" (apartment for people of mixed race) and acted as housekeeper for my father.

So your father was a Jew?

Yes, of course!

Why are you so hesitant when I ask whether your father was a Jew?

I experienced so much discrimination in Graz—the "city of the people's revolution"—between 1938 and 1945, that I only have to hear the word Jew to feel all the old fear.[1]

You'll learn more when I read you extracts from my diary.

Before you tell me about 1938, could you tell me something about the fate of your father's family?

My father, Arthur Ornstein, was born in Vienna in 1878. He was the oldest of eight children of Jewish parents, whose fore-fathers had come to Vienna from Moravia, where their family tree stretched back to the Middle Ages.

They were from the middle class and had jobs to match. His nearest sister Elsa married the editor of the Vienna *Volksblatt*, Max Sonnenschein, whose son emigrated to Israel in 1948 and who now works in a famous museum there (Ohel Sarah). His brother Heinrich was the Honorary Consul in Baghdad and mar-ried a Christian, which didn't please his family. His second sister

---

[1]The Austrian province of Styria was a Nazi stronghold long before the *Anschluss*, evoking the jealousy of illegal Nazis in other parts of the country. A very large proportion of municipal officials in the capital of Graz were Nazi supporters, as were students and faculty alike at the University of Graz. The Styrian party also had strong support in the local army garrison and amongst the police. Local Nazis were actually negotiating with the federal government over National Socialist participation in the provincial cabinet on 8 March 1938, i.e., before the *Anschluss*. In its wake, a few weeks later, Hitler visited the Styrian capital and named it "City of the People's Revo-lution" (Stadt der Volkserhebung). Bruce F. Pauley, *Hitler and the Forgotten Nazis: A History of Austrian National Socialism* (Chapel Hill, NC., 1981), p. 202-205.

Clara didn't marry and ran a kindergarten, and another sister Rosl was a bank clerk until she married Oskar Deutsch.

The youngest son Jacques Ornstein was an engineer and one of the pioneers in Palestine. He helped reclaim parts of Tel-Aviv from the sea and build the railroad along the coast. He lived later with his family in Jaffa, although they all grew up in Vienna before they followed their father to Palestine. He had twins Diti-Susi and David, who had a dance school until recently. David was in the Hagana and later a senior officer in the Israeli police force. They all live today in Tel-Aviv and Haifa.

The baby of the family, Lily Ornstein, got the biggest bite of the cake of life. She married a doctor, Siegfried Diamant, an internist, and she had two sons. They moved to Agram (Zagreb), where Uncle Siegfried had a very popular country practice. The older son, Hans, followed in his father's footsteps and is now the official doctor at the Oberlaa health resort. The younger son, Robert, went to England, studied and was sent as an education-alist to the Gold Coast (Ghana). He got very sick there and had to return to England. He married a teacher and was a professor until his death at the University of Birmingham, where he set up a chair for the study of colonial problems. I visited Bobby in Nottingham in 1949. He was still studying then.

In 1965 I went to Israel to see all the cousins and was most impressed with the development of the country.

Now you've told me of your family's history, I'm very keen to know what happened to you after 1938. You kept diaries— do you still have them?

Yes. Every one of my diaries has its own title, and this one is called "Upheaval." It begins with the motto:

"Nun komm, du Schicksal, um dich zu erfüllen,
   denn siehe, jetzt ist deine Zeit!
Ich kann dich nicht erzwingen mit dem Willen—
   doch warte ich—und bin bereit!"

(Come Fate, take your fill, You see your time has come!
I can't beat you with my will—but I'm ready and waiting!)

When did you start this diary?

On 4 April 1937. It was an omen!

How do you mean?

The coming events already cast their shadows in front of them. Even on 7 April 1937 I was thinking of suicide. I was very unhappy about the spread of rumors of discrimination against me.

What discrimination do you mean?

It's not clear from my diary, but it was about my Jewishness.

I shall begin with 12 March 1938—it was a Saturday. Chancellor Schuschnigg has resigned! Graz has been Nazi since yesterday!

Before that there had been three days of unrest and indignation at the government and its action. Practically every hour there was a new slogan, and things looked as if they would get out of hand and dangerous. Within three days a public opinion poll was announced by the Federal Chancellor, which produced blazing opposition from the Austrian nationalists. Soldiers from Vienna occupied the streets, machine-guns appeared, secret orders from the Communists were passed on—hence the weapons— excitement mounted, and there were repeated requests to vote.

And then suddenly like a bomb exploding came the news: Schuschnigg had resigned!!! There was terrific rejoicing at this news, and a torchlight parade was formed in Graz with 60-70,000 people, not counting the crowds who watched. Everybody was shouting "Heil Hitler!" and "Sieg Heil!" and waving swastika flags. The procession went on until three in the morning, while there were new announcements on the radio every hour concerning changes in the government. Everything changed— Seyss-Inquart became the Chancellor and Kaspar the mayor of Graz.

Whole troops of "BDM" girls went by singing,[2] the whole town was on its feet and lining the streets to receive the German troops with flowers and flags. All the shops were closed.

It was a beautiful day, but there was an ice-cold wind blowing—symbolic perhaps of the fact that now "another wind was blowing"! For me it was too cold and unpleasant among the crowds on the street.

And what was it like a couple of weeks later?

My diary entry for Sunday, 27 March 1938 was as follows: Everything looks different—if only I felt different!

Rolf (second name undisclosed), with whom I was once able to have a sensible discussion on politics, has suddenly become a determined and completely one-sided Nazi. He plays the same tune as everyone now, and won't recognize anyone else as a human being if they aren't like him.

There is already a lot of injustice. Jews and Jewish businesses are barred to customers. You aren't allowed to shop there anymore. It doesn't matter whether the man was a respectable retailer or a cheat, they are treated the same. It must feel like being bricked-up alive! Aren't they human beings too? Is there a different blood flowing in their veins, a blood that's worse than others? Don't they have just the same qualities? Loyalty to family, intelligence, acumen, ambition, perseverance, adaptablity, agility—aren't those merits in a people?

Austria's history for centuries has been full of the mixing of races. The Mongols, the French, the Slavs and the Jews—they've all made their contribution to the highly cultured Austrian, to his lively spirit, his self-appeasement, to his desire to experience novelty, to his love of music, and to his constant dissatisfaction and grumbling.

And even if the Austrians are forcefully annexed and brought into line with the Germans, the mentality of our people will never be so self-satisfied as theirs. The Germans accept everything as serene vegetables.

"That's how we live, that's how we live every day!"

---

[2]The Bund Deutscher Mädchen [BDM] was the section of the Hitler Youth for girls.

Politics? That's what the "Führer" does.

Art? That's what the nation agrees on.

Music? Yes, but only if it makes a terrific noise!

Reading? Recommended literature on the nation.

Thinking? You mean how this hangs together with that? God Forbid! The "Führer" does that as well.

But what is the "Führer" aiming at with his absolute racial purity? The only thing that leads to is inbreeding! What will be the result? A strong, physically well-developed, victorious and united people, a colossal Reich, a pure community according to Plan ABC:

A is for the worker,

B are the leaders and

C are the intellectuals—and no longer accepted as fully valid.

So you'll get an overbreeding of physical power at the cost of brain power. Then the people won't need to think! The less the people think, the easier it is to lead them! And now dear Austrians—to go with them, is to hang with them!

When our people awake from their daydream, we'll be part of them, swallowed up like a grain of dark blue color in a black cloth. Austria may be rejoicing with the German Reich now, but will it still be rejoicing when Austrians try to live with the Germans? Our children will find out.

I'm afraid I'm too much of a cosmopolitan to have any understanding for such a single-minded view of the world.

And what happened the following day?

Monday, 28 March 1938:

There are SS men in front of every Jewish business, telling everyone that an "Aryan" would lose the right to wear the swastika if he shopped there!

I was so upset my knees were shaking. I met Hans and his wife, and they shared my opinion.

But then I met Rolf and I went on with him further. He found it strange that we hadn't got upset over those who had been hungry and imprisoned when the *Volksfront* was still in power. Well, we did get upset when we found out about it, but those people had been fighting for ideas and goals, whereas these people (the Jews) were completely innocent and were now being

publicly branded. Are you going to let those with dirty hands be
pilloried, while honest and respectable businessmen starve, simply
because they have different blood? That's terror, isn't it? Is that
the culture, the justice about which they are writing every day!?

Unfortunately, all this occurred to me later, at the time I was
so angry I couldn't speak. Rolf acted as if he himself had
suffered, but never mentioned that he had eaten "Jewish bread"
for eleven years! Ugh!!!

**You have told me of your first impressions of the March Days,
what happened later? What was your attitude?**

Hitler's personality left one with the impression of a pied-
piper—just how strong, is clear from my diary. Sunday 3 April
1938:

The "Führer" came to Graz!

Adolf Hitler spoke to the people in our town today. It was
a great day for the whole of Styria, an incomparable event for
the people of our capital. During his speech we even cried now
and again. And I felt I belonged to this German "Volk" that
Hitler spoke of. He spoke of the decent people whose hearts belonged to Germany!!!

And we felt German—the whole family! Even if a few paragraphs in the law exclude Father; his heart is German and his
feelings too!! How he suffers from his "non-Aryan" birth. How
Mother is concerned that she might cause offence, because of
course she's pure "Ayran" to the tips of her toes. Only I'm not
bothered anymore, since I read the Nuremberg Decrees and found
out that I could call myself an "Aryan."

So even you were captured by Hitler?

No, no. That was just a passing euphoria. Pretty soon
afterwards my eyes were opened.

Let's continue with your diary entries.

Thursday, 25 May 1938:
The persecution of the Jews is increasing and assuming a
terrible form, although it's rejected by most law-abiding citizens.

They want to destroy my boss (Müller) any way they can. First they tried to get him through the employee legislation, then they used me as a pretext, and now all "non-Aryan" suppliers are withheld until he gives in. They don't seem to realize that they will have to look after twenty employees, if they close his Aryan undertaking down.

Sunday 29 May 1938:

I need have no fears at the moment so far as my business is concerned and if the worst comes to the worst, I'll always find a job. I'm not scared by all this hatred of the Jews—everyone is responsible for his own fate!

And in June?

Tuesday 14 June 1938:

We've just had the first "Strength through Joy" picnic. Mr. Müller invited the whole staff, who have now joined the DAF (the single Nazi trade union), to his vineyard. It was fun, I didn't drink anything, but I played the violin, danced, and recited jolly poems (from my artistic period).

Did you experience personal discrimination?

Of course. I was fired!

After "very important people" started to refer to me as the "Jewish manageress," my dismissal was inevitable. On 3 July 1938 I was fired. But then a prominent person declared that "in my case the racial question really wasn't so bad"—my child was born to an Aryan, and moreover there was my appearance (not very Jewish) and the reputation of my family. The dismissal notice was withdrawn, but I was demoted from manageress to an ordinary employee. I was told, however, that the "racial question" had no bearing on my rights of employment, so long as I didn't want to supervise those who were 100% Aryan. Otherwise I enjoyed all the rights of the DAF.

However, all our worries were not over. Father lost his job in July 1938, although actually everybody had been dismissed, and there was no more cinema in the Schauspielhaus after September (Father was at the ticket office).

I was able to arrange for him to stay at least until the end of July. At the same time I lost my job with Müller Fashions and started a desperate search for a new position, at least so that I could look after my child, whose father didn't pay anything. The financial situation was very hard—a real crisis.

I decided to tell them about my "birth defect" when I applied for jobs, so as not to have to endure any unpleasantness later. That made the whole thing fraught with difficulty. Wherever I was successful on a personal level, I failed as soon as I told them about my "situation." Particularly where the firm had anything to do with armaments, e.g., at Siemens.

How do you remember the rest of 1938?

I describe the events to the end of 1938 in my diary.

Sunday 11 September 1938:

. . . test with Auto-Union turned out all right, but he was afraid of what the people would say after he opens. I could take the job after clearing it with the *Gestapo*—of course for less pay.

This job ended in disaster too—it even went to court with a marvelous result for me: he had to pay me all the notice time that I should have received before I left. Trixner, complete with golden swastika was condemned. Incidentally, he even gave my father a job as a decorator, although he knew that he was a Jew (he didn't have to wear a Star of David—it was a borderline case). I had to work in a back room, so that people passing by didn't see me through the window in the showroom with the automobiles!!

After the break there I got another job immediately with the transport firm Kloiber, Riedl und Schrott.[3] Dr. Sturminger, who first gave me a chance in 1934, has been a friend ever since and has always given me a helping hand.

Wednesday, 30 November 1938.

Today something extraordinary happened!

Father and I were summoned to the *Gestapo*. Father because he was a Jew, and I just for decoration! We found ourselves standing before a twenty-year-old youth, who said by way of

---

[3]NOTE: the mother of Baroness Kubinzky was writer and dramatist Sylvia Kloiber. Her daughter, Herta-Maria, attended the Anderl-Rogge Institute with Gerda Ortens until 1937.

introduction, "So, ain't you disappeared yet?"

A wave of anger swept over me, and I said sarcastically, "Charming!"

To this the youth replied that I'd better not "put on airs" or "they would have to see about us."

I told him that I was in the DAF and that he had no right to talk to me like that. Then he accused my father of having made no provision for his departure (for which of course he had had no need!!), and finally he threatened to send him to *Dachau*.

"Please," my father said quietly.

"Then you'll get fed for nothing!" he continued.

"I can work," said my father without getting emotional, "I'm a trained decorator."

To this the green-clad youth said, "You have to be out of Graz by 15 December—and that don't mean go to Vienna, submerge there, and do nothing!"

"What rudeness!" I hissed angrily.

"Ya don't have to get so upset," he warned me.

"This is a government office, is it not?" I replied, "And in government offices one can at least expect to be treated with a minimum of courtesy."

Then he offered us a chair and said in a somewhat apologetic tone, "We've become used to speaking like that, otherwise you never get anywhere!"

Then he put a sheet of paper in a typewriter in connection with the threat about *Dachau*. However, he seemed to have second thoughts and got another typewriter out and said that it would take half an hour. Father gave him his registration card and told him that he was only here for a visit to put everything in order, and that he'd be leaving this week. That seemed to satisfy the boy and present him with a welcome solution to the problem of what to do with a Jew who'd been a Roman Catholic since 1903 and never done a thing wrong in his life.

He stood up and said as if in inspiration, "I'll give you some good advice, get to Vienna as quickly as you can. It'll be better for you there than here! But we'll come and check!"

"And me?" I asked, "what did you ask me here for?"

"For nothing!" was the informative reply.

After that we left. I was in tears, because I was so disgusted with the manners of these *Kulturmenschen*. Words fail me if I have to make a commentary on the whole sordid affair.

But my father was badly upset. Although he showed admirable self-control, I saw how his lips were trembling and how much it took for him to hold back the tears. It's awful—a spiritual torture that can never be made up for. My poor, poor father!

At the same time Mother applied to the court for the dissolution of their marriage! She's also completely broken and it's horrible to see how one person suffers for another. Father has to leave so that Mother can carry on living. Mother suffers unspeakably when she imagines what will happen to her husband staying with his siblings. And the separation from him is absolutely incomprehensible. It's terrible. . .

In December I received a letter from the DAF with the reasons for my dismissal from Trixner, who claimed that my father did repairs in the local pub! What a swine! He'd said himself he didn't mind—it was just because of the employees. . . and now he uses it as grounds for dismissal without notice.

Daddy misses us very much, he writes. He misses the domesticity of home life.

That was the end of 1938.

And how do you see it all now, fifty years later?

Just talking to you has broken through the barrier of admitting to my Jewish ancestry. The fact that, with God's help, my father was rescued from deportation, that allows me to forgive.

As an "Aryan daughter of mixed race," I was given an apartment with my father and in the next room was a Jewish mother with a little girl who had an "Aryan" father (complicated).

Nevertheless the end was terrible: on the day the Russians arrived, 8 April 1945, my father was hit by a bullet from a concealed Nazi machine-gun nest and he died.

No more terrible things in 1987, in my eightieth year—surely nothing more can happen to me because of my Jewishness—or can it?

"... Certainly everything was for the *Anschluss*. . ."

Conversations with *Rudolf Pieber* on 25 August, 2 and 3 December 1987.

Rudolf Pieber is the General Director of the Styria Sparkasse Bank in Graz. He was born in 1930 and spent 1938 in St. Stephan bei Stainz. He lives today in Graz.

What do you think of when you hear the words 1938? What do you associate with this time?

I was born in 1930, so in 1938 I was just an eight-year-old boy. Of course I can remember the time around 13 March, but I don't know if my memories are of much relevance. Still, three things occur to me.

Firstly, the old farmers in St. Stephan bei Stainz said that if the Germans came, that meant war. Secondly, the Jewish shoemaker disappeared. He was a bachelor. It was whispered that he'd been sent to a camp, but no one knew for certain. And thirdly, suddenly it was important to have proof of "Aryan" identity.

Those are things that occur to me when I hear 1938.

Were people for the *Anschluss* then, in your opinion?

Yes. Everybody was. The statistics show it quite clearly. It appeared to be the only way out of a very difficult economic situation. People were terribly poor then. It had to get better, people thought; more than that they didn't care.

Do you think there is anti-Semitism again after fifty years? Here in the town of Graz?

Not specific anti-Semitism. There is prejudice against the gypsies and against Yugoslavs and other Slavic people. It's just that anti-Semitism is one of the most generalized and exaggerated racial prejudices of all time.

Do you know the magazine *ENTSCHLUSS*? It deals with questions of belief. In the July edition Cardinal König wrote an article on the Christian roots of anti-Semitism. What do you think about it?

Well, I can't say much because I haven't read the magazine. I don't believe anti-Semitism is any stronger today than it was two years ago.

I think that on account of the clumsy remarks and accusations by the World Jewish Congress against our President, emotions have run high—and in an artificial way that would not otherwise have happened.

One has to differentiate. Anti-Semitism is never justified, I want to make that clear. But I would also like to be able to speak freely and not be judged an anti-Semite, if I say, for example, that I didn't like the performance of Mr. Tabori in Salzburg's Kollegienkirche. Of course, I don't say, "What awful things the Jews are performing," but make it clear that it is specifically the *performance of Mr. Tabori* that I don't like— which is unconnected with the fact that he's Jewish. I believe that if I make that clear, I'm justified in expressing my opinion. You can't live by the notion that the Jews are now somehow sacrosanct and that nothing negative may be said about one or the other individual Jew. And then I know that sensible Jews don't even want that, because it would be phony philo-Semitism.

I belong to a different generation from that of my father, which was characterized by a dyed-in-the-wool and unconditional anti-Semitism. I've often asked myself how things could be so oversimplified? On the one side intellectual brilliance, on the other side narrow-minded anti-Semitism.

I've always rejected generalizations like the one that says that Jews have it easier getting into certain positions simply because they are Jews. In my view individuals occupy high positions in society because they have the talent and capability. Frankly, I think the Jews are very capable and hard-working people and that is the reason they reach good positions, and the reason they've provoked envy around them. I'm just against the way the whole subject is focused on today.

How do you mean?

Well, at the moment there seems to be only two problems in the world, doesn't there? Anti-Semitism and AIDS!

Don't misunderstand me, I don't wish to trivialize the problem, but I don't like to see it exaggerated either.

What do you think of the letter of the Linz Deputy Mayor, Mr. Hödl, who claims that Bronfman's views on Waldheim are the same as those of "the Jews in Jerusalem, 2,000 years ago, who allowed the death of Jesus Christ. . ."?

I wouldn't find it so bad if he'd confined his attack to Bronfman himself instead of attacking Jews generally.

Another thing I don't like is the younger generation sitting in judgment of older people, who allowed themselves to be conscripted to the *Wehrmacht* instead of opting for some sort of non-military service. Thirty-five-year-olds suddenly want to establish the meaning of humanitarianism and seek to establish how one should have behaved "if one had been Waldheim." I don't like that at all. They have absolutely no idea what it was like then. They were still in diapers. So were Messrs. Bronfman, Singer, & Co.

Don't you think that the Hödl letter is a serious example of Christian anti-Semitism? Didn't this religious anti-Semitism blend in with Hitler's racial anti-Semitism?

Yes, of course, terrible crimes were committed. Rosenberg's racial ideology was primitive and the most hideous form of anti-Semitism. And the Nuremberg Decrees were diabolical. Yes, of course you're right, there's no doubt about it.

Why do you think there is still anti-Semitism, fifty years after Auschwitz?

I think there are two causes. The basic cause has nothing to do with Christianity, because there was anti-Semitism even before Christ. I don't know why.[1]

The second reason was perhaps because the Jews had "their religion" and "their upbringing," and because of that they were very capable people with a strong sense of solidarity. And just like every capable person arouses envy on the part of the less capable, so did the Jews. It seems to be the law of life: capable people provoke envy. This envy is certainly a root of anti-Semitism.[2]

In March 1941 Archbishop Gröber of Freiburg wrote a pastoral letter of some length and the most appalling anti-Semitic content at a time when Jews were being deported in cattle-cars to Auschwitz. It was his Easter message to German Christians.

What do you think of it, and how is it to be seen in the light of more contemporary developments like the Second Vatican Council?

As a Christian who feels bound to the Catholic Church, I can only say, terrible, awful, terrible. . . it makes one think, I agree with you.

---

[1] See Henryk M. Broder, *Der ewige Antisemit. Über Sinn und Funktion eines beständigen Gefühls* (Frankfurt, 1986), p. 29.

[2] See Alex Bein, *Die Judenfrage: Biographie eines Weltproblems* (Stuttgart, 1980), Vol. 2, p. 209.

According to the new **Suffragan Bishop Krenn**, the Church has to "find its way back," it must be "political" again.[3]
What do you think of that?

Yes, I agree with you completely. That would be a step backwards, which one can't accept!

Cardinal König, with whom I have also conducted an interview, said recently that the Church must also bear a part of the guilt for allowing virulent anti-Semitism to spread. He also said that in the final analysis there was too little resistance to the Nazi terror against the Jews.
What is your response to the Cardinal?
Those are the words of a wise man. Let's hope they weren't spoken in vain. . . they should reach the hearts of the people.

What would you like to say in conclusion?

Well, I can only say that we must ensure that it never comes to another 1938, with all its terrible consequences. And for that it's important that we know our history and that we accept our past instead of trying to suppress it. And that we reject generalizations of all kinds, because they are always unjust!

---

[3]Roland Machatschke in conversation with Bishop Kurt Krenn on the *Mittagsjournal* on 22 August 1987.

". . . Many investigations. . ."

Correspondence with *Otto Pollak* during December 1987.

Dr. Pollak, a physician, was born in 1915. He spent 1938 in Graz and lives today in Tel-Aviv.

You come from an old Austrian family and yet live today in Israel, how did that come about?

It's only today that I understand how the traumatic events of the 1930s put me in a sort of state of shock. Moreover, I think I wanted to suppress everything that I experienced into my subconscious. My memories of that period are now rather sketchy, so I can't give you a complete report, although I returned to Graz in 1948 for four years to finish my studies. I also came back a couple of other times to see friends and visit the graves of my parents, and to erect a memorial to those of my family who died in concentration camps.

My grandfather Leopold Pollak came from Güssing and was one of the first Jews allowed to take up permanent residence in Graz. My father, Counsellor Gustav Pollak was an engineer with the Postal Service in Graz. He was a major in the First World War, in Galicia and on the Isonzo front. He collected a lot of decorations: the Order of Franz-Josef, the Golden Bravery Medal, and the Medal of Honor of the Austrian Republic, in recognition of the building of the new "Tele-Dion" on the Marburg Quay in Graz.

Was there anti-Semitism before 1938?

The climate in Graz even before 1938 was not very pleasant. Particularly when one met people one didn't know. My father was known in the town. Thanks to his popularity and his comrades from the War, my sister and I were not seriously confronted with anti-Semitism before the *Anschluss*.

That changed completely! Thanks to his war record my father was one of the last Jews to be expelled from Graz. However, despite all his protection he had to leave his home and take a room in a "shared apartment"! I was already in Palestine.

In Vienna and *Theresienstadt* his condition got worse and we didn't know what was going to happen to him. In November 1942 my father died in *Theresienstadt*.[1]

My mother was left behind. I don't know the details, but in May 1944 my mother was deported to *Auschwitz*.

My school friends disappeared overnight after the *Anschluss*, and only a few remained loyal. Of course, they were scared of any contact with me because of the swastikas and abusive graffiti daubed on the walls of our house. As I told you, our house was confiscated, and my parents had to move to a room in Eggenberg.

My father's three sisters were also deported. My sister's parents-in-law had to clear out of their apartment overnight. Their furniture was simply thrown out of the window.

My mother's family lived in Yugoslavia, and so they were spared the immediate consequences of the persecution.

What was the day of the *Anschluss* like?

I can hardly remember the day of the *Anschluss*, just Schuschnigg's farewell speech. None of us could grasp that our dear Austria didn't exist anymore. Our whole world seemed to have collapsed. Above all, my father simply couldn't understand what had happened. We were pretty naive and believed that the Western Powers would protest and intervene.

---

[1]Mary Steinhauser & Dokumentationsarchiv des österreichischen Widerstandes, *Totenbuch Theresienstadt—Damit sie nicht vergessen werden*, p. 104.

On 21 March 1938 I was taken into "protective custody." My brother-in-law was caught as he was leaving Vienna and sent to *Dachau.*

I lost contact with my parents—even my father's friends couldn't help since in the meantime they were all put out of harm's way.

I was forbidden entry to all kinds of clubs and associations for students and for singing, etc. Professor Löwi was accused of having a radio in the cellar tuned to Russia!! One heard on the radio that communist cells had been uncovered!

After three months in prison I was released from the Paulustor, released under the conditon that I report to the police two or three times a week and emigrate within three months. I had to sign a written statement that I'd been well treated—the rest I've forgotten.

How did you finally get to Tel-Aviv?

At first I tried to get through Yugoslavia and Italy to Cyprus, but I wasn't allowed to stay in any of those countries and had to return to Graz! Later I succeeded in getting on an "illegal transport to Palestine" down the Danube from Vienna. I reached Palestine with ten Reichsmarks in my pocket and ten kilograms in my rucksack. To pay for my expenses on the trip, my parents had to sell the carpets.

Later I heard they had to sell everything else for "reduced" prices. We heard of all kinds of excesses against the Jews in Graz, but we just didn't want to believe them—we just couldn't accept that people were capable of doing such things. We were so naive!

Of course, I couldn't continue my studies because I was imprisoned, and afterwards I didn't dare enter the University. Moreover, it was about this time that the anti-Jewish regulations started to come out. My father was forced into retirement, and my sister was dismissed from the public service. She and her husband—after he was released from *Dachau*—were forced to flee illegally to Prague, and then after Prague fell to the Nazis, to flee further.

My sister's parents-in-law fell into the hands of some swindler, and they were stopped on the Hungarian border, arrested, robbed of all their possessions, and finally deported to Minsk!

For all this I will get a retirement about three thousand schillings per month as a pension from Austria. At the moment, because I'm still working, I get 1,909 schillings, and I have to pay a certain sum for buying these rights in the "guest pensions."

In any case, with money you can't undo what happened! However, one sees how little Austria has learned from history—with a few praiseworthy exceptions.

". . . a massive demonstration for Austria. . ."

Conversation with *Ditto Pölzl* on 12-13 September and 12 and 14 December 1987. . . ."

Mr. Pölzl was born in 1907. He was in Graz in 1938 and still lives in the city.

You were politically active even in your youth. How do you remember 1938 and the years before? Which political party did you belong to, and what was your function?

I belonged to the Social Democrats until 1934. I was Social-Democratic community leader in Eggenberg, shop steward of the trade union in the Waagner-Biro factory and also an official in the "Young Front." By 1938 I was a communist.

The leftist grouping that tried to reach agreement with Schuschnigg had a big demonstration on March 1, 1938—a massive demonstration for Austria. It was clear to us communists that Hitler was a bigger danger than Schuschnigg. Communists and socialists and all those who were against the Nazis had a great meeting and demonstration at the Freiheitsplatz. The Nazis stood around in lines and took note of who we were. Then after 13 March they knew immediately who their enemies were. They already had their spies in amongst us, observing us, and remembering our faces.

At the time, of course, we were still strong, and there was no counter-demonstration. It was shortly before the *Anschluss*—the demonstration for Austria!

Were you still optimistic then? You didn't believe it would come to a German invasion?

I was pretty realistic. I had the feeling that the "brown flood" could no longer be stopped. I also had conversations with Jewish friends at this time, and I urged them all to emigrate!

What did the Jews say at that time? How did they react?

We already had the reports from Germany that people were being put in concentration camps, but the Jews just didn't want to accept the full horror of National Socialism and so they didn't react. They labored under the appalling illusion that everything would be OK.

Did you have Jewish friends?

Yes, one of my best friends was Richard Schacherl. His father was one of the founders of the Socialist Party, he was decorated for his service as an officer in the First World War, and lived in Eggenberg in a villa belonging to one of his former regimental comrades. It was a deep friendship which survived the worst times. Richard Schacherl was arrested with Isidor Preminger and many other Graz Jews during the *Kristallnacht* and sent to a concentration camp. After his time in the camp, unlike many other Jews, Schacherl was allowed back into his own apartment. His old war comrade had held the apartment for him and remained his friend despite the times.

What I want to say is that there were deep human relations, friendships, between Jews and non-Jews. Richard Schacherl was Jewish, and the owner of the villa who had kept his apartment for him—he owned a printing works—he was non-Jewish, but that didn't make any difference. They remained good friends, old war comrades. The Nuremberg Decrees couldn't separate them!

Did you detect anti-Semitism even before 1938?

Yes, and not just from the Catholic side; there was anti-Semitism also from the socialists. Yes, there was anti-Semitism in the Socialist Party![1]

Moritz Robinson was the chief editor of the *Arbeiterwille* newspaper. Counsellor Dr. Eisler was one of the best jurists that ever practiced under Austrian law, and he was also senior candidate of the Social Democratic Party.

But Jews who returned from emigration in 1945 did not find a happy reception!

Why not?

Because of political opportunism in regard to the Nazi past of many members of the Styrian population. The same goes for Dr. Steigmann.

Were they Jews?

Yes, they were Jews, and two of them left Austria again on account of their unenthusiastic reception. They left the country for which they had really yearned.

It was the same with the Jews from Vienna. They were all important people, and most of them were killed. Those who came back were not well-received.

Were Christian Social Party members anti-Semitic?

Well, the step from Austrian fascism to National Socialism wasn't difficult. You could see it in the development of the *Heimwehr*—in February 1934 they were locked in battle with the republican *Schutzbund*. And we know that the *Heimwehr* then fell apart into a Nazi group and into a Christian Social group.

---

[1] In Voitsberg, at a meeting of artisans in March 1937, there were cries of "Down with the Jews! Out with them!", Stefan Karner, *Die Steiermark im Dritten Reich 1938-1945* (Graz, Wien, 1986), p. 42.

Who do you think contributed the most to Austria's reconstruction?

The most consistent fighters for Austria's reconstruction were the communists and of course those people who had wanted to retain Austrian independence within the Austrian fascist movement. They made a pact with Mussolini and forgot that in doing so they'd rejected the workers who really wanted to fight for Austria.

What position did the communists adopt with regard to the reconstruction of the Austrian Republic?

The communist emigrants who returned from the Soviet Union[2] tried passionately to make it clear to the Russian Bolsheviks that Austria was different from Germany and should be looked upon as a separate nation. Throughout the war Ernst Fischer made propaganda on Radio Moscow for the reconstruction of an independent Austria.

What do you think of the Resistance literature?

This book of Karner's is an honest and very important book, a comprehensive report on the resistance between 1938 and 1945.[3] He shows exactly the people who were Austrian fascists and whose sins were forgotten. He mentions, for example, Dr. Stepan and the whole group of Dollfuss supporters. It occurs to me in this connection—and this is my personal opinion—that he tries to present the arrest of Pawlikowski as something extraordinary. That's regrettable.

Archbishop Pawlikowski of Styria was the only prince-bishop in the Greater German Reich who in my opinion was on the extreme right-wing amongst clerics and was also for a short while in Nazi imprisonment. Karner mentioned the number of resistance fighters who were executed but didn't really relate

---

[2]Eg. Johann Koplenig, Friedl Fürnberg, Ernst Fischer, and Franz Honner.

[3]Karner, *Die Steiermark*.

their individual fates. Why was this? Could it be because most of them were communists and socialists?

I don't think one can write about the resistance to fascism and ignore the period of clerico-fascism from 1933 to 1938.[4]

What happened on 8 May 1945? What function did you have then?

I had been involved in the trade unions since my youth. On 8 May 1945 I entered the first provisional state government. Immediately after the capitulation I was asked by Waagner-Biro to come to the Eggenberg sanatorium, where the later police president Captain Alois Rosenwirth was waiting for me. He asked me to come to the City Hall to help set up a provisional state government. Rosenwirth thought that I could do that in the name of the Communist Party. I told him that I could only come into the new government as a trade unionist.

So the new provisional government was formed in the Graz City Hall composed of the former deputy state premier, Machold, Captain Rosenwith, and the theologian Professor Dienstlader, who had been provincial governor during the years of Austro-Fascism from 1934 to 1938. Representing the People's Party was the tinsmith Josef Schneeberger. Across from us sat the (Nazi) District leader Professor Dadieu and the mayor of Graz, Kaspar.

Dadieu declared that the Nazis were finished and the capitulation had been carried out. He and Kaspar were therefore resigning their positions.

Machold immediately asked what the food supply situation was like, to which Dadieu replied, "There isn't any!"

Professor Dienstlader then asked what power we could rely on to support us, to which I responded, "But Herr Professor, if the Nazis still had power we wouldn't be sitting here."

Dadieu referred Dienstlader to the "Ferdinand" group, which was fighting in the Koralpe.

Then Dadieu and Kaspar retired and we heard someone from Radio Graz who told us that the radio was at our disposal. I immediately took the opportunity to get in touch with an official

---

[4]For relations between the Church and the Nazi Party, and the numbers and origins of resistance fighters, see Karner, *Die Steiermark*, p. 475.

of the municipality I knew, Mrs. Loidl, and had a broadcast written for transmission to the factories in Styria, to the effect that all the Nazi trade-union organizations were abolished and in their place the factory councils that had been in operation before the events of February 1934 should be re-established and strengthened with democratically-inclined people. I asked Machold whether he agreed to such a broadcast, and he said yes. This announcement was broadcast, the first act of the provisional government in Styria.

So when the Russian Occupation forces arrived on 9 May 1945 there were already authorized officials of the new Austria in place. The new factory councils also lasted through the British occupation, until regular elections could be held.[5]

What do you like to remember from this time? What touched you?

I remember Isidor Preminger with great affection. He was the section leader in the Lend workers' district during the worst years of the great Depression. The unemployment then was terrible! And my strongest recollection is that he always gave five schillings from his own pocket to those hungry, jobless men whenever he was with them. He was an enthusiastic supporter of young people. He also did a lot for the white-collar workers as General-Director of the Merkur Insurance Institute. He returned from emigration in 1946 to Graz and has done a great deal for this town since then.

I also like to recall Otto, Ernst, and Walter Fischer. I was friends with all three of them, but my closest relationship was with Walter. He was a doctor—for chest ailments—a commander in the "Schutzbund," and a leading man in the fighting in defense of Vienna in 1934. Walter Fischer emigrated with his wife to the Soviet Union. He worked as a journalist and physician, and was later in the Spanish Civil War. After the war he gave up medicine and dedicated himself to politics. He translated many Russian poems into German and was very gifted in literature. He died a few years ago. I lost a very good friend then.

---

[5]Details on the formation of the provisional government, Karner, *Die Steiermark*, p. 428.

What was your special field after 1945?

After the war I was mainly concerned to build up a unified Austrian trade union federation. In addition I had my job as State Counsellor for Art and Culture. In the second provisional state government I was State Counsellor for Art and Culture for the Communist Party. It was always my concern to help in the reconstruction of Austria and the revival of its democracy.

Are you still a member of the Communist Party?

No. For years now I haven't been a member of the KPÖ.

". . . and ransack everything in the apartment. . ."

Conversations with *Anna Katharina Preminger* on 12 September and 25 October 1987.

Mrs. Preminger was born in 1897 and is a retired businesswoman. She was in Graz in 1938 and still lives there today.

You wanted to tell me about a time that was very painful for you. Did it begin in 1938?

I don't have much to tell you about 1938, because things were not so barbaric in Graz as they were in Vienna. In Vienna Jews had to clean the sidewalks and things like that. I don't think there were similiar outrages here in Graz. However, it was bad enough! Everything's relative in life.

What I do remember about 1938 is after the *Anschluss* SA men used to arrive unannounced and ransack everything in the apartment. As I recall, they were most interested in the books on sex. In particular there was one book that fascinated them called "Das Weib ist ein Nichts!" (The Female is a Nonentity). They took it with them when they left.

These house searches were very unpleasant. Today you can hardly imagine how bad it was. You were on the street and suddenly there were men in front of the house about to enter your apartment. They went through everthing, and there was

nothing you could do to defend yourself. You were completely
at their mercy.

Can you remember anything specific about 13 March 1938?

I only know that we had the radio on that evening, and when
the announcer reported that German troops had invaded the
country my husband said that it was just the announcer "exaggerating"—he was a hopeless optimist! He simply didn't believe
what was happening. But we did have friends and acquaintances
who left that same evening. I had a good friend who left Graz
that evening and emigrated to Brazil.

What was it like then after 13 March?

As I told you, we had endless "visits" from the SA. People
just arrived and searched the apartment. One evening the bell
rang again, and this time they wanted my son and my husband.
I explained to them immediately that my son was not Jewish,
and moreover he had tickets and was about to leave for England.
So they took only my husband and let my son stay. But it was
terrible, imagine a member of your family is suddenly taken from
you. And there's nothing you can do about it.

What did you do then?

I said I wanted to jump out of the window. I was desperate
and didn't know what to do. Imagine, men in civilian clothing
just appeared and without the slightest emotion arrested someone
in your household and took him off. . . that was what it was like
then! I tried to control myself—my son says today, "My mother
was a brave woman."

After my husband left the apartment we had no way of contacting him. Then I got the address, so at least I had the chance
to send him warm clothing. There were a lot of Jewish people
taken away to concentration camps then.

Did that take place during the *Kristallnacht*?

I can't remember exactly, but I suppose it must have already been November.[1]

When did your husband return from his imprisonment?

After three months he was released because he'd organized the emigration of Jews to Palestine. Also other Jews who had had a position in the Graz community were sent home because they'd been concerned with getting Jews out.

What happened to your son?

The day after my husband was sent to the camp my son was able to travel to England. Travel? What I mean is he was able to flee! He had to leave the town as quickly as possible to avoid any new arrests that might be ordered.

So I was left alone, although I had my friends who stood by me wonderfully during this time. But you have to understand, my husband had been arrested out of the blue, and one had no idea what was happening to him. My son left the apartment for an uncertain future.

What was your reaction when your husband was released?

Suddenly there he was standing before me, his head shaven, stooping, a miserable sight.

Dachau must have been terrible for him. The room in which they all had to live was so small that they didn't even have space to stand. They had to squat, practically one on top of another. They weren't allowed to use the toilet and had to spend the entire night in this squatting position. The next day some potatoes were thrown on the floor—that was their meal! That's what it was like in *Dachau*.

How could these people look after themselves? Were they allowed to wash?

---

[1]NOTE: Mrs. Preminger's son, Franz, has confirmed that the arrest took place during the *Kristallnacht*.

There was a "washing facility," through which they had to run—it was the sort of thing they use today for cleaning cars! But that certainly wasn't the worst.

Did your husband tell you anything else about Dachau?

He came back from these three months totally changed. He didn't want to speak about it at all. I think it must have been so humiliating that he just couldn't bring himself to talk about it. He neither whined nor complained in any way. He was always quiet and, thanks to his nature, always able to withstand things. He always behaved with dignity.

How did your friends and acquaintances react?

Certain people with whom we'd been friends suddenly didn't know me anymore. They looked demonstratively to the other side of the street.

What was it like before 1938?

I can think of one episode, long before 1938. It was summer and we were at the Wolfgangsee. We were in the Hotel "Zur Post," in a beautiful restaurant one day, and the landlord said, "I'm sorry, we can't feed you any more. . . we have so many guests." You see it was clear, long before 1938, people complained if they had to sit in a restaurant with "a Jew."

So then we tried to get a meal in the *Weissen Rössl*. We went in, sat down at a table and waited, and waited, and waited, but we were never served.

Where did you stay then?

It was depressing. Luckily we had relatives in this place, so we were able to stay there. From this point onwards we retreated into loneliness. We avoided people and just tried to get some peace.

What did your husband say to you about the future? How did he see the political situation in Austria?

My husband always kept to himself and didn't share his thoughts. He hardly ever spoke to me about politics. Women were not so emancipated as they are today. He had an unshakable optimism about him. He thought that the Nazis would never come to Austria. He had already been in prison between 1934 and 1938 because he was a Social Democrat and a politically active man.

Let's come back to 1938 and the period immediately afterwards. You didn't stay in Graz?

After he got out of the concentration camp, my husband was here in Graz for a while.

We tried to get a visa for England and eventually we succeeded. My husband went first, and I followed later. We both worked there. I took all kinds of jobs. First I worked in a factory on an assembly line. The doors of that building were always closed for us workers, and if a bomb had landed there we'd all have been killed. I was very hungry then—more hungry than I've ever been. I had no money to buy food, and when the other women workers bought something to eat I could only watch. . .

The factory work was very hard and unpleasant for me. At last my husband said he couldn't stand to see me slaving away there anymore. I gave notice and went into business for myself, making women's hats. Luckily English women always wear hats. In order to survive I also gave German lessons.

The English were very generous, in every respect. They helped me a lot, and I think they allowed me to give the German lessons because they wanted me to have an opportunity to keep myself busy.

We also had meetings with other exiled Austrians. The head of this so-called "Österreich Club" was comrade Dr. Pollak. It was through the club that we kept contact with home.

What sort of a club was that?

We talked about politics and had social gatherings. We talked about what would become of Austria in the future. I always hoped that I could go home to Austria. I was so happy when I heard Styrian (German) spoken again. When we went to England we couldn't speak English. But of course we learned the language with time. Reading the newspapers every day was a great help in learning it.

What happened to your son?

My son went to school in England and graduated there. He was interned like many other enemy aliens. (The Austrians were considered then to be "German" since Austria had been annexed to the German Reich). One day he was fetched from his college in Wigan (a town in northwest England) and deported to Australia, where he spent two years behind barbed wire.

Weren't you ever together with your son in England?

As I told you, my son went to England first. Then my husband followed after he was released from the concentration camp. I came last after about a year. I wasn't with my son much in England. My husband lived with him in the family that had helped us get the visa for England. But we were together, all three of us, for only a very short time. My son soon went to school in Wigan. My husband and I lived in London.

One could say that our lives were changed immediately with Hitler's invasion of Austria and that our family life was destroyed.

Did your husband have other relatives who suffered under the Nazis?

He had a sister and a brother, and a sister-in-law. They all died in concentration camps.

You suffered terribly at the hands of the Nazis and had to leave Austria. Why did you come back here?

We always hoped to return to Austria. We loved this country, and after the war we returned as quickly as we could to Graz. My husband, as an active Social Democrat, fought for the eight-hour day and collective wage agreements for white-collar workers. He helped build up the Merkur Insurance Co. and was later General Director. He also founded the sanatorium in Eggenberg.

". . . the terror of this awful night. . ."

Conversation with *Franz Preminger* on 25 August 1987.

Mr. Preminger was born in 1920 and is a Graz businessman.

Can you remember 1938?

I can remember 1938 very well indeed. Very soon after the invasion people were driven out of their homes. Landlords immediately put pressure on tenants, and people came to rely on each other. Those who had no accommodations moved in with those who owned their own apartments.

It was terrible also how many people were fired from their jobs in the civil service and elsewhere. Jewish doctors and lawyers were not allowed to continue practicing. Everything was suddenly different.

Most of our friends remained friends. But of course they became cautious. They hid their feelings, and all had at least one swastika hanging outside their houses.

My grandmother, who was not Jewish, took her life in 1938. She couldn't stand those barbaric times. . . she was about sixty then.

What was the *Kristallnacht* like?

That was the next decisive event after the *Anschluss*. In the evening there were announcements about the "justified anger of the people" against the Jews—that was the *Kristallnacht*. The synagogue was burned down. I can remember that the doorbell rang again, usually they pounded on the door. My father was taken away—"luckily" by the *Gestapo*. I say "luckily" because at the same time one could hear terrible screams coming from other apartments. A good acquaintance of ours, who lived across the street on the Annenstrasse, was badly injured that evening. He was attacked by some of the hooligans who were indiscriminately beating people up. Three or four different organizations came to us and searched the apartment. They wanted to confiscate my passport, I could collect it the next morning, they said.   My mother cleverly talked them out of that, and I was able to keep it. Still, I was told to report to them the following morning. Of course I didn't—instead I cleared out as quickly as I could.

My father had good friends in England. He was a trade unionist, a socialist, and a well-known journalist. He worked for Reuters in England. He found an English Member of Parliament who guaranteed to cover the expenses of our family—that was the only way you could get a visa. My parents insisted that I travel first. I had my passport and it was arranged that I would leave on 9 November by train from Graz, through Germany to Holland and then over the Channel. I was packed and ready to go, and then came the horrible *Kristallnacht*.

Then what happened? Did you leave the city?

Yes, I set off the morning after the *Kristallnacht*. It was the only thing I could do. It was a terrible chaos—hundreds of Jews had been arrested during the night. I'd only experienced the thing—the terror of this awful night—in my Graz apartment.

I can remember I had to change trains in Munich and wait three hours for my connection. I looked around the city a bit and saw all the broken windows and goods lying on the pavement. And everything was daubed with the words "Juda verrecke" (a vulgar rendering of "Death to Jews!").

Then I continued on the train to England without further difficulty. I was of "mixed race," so I didn't have the dreaded "J" stamped in my passport. Nevertheless, it was a shock for me getting to England: my father was imprisoned and I didn't know what had happened to him. After the *Kristallnacht*, he was taken away by the *Gestapo* and sent to *Dachau*. I didn't know what had happened to him before I left, but I feared the worst. It was terrible for my mother, because she didn't know what was going to happen.[1]

What happened to your father?

He had "luck." Because he'd already been in prison after 1934 in Wöllersdorf, he'd gotten to know Nazis who'd been locked up there.[2] A certain relationship developed between them, it wasn't exactly a friendship, you understand, but they shared the same fate at that time. One of these Nazis later joined the *Gestapo* and with his help it was possible to get my father out of the concentration camp after four months. They said at the time that he'd been released so that he could do everything possible to get the Jews out of Austria as soon as possible. The *Gestapo* man got my father a passport and told him to leave Austria (or the "Ostmark" as it was known then) immediately. He went straight away to England and my mother came after.

My half-sister got the apartment, although she was refered to not as a sister but as "so and so." It was actually transferred to an "illegal" (underground Nazi), but it was agreed that she could stay in the apartment. She moved out later and the "illegal" was killed in the war. My sister survived.

My father looked terrible when he arrived in England. He'd lost a lot of weight and his black hair had gone completely white! For a long time in England he woke up screaming in the night, remembering the horrors of the concentration camp.
Did he tell you about his experience in the camp?

---

[1]"In Styria the Gestapo and the SD only received information on the *Kristallnacht* 'action' after the SA and the district Nazi Party leadership. 350 Jews were arrested on the night of 10 November 1938 and brought at first into the local prison before being sent to concentration camps on 11 November. The synagogue and funeral hall at the Jewish cemetry were burned to the ground. Some shops on the Annenstrasse were destroyed." Erika Weinzierl, *Zu wenig Gerechte, Österreicher und Judenverfolgung 1938-1945* (Graz/Wien/Köln, 1969), p. 60.

[2]At this stage the National Socialist Party was still illegal in Austria.

He talked of the terrible things that happened there. Many arrived there already marked for death—in 1938! A lot of people were killed. But of course it wasn't just Jews in this camp.

He has to thank that "illegal," the *Gestapo* man for his survival, the one he knew in Wöllersdorf camp. But that sort of thing was a rare exception!

How do you see it all today?

About thirteen years ago, it must have been, there was a student, to whom I rented a room, and he revealed quite nonchalantly that he knew that I was half-Jewish and that "Jews always gave him a terrible feeling and somehow he didn't know how to get on with them."

You ask me today how I feel? I'm a "Grazer" and many people don't know that I'm also of "mixed race." What makes me uneasy is the things I've heard in the last few years, things that I wouldn't have heard otherwise, things that sharpen my hearing.

"... Thereafter there was only occasional enthusiasm..."

Conversations with *Paul Schärf* on 22 October and 18 December 1987.

Dr. Schärf was born in 1907 and is a former General Director of the Vienna Municipal Insurance Institute. He was in Vienna in 1938 and still lives there in retirement.

Dr. Schärf, you were in Vienna in 1938. What can you remember?

I was employed at this time by the Vienna Municipal Insurance Institute. As it transpired later, there were among the approximately 250 employees in the Internal Service only about ten so-called "illegal" Nazis. I saw the March Days coming and feared for Austria's independence.

On the day that the German troops massed on the Austrian border and Schuschnigg resigned, there was a meeting of the illegal free trades union representatives. There we found out that the situation was hopeless. On the way home on the Ringstrasse I saw policemen already wearing swastika armbands. And when I got home my wife asked me to visit a friend who lived nearby and who was very worried about the situation. When he opened the door to his apartment my friend had tears in his eyes as he told me that Schuschnigg had just resigned. He was very upset and depressed, not least because he had a Jewish brother-in-law. I tried to cheer him up and told him that we would survive even this "thousand year Reich." He was also a colleague from the office and the next day when I saw him at work, he was wearing a Nazi badge! This time it was I who was shocked!

I tell you this to show what extraordinary times they were. Not just extraordinary—crazy times!

What was it like then in your office?

There was tremendous excitement. Nobody worked. One of my directors was a well-known Greater German and an active member of the academic choir "Die Nibelungen." Moreover he never made any secret of his Greater German sympathies. But he had in the eyes of his future leader only one fault—his personal secretary was a Jew! At first we assumed that he would remain head of the Institute. But after the so-called seizure of power on 20 March he was fired and had to find employment elsewhere.

One of the employees who had been a functionary of the Fatherland Front turned up proudly wearing an SS uniform, but it came out pretty soon afterwards that he was half-Jewish. Such things happened at that time!

What was it like in the foreign service?

In the foreign service there were of course more "illegal" Nazis. I remember how we gathered for one of the first receptions in the great lecture hall in order to have to listen to a speech of Hitler's. A lot of female employees were crying, some out of rapture, a lot more out of grief. And we men were also very moved, likewise from different motives.

The tidal wave of propaganda that rolled over us, all the promises that were made to us—you can hardly imagine it today. Starting with the swastikas on every house, the endless marches and parades. . . the people were subjected to overwhelming propaganda. It was massive, clever, and impressive.

Then there was the work creation programs. I remember that before 1938, or was it 1934, I was in a youth group with about sixty members of whom no less than fifty-five were unemployed. People got well-paying jobs almost immediately. German wages were higher, even if the taxes were too.

But the propaganda, that was fantastic. Everything that one had wanted or hoped for, was fulfilled—sometimes even more.

The people were pretty soon ecstatic and the fully-controlled press made sure they stayed that way.

Did you see the rallies in the Heldenplatz?

No. Like me, many people didn't go to those things. My wife, for example, deliberately kept off the streets for two weeks so that she wouldn't have to confront these flag-wavers and greet them.

But then in a city of 1.7 million it was hard to avoid a group of 200,000 zealous Nazis. In Graz I believe the percentage of supporters was even higher. It wasn't for nothing that it was called the "City of the People's Revolution."

What happened next?

Spring came and our employees received, like everybody in the insurance business, a special "Home in the Reich Bonus." Later they were even invited on a trip to Germany, from which they returned in a state of great enthusiasm. They saw the "autobahns," the full employment, and other things which fascinated them. What they didn't see was the rearmament, the debts, the exploitation of Austria! They didn't see that, or they didn't want to see it.

In the summer of 1938 things calmed down a bit. German taxes and German laws were introduced. I remember I started to earn a bit more thanks to German salary rates, but I was paying ten times more in tax. Slowly the negative side of the Nazi system started to become apparent.

In the autumn there was the Munich Crisis and people started to get more anxious. The Jews started to disappear. Actually there were very few Jews at work—or those who had been "made" Jews by the Nuremberg Decrees.

Did you notice anti-Semitism before 1938?

I don't want to boast about it, but apart from the fact that there were Jewish kids in my high school, I had read *Mein Kampf* and was pretty well-informed. I knew what Hitler was going to do with the Jews. I must have been among the first hundred people to read the book. I was interested in the National Socialist Party very early on and had studied their program. There was nothing new there! For me it was all no surprise.

Even in the Vienna colleges there was very strong anti-Semitism before 1934, and the nationalist clubs—above all the fencing associations—always tried to keep Jews out.[1] But that was normal, however bad it sounds!

I graduated in 1926 and so I avoided the whole awful business as a student. By 1930 I'd finished my legal studies.

What did you expect from Hitler?

I was convinced with many of my friends that "Hitler meant war." After Hitler's seizure of power in Germany we had press censorship here in Austria. Certain things were stressed—they tried to create the Austrian people, and, not very cleverly, certain things were imitated—but their efforts didn't succeed.

Did the general enthusiasm for Hitler continue?

In my opinion it gradually subsided. It began with the difficulties experienced in food procurement, in getting clothes and shoes, etc. Everything was bought up by the Germans. Thereafter there was only occasional enthusiasm. Most people were neither politically schooled nor interested, and so they believed what was in the newspapers and what was being constantly preached.

Then the war broke out, and I can still remember my colleagues at work asking me how I knew that there'd be a war. For me it could all be foreseen.

Did you know about the discrimination against the Jews?

---

[1]After 1918 Austrian universities became a breeding ground for German Nationalist and anti-Semitic thinking, manifested most obviously in the demand for a *numerus clausus* to limit Jewish entry. The "Jew" became a synonym for all so-called "antisocial races" (*volks- und rassenfremde Elemente*), e.g., Jews, Slavs, Social-Democrats and Bolsheviks. See Brigitte Lichtenberger-Fenz, "Die Universität Wien und der National-sozialismus", in *Das Jüdische Echo. Zeitschrift für Kultur und Politik* (October 1987).

The discrimination against the Jews, the plundering of shops, the humiliation of the young and old people who were defined as Jews—all that was generally known. I saw Jews on the sidewalks with toothbrushes, being forced to wash off the slogans of the *Volksfront*.

If you "wanted to know," as opposed to deliberately turning your back on the thing, then it was impossible to ignore what was happening to the Jews and what Hitler planned for them.

Did you know anything about the concentration camps in 1938?

Yes. In 1933, after Hitler's seizure of power in Germany, political refugees were already coming to Austria. But I had also read Rosenberg and *Mein Kampf*.[2] So I knew all about it.

What did your family think of Hitler? Were the Viennese happy about him?

My uncle Adolf Schärf, who was later Deputy Chancellor and Federal President, was imprisoned. So one can assume that neither he nor his family were keen on Hitler.

In my family there was only my sister who showed any enthusiasm at the beginning. But she was soon called up to do Labor Service and was treated there as a "lazy Austrian girl." Thereafter her enthusiasm declined pretty fast.

Coming back to the general picture. One had the impression that everyone was contented, but we didn't see the sad people like my wife who stayed at home and didn't even want to go on the streets.

Did you have many Jewish friends and were they afraid?

Yes, I spoke with some after they'd been released from prison or concentration camps—but none of them would talk

---

[2]Alfred Rosenberg provided the so-called intellectual underpinning for National Socialism in his grandiose but little-read *The Myth of the Twentieth Century*, which was an attempt to rewrite history according to the racist ideologies of Gobineau and Houston Stewart Chamberlain.

about their experiences. They didn't want to talk about what happened to them there. You know there are things, experiences . . . about which people won't talk, because they've suppressed them to the deep unconscious, so that they can carry on living. You have to understand that. People had suffered too much.

I have to tell you something else that was typical for this time. In my office we had this Greater German Nationalist for a boss, and he had a Jewish secretary. (At the beginning, we thought, nothing can happen to us because he's certainly a Nazi. But then both of them were fired.)

But in 1935 I had the following experience with this Greater German, and it was typical for those times. I wanted to attend an Organizational Course of the Industrialists' Association, and I had to get my boss's permission. So I reported to him and told him what I wanted to do. He was a very frank man and he asked me quite openly,

"Schärf, are you a Jew?"

I replied, "What sort of a question is that?"

To which he said, "Look, that's a typical Jewish habit. What does a 'goy' do in his free time after school? He goes and plays football, or he goes for a drink. And what does the Jew do? He learns something, he learns. . . he gets smarter, he writes a book, and then the 'goyim' speak badly of the Jews. . ."

". . . But of course, my friend, off you go!. . ."

Telephone conversations with *Edmund Schechter* on 22 October and 18 December 1987.

Dr. Schechter, was born in 1912 and reached a senior level as a diplomat in the United States Foreign Service. He was in Vienna in 1938 and lives today in Washington, D.C.

Dr. Schechter you still feel a spiritual attachment to your old homeland—one can see that from your letters. What was it like in Vienna fifty years ago?

You know in later years I was always commended for making the decision "so quickly." I was able to leave Austria just in time. It was a decision that saved my life! But you know these "compliments" or whatever they were, on my "swift decision-making," were really undeserved. On the contrary—my stupidity was limitless!

I left Vienna, thank God, on 15 March 1938. It was a Tuesday and four days after the *Anschluss*.

But I have to tell you a story from the days before, so that you understand what I mean. At the beginning of March, about ten days before Hitler's invasion, we organized a rally by a Jewish self-defense group. It was modeled on the organization set up by Jabotinsky and his Revisionist Zionist movement in Poland.

Austria's last Chancellor, Kurt von Schuschnigg, was the guest of honor, and at the end of the event I had a chance to speak to him briefly. I mentioned that I always went skiing in March and asked him whether, in view of the tense situation in Austria, he recommended going away. He replied without hesitation, "But of course, my friend, off you go!"

I'm ashamed to say that, despite the fact that I'd been politically active for years, I took the Chancellor's advice. Looking back, the fact that I allowed myself to go off skiing is all the more incomprehensible because my friends and I were active in the Zionist-Revisionist movement and naturally well known to the *Gestapo*.

Only a month before I had brought out a book with the rather conspicuous title of *Kampf um Zion* (Fight for Zion). In the book I compared the liberation struggles of the Irish, Italians, Poles, and Czechs with the efforts of the Jews to establish their own state. The book advanced the thesis that throughout history oppressed people had only achieved freedom and independence through military action and the will to fight. The book's publication came just at the right moment to bring me to the attention of the Nazis and thus into great danger.

How did you react after your talk with Schuschnigg?

Look, I probably wanted to believe everything he said, because the next day I went skiing at St. Anton am Arlberg. On Friday, 11 March, I went to bed with the red-white-red Austrian flag flying over the hotel, and when I woke up the next day, the hotel and the entire valley was a mass of swastikas. Overnight the world had changed!

What did you do then?

On Sunday I traveled back to Vienna by way of Salzburg. The German Army was making a triumphant entry, and the whole population seemed to be in a state of euphoria. Back in Vienna, I at last became more cautious, and instead of going home I took a room in the "Hotel de France" on the Schottenring.

Why didn't you go home?

I guess I'd smelled trouble! I asked someone to call my mother and tell her where I was. I found out immediately that the *Gestapo* had been there looking for me and had been talking to the maid. She'd truthfully told them that I'd gone skiing, as I always did at that time of year.

What happened to your father? And your mother?

My father had gone on a business trip to Romania two weeks earlier. Later he went to Palestine.

My mother was a typical Jewish mom and didn't panic. In the next few days she managed to bring a suit, shirt, shoes, and socks to me in the hotel without alerting the maid. Otherwise I would have had just my skiing outfit, a pair of trousers, and a tuxedo. The tux would have been useful for a job as a waiter, but I didn't use it much in the next ten years of wandering. So I began my flight from Hitler, with practically nothing. The tuxedo in my baggage led to plenty of jokes later on.

What happened to you after you left Vienna?

Yes, well, on Tuesday, 15 March 1938 I took the train from Vienna to Trieste. Fortunately, I had a valid passport in my pocket.

And you know, in these few days after the *Anschluss* thousands of Jews could have saved themselves, if only they'd just taken a train and left everything behind them. . . if only. . . But very few of them did that.

Just before my departure some friends from my Jewish student fraternity and my mother came to see me at Lene Altmann's house. Lene Altmann was the fiancee of one of my best friends and they lived near the Südbahnhof, which is where my train left from. We had an evening meal together, and then they all came to see me off at the station, so that my mother would not be left alone. It was a difficult parting. Fear and uncertainty hung over all of us!

My mother didn't know whether I'd made it over the border until the next day when she received a prearranged signal from me.

This train trip must have been very oppressive for you. How did it go?

There was an attractive young woman in the train with her two small daughters. They looked "non-Jewish." Just before we reached to the border, I stuck a piece of paper in her pocket without her noticing. It had a telephone number and the request that she inform my friend that I'd been arrested—if that was what had happened.

As everything went all right and we entered Italy, I told her what I'd done. I apologized and asked her to return the slip of paper. She read it and suddenly began to laugh—it turned out that she was also Jewish.

From Trieste, after a few weeks, I managed to get to Paris, where my mother joined me in May 1938.

My activities in Paris are another story.

In 1940, after the beginning of the German invasion of France, I was mobilized as a "prestataire" (auxiliary formation), and sent to Brittany with the French Army. There we were captured by the advancing Germans. However, after a week I was able to escape and, after crossing the whole of France, I reached Marseilles in unoccupied France.

I found out there that my mother had been able to leave on a ship for England, but the boat had changed course and gone to Casablanca instead. In the confusion I was able to get to Casablanca too. After seven adventurous months we got our permits for the United States and arrived in New York, via Lisbon, in May 1941.

This is a sort of telegram-style recapitulation of three difficult, dramatic and sometimes incredible years.

What happened to your father? And how did your mother get out of Vienna?

My father, as I said, had made a business trip to Romania shortly before the *Anschluss*. He traveled from there to Palestine. I never saw him again. He died in Israel and is buried near Tel-Aviv.

As for my mother, relatives in Paris helped her get a special visa, and she just managed to save herself. She left with just her handbag and had to leave everything behind her.[1]

You live now in Washington DC with your wife and son. You are an old member of the Vienna "Kadimah"—can you tell me something about this student fraternity?

This fraternity was founded in 1882 and is the oldest Jewish fraternity in the world. The "Kadimah" arose from a turning point in modern Jewish history when assimilation among West and Central European Jews had reached a high point, while in the area of densest Jewish settlement in Russia there were bloody pogroms. It was a period in which anti-Semitism found a new impulse, even in the so-called enlightened parts of Europe.

The object of the "Kadimah" was to counter assimilation and propagate the idea of a Jewish national identity. Its first task was to protect Jewish students. The "Kadimahners," and other Jewish fraternity members were enthusiastic supporters of Theodor Herzl and his ideas. His book *Der Judenstaat* made a deep impression amongst the "Kadimahners" and he was made an honorary member. In his diaries are numerous entries that document the enthusiasm of young Jewish students in the early days. This was when modern Zionism began.

The first phase of the Jewish fraternity ended with the collapse of the Austro-Hungarian Empire in 1918. They had been practically inactive during the First World War, as all the members of military age had been called up to the Army. But after 1918 the fraternities were revived, and they exercised an increasingly Zionist influence on the Jewish community in Austria.

Between 1918 and 1938 the parties were polarized into Christian Socials and Social Democrats. Traditional anti-Semitism fused with the more aggressive Nazi racist anti-Semitism. The universities in Graz and Vienna fell steadily under Nazi influence, and Jewish fraternities had to fight almost daily for the rights of Jewish students.

---

[1]In Edmund Schechter's *Viennese Vignettes* (New York, 1984), he devotes a chapter to his escape from Vienna and the March days in 1938.

Were you active then?

At the end of the 1920s and beginning of the 1930s I was "Chargierter" (leading member) of the "Kadimah." The Nazis saw it as their task to eject us from the university, so there were fights on a pretty regular basis.

In the 1920s the Jewish journalist Hugo Bettauer had written a sensational book entitled *Die Stadt ohne Juden,* in which he described a Vienna of the future from which all the Jews had been driven. The book sold well, in fact it was a best-seller. The trouble was none of the Jews in Vienna took its message seriously. No one thought the book's ghostly prophecy would ever come true.

In 1930 there was a deep ideological split within the Zionist movement. On the one hand there was the cautious and restrained approach of Chaim Weizmann, the president of the World Zionist Organization. On the other hand there was the revisionist approach of Vladimir Ze'ev Jabotinsky.[2]

In 1935 there was a world congress of the Zionist-Revisionist movement in Vienna. Jabotinsky put forward the ideas of militancy, self-discipline, and self-reliance—ideas which finally led to the foundation of the state of Israel.

What relationship do you have today with the Kadimah?

We are getting fewer in number, but I can tell you that the feeling of brotherhood has never changed, right up until this day. After fifty years my closest friends are still "Kadimahner" and "Masadenser"—I began my militant Zionist activities in high school with the "Masada" (a high-school students corporation). Now we are spread across the face of the earth, in the United States, Latin America, Australia, England, France, and Israel. We were driven by Hitler into every corner of the world, but we never lost each other!

It's a fact that in a few years there won't be any more Jewish fraternity students. There will be no one to bear witness to the important role that the Jewish students played in the Zionist

---

[2]Some details on Jabotinsky and the Revisionist movement are given in Schechter's, *Vignettes,* p. 70-72.

movement. Two years ago I had an idea: on my annual trip to Israel I presented the mayor of Jerusalem, Teddy Kollek (who also happens to be from Vienna), with a proposal to name a street in Jerusalem after the "Kadimah"—Rechov Kadimah as it is known in Hebrew—and in that way to honor the memory of the "Kadimah" and all the other militant Jewish fraternity students.

And did Teddy Kollek agree?

Yes, Kollek and the Jerusalem city fathers accepted the idea with great enthusiasm, and we were very grateful.

You said that you received a great personal surprise on 19 March 1986, what was that?

In March 1986 there was a gathering of all the surviving alumni (*Alte Herren*) of the "Kadimah" and other similar fraternities from Vienna, Graz, Prague, Cernowitz, Riga, and Basel. They were all witnesses to the naming of Kadimah Street in Jerusalem. The ceremonies began on 19 March 1986 and happily the children of the second generation were also there to be initiated into the "secrets" of their fathers. The great surprise for me was a speech made by my son, who is twenty-eight years old and works in a political consulting firm. Only my wife knew about his planned speech, and it was a complete success. I don't have to tell you how proud and happy I was!

The ceremony closed with the unveiling of the street name plate by the oldest "Kadimahner" present. The plate is inscribed, as is usual in Israel, in Hebrew, English and Arabic, with the following words: "Kadimah," Fraternity of Jewish Students, founded in Vienna in 1883.

At the end we remembered those brothers who had been murdered by the Nazis in the Holocaust, who had fallen fighting Hitler in the Allied armies or who had given their lives in the Israeli Army for the freedom of Israel.[3]

---

[3]Cf. Harald Seewann, *Die Jüdisch-Akademische Verbindung Charitas Graz: Ein Beitrag zur Geschichte des Zionismus auf Grazer akademischen Boden* (Graz, 1986).

". . . Jud, Jud, spuck in Hut, sag der Mutter, das ist gut. . ."

Conversation with *Karl Schiffer* on 23 August 1987.

Karl Schiffer was born in 1910 and is a retired chief editor. He was in Graz in 1938 and still lives there.

Can you remember 1938 and the period before?

In order to make the events of March 1938 in any way comprehensible, I have to describe the situation before 1938.

I went to a Jewish elementary school and grew up with the anti-Semitism that always existed here. Graz was a sort of frontier town. German Nationalism was very strong among the upper classes. There were lots of associations that were proud to have "Aryans-only" paragraphs in their constitutions. Many of them didn't take Jews.

It was in 1926, I think, and the GAK (the Graz Sports Club) didn't take any Jews. There was a Jewish Sports Club—the HAKOAH (it means "strength" in Hebrew)—in Graz and Vienna. Their soccer team got into the First Division and had to play against the GAK. I was at the GAK playing field—it's the same place today—and the two teams had to exchange pennants as usual and shake hands before the match. The HAKOAH captain —I can even remember his name, it was Isi Gansl—and the GAK

captain, who was called Diamant—they had red-white-red outfits
—approached each other with their pennants. (The HAKOAH
pennant, incidentally, was blue and white with a Star of David).
Isi Gansl held out his hand to Diamant, who turned and spat and
went off! There was terrific applause from the GAK supporters.

But the referee was a sportsman, and he called Diamant back
with his whistle and said, "If you don't shake hands with Gansl
immediately, then the score is 3-0 in favor of HAKOAH!"

The latent anti-Semitism was quite clear to me in these years.
If someone says he didn't notice anti-Semitism at this time, then
all I can do is cry. You have to see it in differentiated fashion.
There was no extremism, of course, but there was this strong
Catholic anti-Semitism. It would be false to say that authorities
—the governments at federal and state level—were anti-Semitic,
and of course there was a huge difference from what came later
(after 1938).

Did you notice anti-Semitism as a child?

Yes, I can remember that people called after me, "Jud, Jud,
spuck in Hut, sag der Mutter, das ist gut!"

What was the religious anti-Semitism like?

I remember the reproach: you crucified our Lord Jesus! So
then I asked the question, "INRI, what does that mean?" It means
Jesus of Nazareth, King of the Jews. Jesus was a Jew, how does
that work out? I often asked myself that question when I was
young; it occupied my thoughts.

But one has to differentiate. There was also a strong Social
Democratic workers' movement, which was the only open movement that I found not to be anti-Semitic. All other parties were
anti-Semitic. Only the Social Democratic Party took Jews as
members. But despite this fact, tragically many Jews supported
the Christian Socials—and later even the Fatherland Front.

The Nazis later found the documentation, and many officials
of the Fatherland Front were actually sent to concentration
camps!

How was that possible?

The situation was wholly misjudged by middle-class Jews, who refused to take the threat seriously. Hitler came to power in Germany in 1933. One could see what was happening—that many Jews were being sent to concentration camps. But the Austrian Jews just thought: Dollfuss is against the Nazis. They knew that he'd set up a "corporate state" and that parliament had been suspended.

But then even someone like Karl Kraus—and this is one of the most terrible things—a far-sighted, imaginative writer, even he supported Dollfuss. He did it because he, falsely, perceived Dollfuss as a barrier against Hitler.

The Christian corporate state of Dollfuss and Schuschnigg certainly had Jews among its supporters. They saw the Dollfuss regime as a defense against the Nazis. This is the only explanation for the thanksgiving services in the synagogues for Dollfuss' escape from assassination by the Nazis in October 1933.

Was this period before 1938 a preparation for what came later?

Yes. Without the period before, you can't understand 1938.

And another thing: the workers' movement—that was 46% of the electorate—they were Social Democratic. These people were ready to fight Hitler, but they were sitting in jail. It was Austro-fascism that made possible the *Anschluss* and what followed.

Were you in Graz in 1938?

No. I wasn't in Graz in 1938. But I can tell you what happened to my family who were in Graz at this time.

Immediately after the *Kristallnacht*, my brother Dr. Benno Schiffer, who was a lawyer in the Andreas-Hofer-Platz in Graz, and my cousin Dr. Walter Gartenberg, who was also a lawyer on the Münzgrabenstrasse (today his name is Gardner and he lives in the USA), were deported to *Dachau*. Neither of them was politically active.

I have to go forward a bit here. I was in Vienna at the time, and I often discussed the situation with my brother. I told him that if Hitler invaded Austria, he should get out of the country immediately with just a briefcase containing the most important things. He should leave everything behind, because Hitler meant death—mass murder. He just laughed—that was 1937—and said, "What's the matter with you socialists and communists? If Hitler really does come, then I'll be busy as a lawyer defending and representing the Jews. . ."

My brother was a liberal democrat, unfortunately—I know it sounds a bit presumptuous—a democrat without a sense of history.

What happened then in 1938?

Well, as I predicted.

My brother's office and apartment were confiscated. My brother was put in a concentration camp. Luckily his wife was not Jewish. He got a so-called Shanghai visa at enormous expense, which got him out of the concentration camp. He just wanted to get out of the camp, not necessarily to go to Shanghai. After six bitter weeks he was able to flee from *Dachau* to Italy.

My sister had been able to get to Switzerland under the most difficult circumstances and was able to carry on from there to England with the aid of an "affidavit." The former secretary had to work as a maid. But she was lucky, hundreds of thousands of people died the most miserable death trying to flee.

My brother, the lawyer, was able to go to England thanks to the job my sister had got. He got a job there as a servant and looking after dogs. He suffered unspeakably that he couldn't live in Austria anymore.

It's a remarkable thing that my brother, despite his great love for Austria and despite the fact that he had the opportunity after the war to get his Graz law practice back, couldn't bring himself to return to his beloved homeland.

Why not?

He once told me privately the reason and then never spoke of it again.

It seems that when he was at *Dachau* he met this merciless SS bully who tortured and sadistically killed Jews and communists. And this thug had been one of his best friends at school!

This terrible discovery really affected my sensitive brother, and he never got over it. He wasn't a religious Jew and he wasn't a Zionist. He was a keen mountain climber and a Styrian—a true Austrian who loved his country above all—but this country had been "defiled."

Oh yes, there's something else that's interesting, about the (Nazi) District Captain, Professor Dadieu.

I was with the "Sozialistische Jungfront"—a Social Democratic association for young people. I had a good friend, the architect Herbert Aichholzer (he was later beheaded by the Nazis as a communist). This man was a student friend of Dadieu's. Aichholzer believed that one should talk to Dadieu, because although he was a National Socialist, he placed more importance on the "socialist" part than on the "nationalist."

I invited Dadieu to my apartment and he accepted—the invitation of the Jew, Karl Schiffer!

He came and found himself in the colorful company of socialists like Ditto Pölzl, Willi Scholz, Primus Unterweger, Gartlgruber, and Dr. Fischer with Otto, her husband. We talked for a long time and at the end we had the impression that Dadieu had been "converted"—he'd become a socialist.

That was 1932 and we'd made a mistake. He hadn't "converted" in our apartment, because immediately after Hitler's invasion he became one of the top people in the National Socialist government—he was District Captain!

How do you see it all after fifty years?

I'm shocked by the action of the Austrian Veterans' Association as much as by that of the former Education Minister Piffl-Percevic, who talks about the borders of the homeland, and where the frontline was and why Austrian soldiers defended the homeland. This sort of thing is against the Constitution. The Styrian State Counsellor—the economic counsellor—wants to be put on the "watch list." That's absurd. Shouldn't this man, of all people, be trying to foster good relations abroad? With the USA? A Deputy Mayor of Austria's third city (Linz) writes an apparently anti-Semitic letter and remains in office?

There's so much talk, and nothing's done. For me and for many other good Austrians, that's very depressing. So I have to say, fifty years after is for me not a pretty sight.

". . . I don't believe in collective guilt. . ."

Interviews with *Richard Schifter* in May 1988, May 1989, May 1990.

Mr. Ambassador, you are head of the Human Rights Section at the State Department in Washington, so you have dedicated yourself to human rights. Human rights are the inalienable birthright of every individual, not by virtue of his citizenship but because he is a human being. You had to leave Austria in 1938 because you were a Jew. What are your thoughts when you think back to Austria today?

I have thought a great deal about the phenomenon of Catholic anti-Semitism in Austria.

Do you have any particular memories?

Yes. I will never forget how as a six or seven year old in Vienna—that was around 1930—a kid at my high school told me that "the Jews killed Christ" and therefore they were "guilty." I went home and asked my parents about this incomprehensible accusation.

I remember also that one had to be very careful in certain neighborhoods in Vienna if one looked Jewish to avoid being beaten up by gangs of youths.

I can tell you something that I once told President Ronald

Reagan. When I was about eight years old and was walking with my father through the Boltzmanngasse in Vienna—that was where the Consular Academy was located (today it's the American Embassy)—I said that one day I would like to attend that school because I wanted to be a diplomat. I can still remember my father's words: "You must stop talking about a career as a diplomat, such a field is closed to Jews. . . you can forget it."

Fifty years later I really was a diplomat.

You have had an extraordinary career in America. Do you still have contacts to Austria? How do you feel about Austria today?

I have no hatred. And I don't believe in collective guilt, only the guilt of the individual. I judge people as people.

Do you still have personal memories of 1938?

I remember it was October 27, my parents' wedding anniversary. They were asked to report to the police and then did not return home. . . I remember my teeth chattered the whole night from fear.

You left Austria in 1938 and fled to America. You never saw your parents again. You were suddenly in another country and entirely dependent on yourself. You speak English without an accent, how is that possible?

I had an excellent speech teacher at my high school and carefully followed his instructions. I remember that I was just fifteen and worked for a tailor as a delivery boy. When I was making clothes deliveries I practiced the speech exercises as I was walking along the street.

Do you believe in God? Are you a religious person? What is the secret of your successful career?

I believe that people should show respect to one another. That, I think, is the essence of religion.

I lead a happy family life; I have been happily married for 42 years, I have five children and eight grandchildren. Perhaps that is the secret of my professional success.

And when you think about Austria. . .?

For me, your president Dr. Waldheim was never a problem. I would not have put him on the Watch List, although it may have been legal to do so within the terms of the Holtzmann Amendment. But even here one could have interpreted the Holtzmann Amendment in such a way that Waldheim did not have to appear on the Watch List.

The problem for me lies elsewhere. Why Kaltenbrunner? Why Globocnig? Why Eichmann? Why Seyss-Inquart? Why Hitler? Why were all these people Austrian? Why were Austrians so over-represented in the Holocaust?

Is it because on the one hand one told children to love Jesus, and on the other hand that "the Jews" killed Jesus?

But I believe there will be improvement. I consider the actions of the Second Vatican Council most important. In my view Pope John XXIII was a great human being and a most important figure in the Catholic Church. The declarations of the Council have brought about a most significant change in the Catholic rank and file. Still, after two thousand years you cannot change Church tradition overnight—that is something for future generations to achieve.

"... Perish Judah. . ."

Conversation with *Gertrude Scholz* on 1 September 1987.

Gertrude Scholz was born in 1919. An accountant, she was in Vienna in 1938 and lives today in Graz.

What do you remember from 1938?

I graduated from high school in 1937 in Vienna. In the autumn of that year I enrolled in the Philosophy Faculty at Vienna University. In May 1938 I got a letter from the Dean's Office with the following:"Your request to be admitted to the Philosophy Faculty for the 1938 Summer Semester cannot be granted because of the prevailing *numerus clausus*. However, you are at liberty to reapply for the next semester."

My world fell apart with this letter.

Something about my family: my sister was born in 1923 in Vienna. My mother was also Viennese. My father came from Rust in the Burgenland. My ancestors all came from Vienna. In 1938 my mother was a housewife, my father was commercial director of a chemical firm in Vienna.

He lost his position immediately in 1938. My sister wasn't allowed to continue at school. She was fifteen and wanted to teach handicrafts. She had to go as a maid into my aunt's household. From then on we all had to contribute something to stay alive, since my father's income had ceased. And my aunt was not allowed to hire an "Aryan" maid anyway, so for the time being we found a "solution."

I tried soon afterwards to get to England. I had a reply to my letter from the German Jewish Aid Committee, in which I was told that I had been put on a waiting list for a position in domestic service: "We will try to find a suitable position for you; however, you must be patient, for there is a strong demand for such jobs." Yes, I certainly had to be patient!

There was a Dutch philanthropist called Gildemeester. This man had helped people in the First World War—above all undernourished children—and brought them to Holland. In 1938 Gildemeester founded an Emigration Assistance Action in Vienna for non-Mosaic Jews. After I got the sad news from the University that I couldn't continue my studies, I tried to get work abroad by various means. Some people answered, as I mentioned, others not. So I tried to get a position with Gildemeester.

Did you get one?

I was lucky and got one. On 15 November I received a letter from the temporary head of Gildemeester's office to say that I had an honorary position as an assistant in the Emigration Assistance Action with responsiblility for procuring documents.

It said that the person named here "is working in the interest of the German Reich on the emigration of Jews from the 'Ostmark' (Austria). We request that the named person and other members of her family be allowed to remain in their apartment."

That was very important. It meant that we could look upon our apartment as fairly safe. Perhaps this letter saved our lives.

Do you have any special memories of March 1938?

I had an unforgettable impression standing in the Vienna Heldenplatz as a Jew and watching the people. It's hard to find the right words to describe the excitement there. . . they were shouting, they were going wild, ecstatic about their *Führer*, contempuous of the Jews. When I heard the words, "perish Judah!," I knew there was no future for us Jews in Austria.

Whenever I stood in the Heldenplatz I asked myself the

question: How could the German Jews continue to live in Germany after Hitler's seizure of power? Why didn't they emigrate? Were they asleep? That was the question I asked myself continuously.

Did the city start to look different soon after Hitler's invasion?

I remember very well. Even in the first weeks after Hitler's invasion—I saw it myself—truckloads of SA people rode down the streets (I remember exactly: Wallensteinstrasse, Taborstrasse, the city center, Gaussplatz, etc.) and smashed the windows of Jewish shops, broke down the doors, plundered their contents, and painted swastikas on the walls. It was unbelievable how people behaved in those days. They reminded me of the rabbit before the snake.

Even in the first week after the *Anschluss* many Jews were deported to *Dachau.* I know that because my parents' best friend was sent there. But he didn't get there. His friends were informed that he had "died"; if they wanted, they could have the (burial) urn. . . This man was between forty-five and fifty.

At first they took the men only. SA men (they never came alone) arrived at the door early in the morning and took whomever it was away without any comment.

How did your family fare? Did they work?

The brothers and sisters of my father were Zionists (although my father was not), and they'd already gone to Palestine in the 1920s. Immediately after the *Anschluss* they wrote to my father and obtained an immigration certificate for my parents and my sister. My sister was to be enrolled at Jerusalem University with me. My report card from the University of Vienna was sent and then we waited. . .

I worked at Gildemeesters. I remember we received a small expense allowance, although that wasn't planned. Whether the head of the office there, Galvagni, who was loyal, knew about it, I can't say.

In November after the terrible *Kristallnacht,* the Jewish Passport Office was opened in the Palais Rothschild in the Argentinierstrasse. That meant that Jews could no longer get their passports at the District Office but had to go to the so-called Jewish Emigration Office in the Palais Rothschild.

I was transferred there and was responsible for document procurement. My work consisted of checking all the documents that were necessary to get a German passport. The people—all "non-Aryan" Christians—often had to line up night and day. Every day only a certain number of people were admitted. It all depended on the entirely arbitary decisions of the SS. It was unbelievably humiliating!

Did you ever meet Eichmann there?

Yes, at this time I made the acquaintance of Eichmann. Everybody working there was introduced to him. I can remember that he received me in a huge state room. I wasn't allowed to approach the desk where he sat, because several meters before it there was a line beyond which one wasn't permitted to go.

"One shouldn't get too close to Jews," because they had, among other things, "an unpleasant smell," they "stank."

Through Eichmann's harsh methods the Austrian Jews were deprived of every illusion of human dignity in the Third Reich.

In December 1938 there were the first transports of children to Holland and England (with the help of the Hebrew Community in Vienna and Gildemeester). These transports were only for children up to fourteen years of age. My sister was on the first transport, parents were not allowed to see their children off at the railroad station.

Every child had his name and age written clearly on a card around his neck. The older children carried the little ones who were crying. I was allowed at the station. It was ten o'clock in the evening, and the train stood at an end platform to the side. I think the Red Cross provided the assisting personnel who traveled with the train. Thanks to Gildemeester I succeeded in being among the personnel at the station who prepared the children for their journey into the unknown; my sister was there too.

Then I had a bad throat infection which kept me in bed for four weeks. During this time I received the offer of a position as a "governess" with the Ravenscroft family in Birmingham, England. Through my long illness I was able to leave Gildemeester, and I planned to leave on 28 February 1939 for England. My parents brought me to the station, and we said our sad farewells.

My father told me not to look out of the window, but to look forward, not back. . . . I suppose I'm superstitious but I think that's the reason I came back.

I can remember too that in order to get a passport, it was absolutely necessary to have a tax release certificate. But this document had only a month's validity. If one didn't manage to emigrate in that time, the thing had to be reapplied for. It was a continuous fear and worry, a continuous changing from hope to desperation, and back again.

So I got to England. From 1 March 1939 until February 1941 I worked as a maid. Among other jobs, I worked in England as a cleaner in a maternity home and a lathe operator in a factory.

What happened to your parents?

In July 1939 my parents emigrated to Palestine. My sister was able to continue on from England to Palestine because she was entered on my parents' entry certificate, although special permission was needed from the English King.

Both my maternal grandmother and my uncle—her son—were sent in August 1942 to *Theresienstadt*. She was eighty-two years old! They both died there.[1] My grandmother's brothers and sisters were all killed, together with their relatives. To complete the picture I should tell you that my uncle, Siegfried Landesberg, fought for his country in the First World War and was decorated for bravery. He was badly wounded and lost a lung on account of his injuries. He was an invalid for the rest of his life. My grandmother told us in her last communication from *Theresienstadt* of the "passing away of her son."

My grandmother's father was a military doctor. She had ten brothers and sisters—my great aunts and uncles. I knew them all well including their children and grandchildren. I loved them all. . . all but three of them were killed.

---

[1]See *Totenbuch Theresienstadt*, p. 78. "Landesberg, Agathe, born Stein 28.2.1866, died?"

Do you have a family?

Yes. I have two grown-up children. My daughter lives in England, she's forty-six. My son lives in Graz and is forty-two. My husband has already died. My parents were assimilated Jews and weren't religious.

You've suffered unspeakably. How do you look back on it all today?

In comparison with other people I experienced "nothing." I wasn't in a concentration camp and I'm still alive today, fifty years after.

But what happened to my loved ones? What were their last thoughts—I always ask myself that question.

"...I believe in the good in people..."

Conversation with *Hans Sipötz* on 30 December 1987.

Johann Sipötz was born in 1941 in Pamhagen, the son of a railroad worker. A teacher by profession, since 1974 he has been a state member of parliament for the Austrian Social Democratic Party, and since October 1987 governor of Burgenland.

Mr. Sipötz, naturally I can't ask you about your memories of 1938 since you weren't born then, but I can ask about some contemporary political problems that are connected with this year.

How will you observe the year 1988 bearing in mind that it's "Fifty Years After"? And how important was 1938 for the Burgenland?

There will be many events, commemorating what happened fifty years ago. 1938 meant not only a change in the Burgenland's political structure, it meant the end of the Burgenland as a state. Because in this year its territory was divided up between Lower Austria and Styria. Of course, we will stress those aspects of 1938 that were peculiar to Burgenland, the things that happened there that year.

Mr. Sipötz, you were a teacher and you taught history. How did you handle the period 1938 to 1945 with your students?

I dealt with all the material thoroughly in the appropriate class, right up until recent times. I never left periods out, and every aspect was mentioned. I always tried to show what actually happened, how the people then were led astray. I often noticed that my students were really affected by it.

Do you think that, in so far as *Vergangenheitsbewältigung* (coming to terms with the past) since 1945 is concerned, things have been neglected? And that there's a lot to catch up?

I see *Vergangenheitsbewältigung*—if one uses that word—only in terms of making people aware of the terrible crimes that were committed then. They must know just what happened then! All the facts must be laid out, without emotion, and in every case I'm against apportioning blame—that always leads to resistance.

Were we "liberated" in 1945 or did we lose "our war"? How do you answer this question when it's asked by fellow citizens, students or young people?

I think we should remember that a great many people were soldiers. And the overwhelming majority had nothing to do with the Nazis. The soldier in captivity was bound to view the situation in which he found himself as one of defeat.

Do you think that Austrian soldiers who fought in Hitler's army can fall back on the concept of "fulfillment of duty"? And if so, how can this argument be reconciled with the Moscow Declaration of 1943?

One has to formulate it differently. One has to add that it was a "forced fulfillment of duty." Otherwise you exclude free will. And that did not exist. People had no choice, if they didn't want to risk their lives.

There were Jewish communities in your state until 1938, self-governing bodies that were recognized by the authorities. What's it like today?

Yes, Mattersburg had until the beginning of the century, and Eisenstadt-Unterberg until the *Anschluss,* autonomous Jewish communities with a Jewish mayor and notary.

The Jewish communities were Eisenstadt, Mattersburg, Kobersdorf, Deutschkreutz, Lackenbach, Frauenkirchen, and Kittsee.

But there were also older communities in south Burgenland at Rechnitz, Guessing, and Schlaining. Schlaining transferred its community status to Oberwart in 1929.

Today there are no Jewish communities anymore.

The *Anschluss* hit the Burgenland Jews particularly hard. The people of the "Sieben Gemeinden," for example, had been close to the land and people of this frontier region for centuries. They'd given their blood for Burgenland like other citizens of that state who looked upon it as their homeland. Yet they suffered unimaginably with Hitler's invasion of Austria. They were registered and deported. Under beating and unspeakable threats, the more prosperous Jews were compelled to sign away their entire property to the German Reich. These people were dispossessed and driven out. But even this process was too slow a solution of the Burgenland "Jewish Question" for the local Nazi bosses, and they adopted a policy of immediate deportment. The Jews were repeatedly driven to the Yugoslav border, where they were repeatedly driven back by Yugoslav border guards.[1]

You say there are no more Jewish communities in Burgenland. Is there anti-Semitism there? And how do the Burgenland people treat minorities like Hungarians, Croats, or Gypsies, for example?

I think that it is precisely because the Burgenland developed as a border region that there was always a strong measure of tolerance amongst the people. We have a relatively large Croatian

---

[1]Jonny Moser, "Die Vertreibung der burgenländischen Juden", in *Das jüdische Echo. Zeitschrift für Kultur und Politik* (October 1987), p. 78.

minority—20,000 to 30,000—and also a Hungarian-speaking one.

But there are not only language groups, there are also religious minorities. We have a large percentage of Protestants. We can say that there is really good cooperation between the different groups.

If you ask me if there is anti-Semitism in our state, then I would have to tell you that I haven't noticed it. But of course I can't see into the hearts and minds of every single individual.

Has the damage caused by rowdies in the Jewish cemetery at Eisenstadt been cleared up? It was said that children were responsible!?

I personally believe it was children and not any kind of political organization. In the last few years there's never been any incidents of any kind. Most of the Jewish cemeteries have survived in good order.

Ottilie Matysek has said that the Protestants in Gols are still Nazis. What do you say to that?

I don't believe that. The Protestants just have a stronger relationship with Germany. But that's a natural consequence of their religion. In earlier times they would have joined the German Nationalists.

What do you think of the FPÖ member Dürr, who has gained notoriety through the neo-Nazi brochure *Sieg*? What do you think of his remark on TV that he could not say anything about Auschwitz because he wasn't a historian? Would such a man be acceptable to you as a negotiating partner?

First I'd like to say that since Steger's departure the FPÖ has left the liberal camp and is without doubt becoming more nationalistic.

Up until this television appearance Dürr hadn't done anything worth mentioning. I was appalled by his remarks on this occasion. I didn't know this *Sieg* journal. Of course he knows about *Auschwitz*, he just won't recognize it. I would only deal with him if he appeared in some form of self-defense organization.

What would you do if *Sieg* were distributed in front of schools?

I'm no legal expert and I'd have to take advice. I'd take the appropriate measures within the framework of the law.

What would you like to say about the memorial year 1988?

That we will try and commemorate 1938 in appropriate fashion. As I've already said, my primary aim is to give the facts in an unemotional way to schoolchildren, with the help of eye-witnesses and accompanying discussions. Trips to Mauthausen are also planned. The seductive nature of National Socialism must also be emphasized so that young people are aware and alert to the dangers. Alert to the danger of propaganda. Many events are planned, and as far as I know the Chancellor—who also comes from Lackenbach—will also visit Burgenland. Despite all the terrible things that have happened, I believe in the good in people, and it will be in this vein that I will appeal to my fellow citizens.

I think that it's important that something happens inside the individual. People must be made aware what it means for a neighbor to suddenly have his apartment taken away from him, to be deported, to no longer be greeted on the street. All these tragic things must be made "clear" to people, above all young people.

". . . I was against it through and through. . ."

Conversation with *Kurt Skalnik* on 9 November 1987.

Dr. Skalnik, born in 1925, was in Vienna in 1938. Today he is head of the Press and Information Service of the Presidents' Office.

Dr. Skalnik, you were already a teenager in 1938. How do you remember that year, as a growing boy?

I was, as you know, just thirteen in 1938. I grew up in a politically turbulent time, if you think of what happened in the thirties. I remember 1933 when for the first time there was no Socialist march around the Ring. They were only allowed to walk. I remember, too, the Spanish Riders lining up. And the artillery fire in 1934. . . the first night everything was dark. . . yes, well, those are memories from my youth. It was a time when politics even got into the schools.

Which school did you go to? Did Jewish children go there too?

I went to the Vienna High School IX—the Wasagymnasium. There was a branch of the youth organization of the Fatherland

Front there. They had the rather pompous name of "Studenten-freikorps."[1]

Some interesting people came out of this organization—some are still alive today. We met when we were still in short pants, so to speak. For example the Molden brothers, Fritz and Otto, or the recently retired Vice President of the Administrative Court, Dr. Jurasek, or the Mayor of Klagenfurt, Guggerberger. The list is quite long. I can't remember how I got involved in this organization.

Did you suffer under the economic conditions in these years?

I could really sing a song about that.

My father's business went "belly-up" in the crisis. He found a job as a school teacher. He was already over forty and had to start again with a new profession. He had to start studying again and take exams. . . and look after a family of three on 150 Schillings a month. You can't exactly live it up on that.

Something else occurs to me: we got goose drippings (fat) at the entrance to the Schottenkeller. It was cheaper than pig drippings, and these goose drippings were on the table every day of the week. Every night we had tea and bread with goose drippings!

Let's return to 1938. Do you have any special memories of your school days?

There was a youth leader there who was a driving force in political and spiritual matters. He had what you'd call today "charisma." He was about seventeen, and for me, as a thirteen-year-old, he was someone to look up to. We were a very patriotic Austrian group, above all very anti-Nazi.

Could one say then that your circle of friends and acquaintances were against the *Anschluss*?

---

[1]The *Freikorps* or Free Corps, were independent militias formed in Germany and Austria after the First World War. Composed largely of veterans from that war, their purpose was to combat Bolshevism and left-wing insurgency.

Yes! Look, my family were not very political. My parents voted for the Christian Socials, but they were struggling to recover their livelihood, their economic position. There was a sound Austrian tradition in our family, and we certainly weren't "greater German."

Did your parents contribute to your political development?

No. My parents didn't influence my political development in any way. On the contrary, they were very reserved as far as politics were concerned.

Do you remember the day of the *Anschluss*? Do you have a particular memory?

This day remains very clear in my memory. I can see the Judenplatz. Groups of young people assembled from the different high schools in the early afternoon of 11 March. It was a demonstration for Schuschnigg and his plebiscite on Austria's independence. The slogans were the same as those in Parliament: "Bis in den Tod: rot-weiss-rot!" [Until Death: Red-White-Red!]

Yes, I was also shouting these words. Then we marched over Wipplinger Strasse into the Hof (a large square). Suddenly there was trouble. All the junior school kids—of which I was one—had to get home quickly. It was the time when the plebiscite was abandoned.

Did your life and that of your family change with the *Anschluss*?

Yes. It was a real shock for me. And my family was very depressed. We felt intimidated. The name of Austria was totally eliminated, and I can remember how much it hurt to see the name AUSTRIA painted over, even on the railroad cars.

Those are things which come to mind. It probably sounds pompous and clever, but I was never attracted to the so-called [Nazi] "new age." I suppose I could say I was against it "through and through." I even avoided going into the Hitler Youth.

Did you have the impression then that everybody was Nazi, or were there people in your circle who were sad at what was happening?

We lived in our own little world. We retreated into it. There were some who had originally been enthusiastic about National Socialism, but they soon turned their backs on it.

Were there resistance fighters in your circle?

My friends and I were all, more or less, "subversive." The *Gestapo* was in our school several times.

What happened then to the Jewish students?

In the Wasagymnasium we had more Jewish kids than Catholics. There was a sort of "Apartheid." I didn't have any close personal relationship to a Jewish school colleague. It had nothing to do with race or religion. It was rather because the Jewish kids tended to come from more prosperous families.

Interestingly it was we who had to leave the school suddenly, and the Jewish students remained in the old school where we'd previously all been together. We Christian kids were sent to the G.19, and the Wasagymnasium was reserved for the Jewish students. We were suddenly ripped apart and we didn't know what their fate was.

Like I said, I had no close Jewish school friends. Of course we found out later what had happened.

Did you know in 1938, before the *Kristallnacht*, what was happening to the Jews? Did you see the humiliating way in which they were treated, for example, how they were made to clean the streets with buckets and brushes?

Yes, I saw that. But, as you know, I was against the whole regime and naturally I was against their methods. People were very scared. . . and what could a thirteen-year-old do? I can only remember that when one saw such things, and I can only speak for myself, I just got out of the way. It was depressing.

You saw that yourself then—Jews, including old people, being forced to clean the streets in humiliating fashion while people stood around and jeered?

Yes, I saw that. . . I saw Jews being mocked and humiliated.

And your Jewish school colleagues, you lost contact with them altogether?

Yes. We were too busy with our own personal quarrel with the regime. The Nazi propaganda was so intensive, you wanted to crawl into yourself. . . that probably sounds very clever, but it really was so. I never believed this Reich would be a "thousand" years old. I always hoped it would come to a quick end.

I volunteered for the German Red Cross when I was fifteen.

But shouldn't you have joined the Hitler Youth when you were 13?

I went once and saw what was happening. It made me sick.

Why did it make you sick? Weren't most people enthusiastic? The sport and this "togetherness," so many people have said.

I had already experienced that, but under different auspices. As I said, I was against the Nazis through and through. Of course I have friends today who were enthusiastic Hitler Youth members back then. I don't hold it against them. But for me, I have to say I'm sorry, in other words, I'm not sorry! I wasn't.

And what about your parents? Were they enthusiastic?

No, on the contrary. But my parents tried to make the best of the situation. My father tried to calm me down.

"What do you want?" he'd say, "you can't emigrate."

Actually there were various ways to offer resistance, to express one's rejection. For example, one could show great affection for the professor of religion. He was replaced pretty soon with another, who in turn was also replaced.

Eventually we had a professor who called upon us to pray for the *Führer*. The class refused to do so, so he prayed on his own.

This professor of religion wanted you to pray for the *Führer*?

Yes. Actually he was always accompanied by his cook. I can't remember exactly but I think that was 1940 or 1941.

The *Gestapo* came to the school all the time. Even before the beginning of the war there were radio broadcasts from abroad, for example from France, they had the slogan, "Hang on, Austrians—Austria will be free again!"

Did you listen to foreign radio broadcasts or read foreign newspapers?

I never saw foreign papers, but I listened to foreign radio broadcasts.

Do you remember the *Kristallnacht*? In Vienna terrible things happened didn't they?

Yes. I lived in the 9th District and that was the fashionable Jewish area.

Did you have any idea what was coming?

No. You know that *Kristallnacht* was a planned retaliation for the assassination of von Rath.[2] That night I saw the synagogue on Müllnergasse burning.

How did you become aware of this terrible *Kristallnacht*?

In the afternoon—I can't remember when exactly—I saw shops that had been destroyed and daubed with slogans.

---

[2]Ernst von Rath was the counsellor in the German Embassy in Paris shot by the young Polish Jew, Herschel Grynszpan. For details see Erika Weinzierl, *Zu wenig Gerechte. Österreicher und Judenverfolgung 1938-1945* (Graz/Wien/Köln, 1969), p. 55.

What did you feel?

It's not possible to recapture such feelings after fifty years. But then one hardly expected anything else from this mob.

Did you know people who were deported to concentration camps? Who died there?

There was one personal tragedy that had nothing to do with the *Kristallnacht*, but that took place in the last days of the war. A relative of mine who was connected to the Polish resistance was betrayed, arrested by the *Gestapo*, and sentenced to death. He was taken to Stein, where he was shot in April 1945. The director of the prison, who was an Austrian patriot, wanted to let all the prisoners go free. But a SA man from Krems told the SS, and they came and had the prisoners shot—right at the end of April 1945.

These men were condemned to death after the war by an Austrian court and hanged, but that didn't bring back any of those who had been murdered.

But it has to be said that the people in Austria with blood on their hands were later called to account. It's important to say that!

Did you know anything about the concentration camps?

I knew about *Dachau* already in 1938. I can remember that it was talked about, how people were treated terribly there.

Mayor Schmitz, who was, incidentally, my first general director of "Herold" Publishing after 1945, had to dig a whole pile of dirt to one side and the next day he was made to put it back again.

Whether that's right or not, I don't know, but that's what they said then in Vienna.

Did you know what was going on already after Hitler's seizure of power in 1933?

Yes, and in these years from 1933 until 1938 Austria was receiving German émigrés. Anti-Nazi Catholics and Jews came in those years to Austria. Thus we found out what was going on in Germany.

Would you like to say anything in conclusion? Something for young people, fifty years later? Should we learn from history?

Certainly one should learn from history and be alert to every kind of injustice and totalitarianism, irrespective of whether it comes from the right or the left.

"... that no one ... must feel afraid ..."

Conversation with *Alfred Stingl* on 23 November 1987.

Mr. Stingl was born in 1939 and is presently the mayor of the city of Graz.

Wilhelm Keppler, Hitler's Special Representative in Austria, reckoned that about 80% of the population of Graz sympathized with the Nazis at the end of February 1938. There were open demonstrations of support for the Nazis before the *Anschluss*. What happened in Graz was decisive for Styria and stoked the fires of discontent throughout Austria. They called it the "City of the People's Revolution."[1]

In March 1938 there were still around 1,700 members of the Jewish community. It seems a historical fact that before 1938, despite apparent attempts to combat anti-Semitism, there was no area of life in Graz that was completely free of anti-Semitic feelings—whether it was mere indifference to the

---

[1]Karner, *Steiermark*, p. 44.

fate of Jews, sympathy for anti-Jewish measures, or active racism to the point of participating in their murder.[2]

Jews were abused, stripped of their rights as citizens, driven out of their homes and, in many cases, murdered in concentration camps. Today there are hardly a hundred Jews left in Graz!

The latest Presidental election campaign (1986) has led to a revival of anti-Semitism in Austria, and precisely at this time, Mayor Stingl, you accepted an invitation to visit the Jewish community in Graz. You are the first mayor of this city since 1945 to make such a visit. Why did you make this visit, which was so warmly greeted by the Jewish community?

With this visit, and representing all the citizens of the city of Graz, I wanted to demonstrate our honest efforts to achieve social peace—above all peaceful cooperation among all religious and racial groups. I am of the opinion that we know very well what our history is. None of us can deny the facts of history. Instead we should accept that we can learn from this history—from this history that led to such tragedy.

I want to help produce policies that will sharpen our perception of human rights. Mutual friction and hatred must be ended! The protection of individual freedom must take the highest priority. The rights of all Austrians must be guaranteed, irrespective of race, sex, language, religion, or political conviction. While we must take notice of what is happening in other countries of the world, we must also watch our own society, above all, take note of what is going on in our immediate environment. We must continually ask ourselves whether our policies live up to our concepts of human rights and the dignity of man.

In the (Graz) City Hall we are concerned to create an atmosphere of understanding, tolerance and respect for other people.

As the mayor of this city I want to ensure that no one—and that especially includes our Jewish fellow citizens—must feel afraid. That should never happen again!

---

[2]Dieter A. Binder, "Das Schicksal der Grazer Juden 1938," in *Historisches Jahrbuch der Stadt Graz* (1987), p. 2.

I visited the Jewish community with my friends because I knew that this was an important historical site. The spiritual and religious center of the cultural community stood here, an architecturally important synagogue, which fell victim to the barbarism of the Nazi system.

I was aware of the honor of being the first mayor since 1945 to visit the home of the present—much reduced—Jewish community. A place that bears witness to the burden of history! I am hopeful that we will be able to go into this year of memorial (the fiftieth anniversary of the *Anschluss*) in the spirit of bipartisan understanding. This memorial year should be observed by the generation that now carries responsibility, without presumption or self-righteousness. Our unwavering intention should be: no more fascism, and vigilance against all forms of intolerance and violation of human rights.

". . . who were to be got rid of, in the event of the worst happening. . ."

Conversations with *Alfred Sturminger* on 6 and 20 October, and 5 November 1987.

Dr. Alfred Sturminger was born in 1903 in Vienna. In 1938 he was in Graz as a director of the firm Kastner & Oehler. After 1945 he was General Director of Meinl AG.

Dr. Sturminger, how do you remember 1938?

On 12 March 1938 seven men armed with dog whips took me from my home. My daughter, whose third birthday we were celebrating, showed aggressive tendencies even at that age and bit the leader in the knee.

I was told I was being taken into "protective custody." When I asked them why, and from whom I was being protected, I received the informative answer, that it was only called that, which didn't surprise me.

Do you think the Austrians didn't defend themselves against Hitler's invasion?

It's always said, not without reproach, that many Austrians cheered when Hitler came. Of course, many did, too many. You could see them. But you didn't see the ones who didn't cheer, and certainly you didn't see the 60,000 people who were imprisoned within the first forty-eight hours.

You were in Graz in 1938. What do you remember of the city from this time?

Even in Graz, the "City of the People's Revolution," there were so many people in prison that, for example, in my cell, which was a single cell, there were seven people lying on the floor. We drew lots every day as to who would have to sleep next to the "can." It all took place in the former police headquarters, which was now occupied by the SA and the SS. There were only a few policemen allowed to remain in service, chosen on an individual basis.

One day one of these policemen stuck his head in at the door of our cell. He was an old man with a walrus mustache, and he whispered to us, clearly very scared,

"Excuse me, gentlemen, I have to shout at you."

It was meant in a friendly manner. We showed him understanding. It was a scene that told one a lot about human beings. You see, even the older members of the police force were in danger, and outside he had to play the hard man. He was our guard, but he was unhappy and thereby showed us his humanity.

We were all in this situation for the first time, and so we had no experience. Then we had the "good fortune" that a "professional" was put in with us, a communist who had been imprisoned several times before. This man was a real refreshment for us amateurs. He knew, for example, how to make the cell door stay open longer for ventilation, he produced cigarettes like magic—he knew all the tricks. Moreover, he provided good material for conversation since, as a communist, he was able to take far more liberties than we others; because, at the beginning at least, the SA tried to win these people over.

In the evening there were the daily "rounds," as in a hospital. An SS leader followed by a bunch of SA men went from cell to cell. When we heard them coming we stood up, so that we wouldn't have to stand up in front of them. Every day the leader asked us why we were there, to which we didn't answer.

Only our communist answered, "because I always come too late."

At first he'd been on the extreme left and was twice imprisoned. Then he was apolitical until he decided, too late, to support the Dollfuss-Schuschnigg government. Now he was happily back "inside." And when he eventually decided to serve the *Führer*, then doubtless he would be too late again. Then of course he got yelled at about the "Thousand Year Reich," to which he gave the classic answer, "Yes, of course, world history is going to stand still." This remark became a standard quotation in our family and was a comfort to us at critical moments.

I can remember another dialogue of his. In answer to the SS man's usual question about whether everything was OK, our Red friend said, "there's a bug over there."

"OK, kill it!"

"Well, I don't know whether I should—you see it's brown."

Then he was cursed violently and told to "get on with it!"

He squashed the bug flat and said loudly, "look here, from the outside it's brown, from the inside it's red!"

If it's possible the human being will adapt himself to any conditions. I'm no psychiatrist but I'd attribute it to the instinct for survival.

What did the prisoners do during the day in your cell?

We tried to divert ourselves from our predicament by telling stories about our different jobs.

One of our cellmates, Frederic de Zsolnay (a relative of the Zsolnay publishing family) found a way to play chess. From bread and water we made chess pieces, which we distinguished one from the other by means of bits of matchsticks. We were lucky that one of our cellmates had a handkerchief with exactly the same number of squares on it as a chess board. We washed it and pressed it as well as we were able, and in no time I was checkmate. I've never played as much chess as I played then, because I never had so much time, either before or since.

Do you remember anybody famous who was in prison then?

In the next cell there was a man who was not exactly unknown—it was Bishop Ferdinand Pawlikowski. But he wasn't imprisoned for long. An order came from Berlin that he wasn't to be held too long.

One day the cell door was opened and an old "Geldbrief-träger" (a man who delivers money orders) with full pockets was pushed in. It transpired that he was the first prisoner of the new era. A young colleague of his had provoked him by continuously giving him the "Heil Hitler" salute, which of course he had to return. Finally he got sick of it and interrupted the youth with the famous remark of Goetz von Berlichingen ("lick my behind") which landed him in prison with us.

Then there was another case that I'll admit gave us immense satisfaction; we didn't get much pleasure at that time, as you can imagine. The Nazis, when they were still illegal (before the *Anschluss*), had managed to slip one of their own people as a spy into a local office of their opponents, the Fatherland Front. When the Nazis took over the *Gestapo* arrested everyone there, but their own spy, despite his protests, was also put in prison. Whenever we had the "rounds," this unlucky wretch would declare his innocence, but it didn't do him any good.

"Yeah, we know, you can tell that to your grandmother," was all the response he got.

In short, he didn't get out of prison a day before us, which caused him ever increasing bitterness, and gave us an unedifying, but nonetheless especially enjoyable measure of *Schadenfreude*. Perhaps he was one of the first to be "cured" [of National Socialism].

What sort of feelings did you have during your imprisonment?

The worst thing about our situation was the fact that we had really no idea of what they were going to do with us. We weren't interrogated, we weren't accused—nothing. They just wanted to let us rot and wear us down. We would all have liked a fixed date.

Then one day we were told, "Everybody down in the yard." When we asked what was happening, we were told, "I don't know, either you're being released or sent to a concentration camp."

In the end we were told we would be released but would have to sign a declaration which read, "I take notice that if I continue subversive activities against the state, I will be sent to a concentration camp."

I told Dr. X, who gave me the declaration to sign, that I couldn't sign it because up until the *Anschluss* I'd never been engaged in subversive activities against the state, and since then I'd been in his "protective custody." (In contrast, he had been an illegal Nazi while an Austrian police official.) I was particularly worried that the word "continue" could be used against us later. It needed a long argument before he finally replaced "continue" with "commit."

What occurs to you in retrospect from this time in prison?

You wouldn't believe what we looked like when we were released; it was good that we couldn't see ourselves. We'd worn the same clothes for two months, had eaten and slept on the floor, and were only able to do the minimum amount of washing. Everybody had a wild beard and stank.

Then we had another piece of "Austrian" luck. We didn't want to go home through the town in these clothes. There was an old policeman on guard at the gate; he knew who we were and he got us taxis and we rode home.

There's something I'd like to add to my "prison memories." Of course it was a shock, and the worst thing was the uncertainty about what they would do with us. But what was that in comparison to the terrible fate that hundreds of thousands—millions —had to suffer?! Yes, even though I lost my job, was banned from Styria by Gauleiter Ueberreiter, was summoned endless times to the Vienna *Gestapo*, and at the end was put on the list of people who were to be "gotten rid of" in the event of the worst happening, the so-called "K-Fall," despite all this, I have to be thankful that I'm still here to recall my memories!

I don't want you to misunderstand me.

You wanted to tell me about Mrs. Pavlin—who got an "invoice" for the execution of her husband. How did that happen?

There was a certain Mrs. W who worked in my office anonymously. She worked so hard and was so keen, that I often thought of a book I'd read in my childhood called *Blinder Eifer schadet nur* (Blind Eagerness Only Hurts You). She was friends with the wife of a very prominent leader of the illegal Communist Party, Mr. Pavlin.

One day Mrs. W told me that Pavlin, together with a Graz architect called Aichholzer, had been condemned to death. I told her that I knew Aichholzer slightly. She immediately told her friend Mrs. Pavlin, that on her next—probably last—visit to her husband, she should tell him that I sent greetings to his comrade Aichholzer.

The next day the lawyer Dr. Paulick, who was a friend of mine and who had been appointed as Pavlin's defense attorney, told me that Mrs. Pavlin had been arrested while visiting her husband. A watchdog had overheard her passing on greetings to Aichholzer from someone, but he hadn't caught the name. They had arrested her so they could get it out of her.

Three anxious weeks went by as they "worked" on her to get her to talk. But she withstood the interrogation and said nothing. They had to release her, all the more so as the execution of her husband and Aichholzer was about to take place.

I would like to take this opportunity of remembering, in gratitude and respect, the brave and courageous way she protected me—without even knowing me—from an awful fate.

Shortly afterwards the two men were executed by guillotine in the Vienna Landesgericht, along with twenty other people whom I knew personally, among them a seventeen-year-old boy. 1,184 prisoners were executed in the Vienna Landesgericht alone.

Then there's something I wouldn't have believed possible if I hadn't seen it with my own eyes and held it in my hand—the bill that Mrs. Pavlin received for the execution of her husband, complete with an enclosed money-order transfer form (a slip with which she could pay the money).

You've told me a great deal about 1938, what was it like during the war?

As I told you, at the time of the *Anschluss* I was arrested by the SA and the SS. I spent some time in prison, I was relieved of my position, and was banned from the Gau (District) by the (Nazi) Gauleiter.

Later I was more or less tolerated in the branch offices of the Julius Meinl concern. After 1945 I became general director of Julius Meinl in Europe.

To come back to 1938 in Graz. Did you notice anti-Semitism? What were the political views of people in Graz?

Look, if you ask me, then I'll have to tell you: it all began in Graz. Eight days before the *Anschluss* there was already a swastika flying over the Graz City Hall, and Austria still existed then!

Do you mean that there had been enthusiasm for Hitler even before?

Partly, yes.

And what about anti-Semitism?

That's been around since Pontius Pilate. . . there have always been anti-Semites.

Graz was called the "City of the People's Revolution" and they had it pretty lenient. I can remember I traveled to Graz once on the bus and got into a conversation with a very respectable old lady, and suddenly she started going for the Jews.

When was that?

Around 1937.

So, already in 1937?

Yes. I asked her whether she'd had bad experiences with Jews. She said she didn't know any. . . had never seen a Jew in her whole life. . . had never met a Jew. . . thank God!. . .[1]

---

[1]"The most important difference between anti-Semitism and xenophobia is that in the latter case you have to have foreigners whom one can see, hear, and smell. However banal it sounds, it is a fact that there can be no xenophobia without the presence of foreigners in the immediate environment.

Why did you leave Graz after 1938? You liked the city, you had a good job with Kastner & Oehler and you'd lived in Graz since 1929?

I wouldn't have left Graz if I hadn't had to. I liked Graz very much, but as you now know, I was arrested. . . I was very satisfied with my position as a director of Kastner & Oehler and got on well with the bosses—Franz Oehler as well as Albert Kastner.

Why were you arrested actually?

Look, in Graz everybody knew everybody else. I was, after all, a director of a Jewish department store. Mr. Oehler was decorated with the Golden Bravery Medal, which was the highest award one could get after the Order of Maria Theresia, and he was severely wounded in the First World War. Nonetheless he was caught by the Nazis in Agram and died in a concentration camp. . . that was what it was like then!!

Apart from my position, everyone at Oehler's knew that I wasn't a Nazi. I never made a secret of it. I come from an old Austrian family. Cardinal von Rauscher of Vienna was my maternal grandfather's cousin, and he married Emperor Franz Josef to Empress Elisabeth.

And there was a big difference in my view: in Germany the National Socialist Party was a legal political party, while in Austria it was treason to belong to it.

During the war you were spied on, arrested, and interrogated. How do you see the situation today, fifty years later?

This is not the case with anti-Semitism. People who have never seen a Jew in their lives can be passionate anti-Semites. In fact the absence of real experience of Jews is often a precondition for the development of anti-Semitic beliefs. Anti-Semitism can exist very well as a collective phenomenon without the presence of Jews; in countries in which there have been for a long time no more or very few Jews—in Poland or West Germany for example—there is still a very real degree of anti-Semitism, an anti-Semitism without Jews." Taken from Henryk M. Broder, *Der ewige Antisemit. Über Sinn und Funktion eines beständigen Gefühls* (Frankfurt a.M, 1986), p. 26.

You know 1938 was especially difficult for me because it was the first time in my life that I was imprisoned. I had policemen on both sides of my family—my father was court counsellor to the police, my grandfather was police president, my brother was also with the police. So I was the only one in our family who, instead of locking up others, had been locked up himself. And that was a disturbing situation. But that's all in the past.

Don't let us hang our heads, even if the world doesn't seem so wonderful. In 1945 we all held together in Austria, why can't we do it today? Cooperation is necessary.

To return to the war—you wanted to tell me about 20 July 1944. Were you in Vienna then?

Everybody knew that morale among the population was low, especially after the defeat at Stalingrad—except those who wouldn't accept the truth.

And the fact that Hitler's obstinacy had made him personally responsible for the scale of the debacle at Stalingrad had the effect of undermining his much-vaunted reputation as the "greatest general of all time" (Goebbels). There was clearly a crisis looming up.

The news that German generals had come to Vienna to contact the Austrian resistance, that the deputy head of the British Secret Service was in Vienna (in the middle of a war), and that it was possible to carry out political transfers through the highest ranks of the reserve army—all this was taken by our group at first to be unbelievable. Until we received more and more evidence that it was so.

Shortly before the 20 July assassination attempt (on Hitler's life), I was with the former mayor of Vienna and leading Social Democrat, Karl Seitz, in his apartment, when, to my surprise, Carl Goerdeler arrived.[2]

---

[2]Carl Goerdeler was a former Mayor of Leipzig and after 1939 the leader of the non-communist (German) resistance to Hitler. He would have headed a provisional government of Germany in the event of a successful coup against the Nazi dictatorship. As it was, he was arrested and executed after the failed July plot.

On 19 July I was summoned by Consul Julius Meinl to his estate at Prerau in Lower Austria. The *SS Oberführer*, Mayer, had also said he would come. He was a *Waffen-SS* general and *Staatsrat* from Hamburg, where in the coffee trade there he'd been known as *Pleite-Mayer* (bankrupt Mayer). He'd been placed in the Meinl concern by the Berlin *Gestapo* as a Nazi watchdog with the position of Vice President. Unbeknownst to us, the chief of the Vienna *Gestapo* also said he'd come.

During the meal the assassination attempt by Stauffenberg was announced on the radio, the news of which, of course, went round the table like a bomb. Everything was dropped and left where it was, as everybody had "to get back to Vienna as quickly as possible." *Staatsrat* Mayer drove back with Consul Meinl, while I—because it was practical—rode back with the *Gestapo* chief. The trip was macabre, neither of us knowing what had really happened. Of course, the meeting between Seitz and Goerdeler was going through my head, and the thought that if the assassination attempt had failed, the *Gestapo* chief sitting next to me would hand me over to the executioner. Of course, everbody knows how the whole thing turned out. Goerdeler was executed, Seitz was imprisoned, and my presence at that meeting was fortunately never made known.

Only a very few Viennese know that the military command had already locked up the Nazi bosses (Schirach, etc.) in the War Ministry building in Vienna.

We now know practically everything about Hitler's revenge, carried out by his chief executioner (People's Court President, Roland) Freissler—although perhaps not what an eye-witness, the SS representative with the *Abwehr* (German Military Counter-Intelligence), *SS-Sturmbannführer* Eistert, told me. The head of the *Abwehr*, Admiral Canaris, whom I also knew, was hanged three times on Hitler's orders. At the point when he was about to die, he was cut down from the meat hook, brought back to consciousness, and hanged again. The whole thing was filmed according to Hitler's wishes and shown to him.

You were with Meinl already during the War. This concern qualified as "important for the war effort" and an SS man was put into it. How was it then? You told me that you were

able to see secret documents not intended for your eyes. What was in these documents?

Because the firm was designated "important for the war effort" we had this "counter-intelligence representative" from the *Gestapo*. He had the rank of *SS-Hauptsturmführer* and his office, consisting of three rooms, was adjacent to mine, much to my disappointment. In practice he had the function of a political commissar. Through certain circumstances I succeeded in laying my hands on some documents of this "counter-intelligence representative." I can show you this little *Gestapo* booklet "Guidelines for the Security Activities of the Counter-Intelligence Representative". This secret article, as it was officially called, consisted of seven pages of instructions. I also found in the dossier a list of "recruited" spies (informers).

I can give you a copy of a letter that the "counter-intelligence representative" of another of our branches, in Warsaw, wrote to his colleague in Vienna, our SS man, Eistert. This letter shows what kind of methods the *Gestapo* used to force people into betraying their colleagues and work-mates.[3]

Would you like to tell me something about the end of the "Thousand Year Reich" and your "permit" from the Russians?

I told you that the Vienna *Gestapo* required from our "counter-intelligence representative" the names of people who were "to be gotten rid of" in the event of the worst happening. Our *SS-Obersturmbannführer* Eistert complied and provided a list of six names, of which mine was in second place.

---

[3]This letter, dated 22 January 1944 and directed to Eistert at the Julius Meinl AG in Vienna, dealt with the acute need to ascertain the mood among the company's work force and its attitude to the prevailing political/military situation. A certain Polish woman had sought to achieve relief for her husband, who was gravely ill in a concentration camp, and the SS representantive in the Polish branch of Meinl's agreed to help her if she agreed to take employment in the firm with the specific assignment of spying on her workmates and providing the *Gestapo* with information. Eistert was called upon to help the husband in the concentration camp.

One can easily imagine that a dictatorship that collapses in panic and fear will resort to a wild shooting spree as it goes down. But that the whole thing be arranged in bureaucratic fashion, with typed letters, saying who was to be "gotten rid of"— that is really something else, beyond comprehension.

So it was a welcome development, for us "doomed ones," that our presumed executioners, our SS heroes, shook with fear and took to their heels. They "commandeered" two trucks, packed all their secret documents in boxes, seized a load of supplies (mainly alcohol) which had been reserved for the Army, and roared off towards the west.

After a while I got permission from the Russians to drive to Linz and Salzburg in order to bring some order to the administration of the firm's branches there. In Linz I was told that our fleeing heroes had unloaded a couple of boxes to give them more space for food and drink, until they set off again. I succeeded in finding these boxes and had them delivered to my hotel, where I spent the whole night reading these secret documents.

I was close to losing faith in humanity. Of course, I'd expected to find evidence of denunciation, but what really shook me was that people whom I thought I knew had been prepared to deliver others into the executioner's hands. Apart from that I found secret minutes of meetings, instructions for the press, and a lot of material on secret operations, personal files, lists of people who carried secrets, lists of informers and diagrams of spy networks etc. It was enough to make you throw up!!!

How did you get over it all? Your faith in humans was restored surely?

Well there were inexcusable denunciations, but I also found evidence that some of the people only cooperated under pressure and blackmail, and that helped bring me out of my depression.

It wasn't easy to get this *Gestapo* material back over the demarcation line without it falling into the hands of the Russians. Some people took big risks helping to do that.

When I think how many people risked their own life and liberty to help others—I knew many—you have to be thankful to them.

Evil is loud, good by contrast is quiet, so you get a rather distorted picture.

You wanted to give me some details of the firm for which you worked for so many years?

The firm I worked for had to try and defend itself during the Nazi dictatorship against all manner of unreasonable demands. It had branches all over Europe, in eight countries, and so the Security Service (SD) wanted to set up a spy network in hundreds of shops. It cost a lot to prevent this.

One day as the air attacks against Vienna were increasing and complaints were getting worse, it was proposed that we convert a candy factory that we owned into a "collection center for corpses"—as it was called. Again, it took a lot of effort to head off that plan.

In both world wars there was a clear symptom of how bad the situation was: when we were ordered to use turnip schnitzel instead of coffee, it was bad. But when we were ordered to use turnip remains, then we knew that the end was near.

In 1938 Hitler came and occupied our country. What would you like to say in conclusion?

Hitler didn't just annex Austria in 1938, he also attempted to rob our homeland of its name and to degrade our country to an *Ostmark*.

The collective suffering during the Nazi dictatorship and war have brought Austrians of different political beliefs nearer to each other. Those in concentration camps swore that if they survived they would build a new Austria together. The unfortunate civil war of 1934—a war between brothers would be a better description—should be healed and the graves filled with the collective hope and suffering. The Occupation after 1945, the piles of rubble, the hunger—they welded the people together and the "economic miracle" is the witness.

And you think that the Austrians paid for the "most expensive goulash in world history." What do you mean by that?

Yes. As you know, Hitler ordered his troops to invade Austria on the Ides of March 1938. As a propaganda exercise the so-called "Bavarian Charity Train" was sent to Vienna to distribute free goulash to the "suffering" population. But I discovered in the course of my researches that this train was filled with goulash only after it had crossed the border, in other words, in Austria.

The astoundingly large gold reserves of the Austrian National Bank weighed 78,300 kilograms and were deposited partly in Switzerland and partly in the United States. But the Nazis found out how to steal them. And in addition, Austrians were compelled by the Nazis to deliver up all their gold by 30 June 1939 or else face very severe penalties. That maneuver brought in a further 13,000 kilograms of gold, making a total of 91,000 kilograms of gold that fell into the hands of the Nazis.

I think I've answered your question.

And I'm convinced that the Austrians have learned from their recent history: two dictatorships are enough!

"... my son very often grumbles at me..."

Conversation with *Theresia Szyszkowitz* on 3 October 1987.

Theresia Szyszkowitz was born in 1911 and was in Graz in 1938.

What were you doing in 1938?

At that time I was in my father's office in the Taggermühle in Graz. I worked there as the youngest daughter and understood the economic situation very well.

For example, the bakers could hardly pay for the flour that we delivered. Times were hard. We had to pay cash to redeem the wagons arriving at the station with goods arriving from America. Settling up quickly was important because one paid a lot to have the wagons waiting. We only rented the mill and we often had to go to the community to get the necessary money. As far as I can remember, the people we got the money from were called in my family, *Getreidejuden* (Grain-Jews). There were about five or six firms. For example, I remember the Latzer Brothers, Neufeld, Lustig, and Heinrich Latzer. These firms often lent us money so that we could redeem the wagons from the station. That was what is was like between 1935 and 1938.

You wanted to tell me why your family became Nazi?

Yes, in this firm there were a few nice Jews and a few who—like everywhere—were not so nice. There, it seems we found the not-so-nice ones only. Also, my father was a so-called "Greater German" when he was a businessman in Donawitz. My mother worked in the Catholic kindergarten. When I was a little girl I was with the Scouts. I went to Germany with them a number of times and we performed Styrian dances and songs. I was about fifteen or sixteen years old then and can remember our teacher saying "Heim in das Reich, heim ins deutsche Volk!" (Home to the German Reich, to the German People!). I remembered that well.

That was in 1926 and one dreamed of the "Greater German" idea. In our family, too, especially when things were going bad. My father hoped that there would be economic improvement with the *Anschluss.*

Did you have any Jewish friends?

No. We only did business with Jews

Were you personally anti-Semitic?

No, I wasn't. I think we were just indifferent.

Did you already know, after Hitler's seizure of power, what was happening to the Jews?

No, we didn't know that. Nobody could foresee the end. We knew that Hitler always spoke of the "German race" and wanted to maintain it, but we didn't think what that would lead to.

Did you know about concentration camps?

At first we didn't know, and later we didn't want to know.

Did you consciously suppress it?

Yes, we suppressed it! And we never even had the courage to listen to a foreign radio station. We were scared we would be caught.

And this passivity, this refusal to accept reality, this refusing to look, refusing to hear: my son justifiably reproaches me for it all today.

What did you think about Hitler's ideas and plans?

We didn't read foreign newspapers, we didn't listen to foreign radio stations, we were in the truest sense of the word, credulous. We didn't think for a moment that Hitler could want anything "evil."

Had you read *Mein Kampf*?

No.

What are your memories of 1938?

On the day of the *Anschluss* I didn't see a single unhappy person. Everybody I knew was happy and enthusiastic. I can't remember the details any more, but the impression I have is one of ecstatic people at the Hauptplatz and in the Herrengasse. I watched it all from the Café Nordstern. I had a good view from there.

Did you read about Jews being banned from certain professions in 1938? For example, their exclusion from the legal profession?

No. We didn't want to see anything unpleasant. We just hoped that it would get better. We just thought about our economic situation. Nothing else interested us.

Did you ever speak with Jews?

Yes, once, before 1938 with a young Jew in the firm. This Jew said to me, "I wouldn't even buy a single pencil from Germany."
When I asked, "Why not?" he just said "No, I won't do it!" That was before 1938.

Didn't you ever wonder where the Jews who once lived in Graz had gone?

We thought they had traveled, moved away. There were a few, sure, from whom we bought things because they were emigrating.

Weren't you aware of any discrimination against the Jews?

Oh, yes. The Jew Lustig told me that the Nazis had beaten his father so badly the previous day that he was lying in the next room—I happened to be there to buy something. That was the first time I heard of mistreatment of Jews, and it was a shock for me. Before that I never thought of what could happen to the Jews.

We cut ourselves off totally. That is the terrible thing when I think about it today. It would never have occurred to us to mistreat Jews, but the Nazi propaganda did an excellent job of making the people believe everything they were told, so that they didn't react. The motto was: turn off, suppress, don't believe anything that you don't hear on the (Nazi) radio or in the (Nazi) press. We were impressed with the road building and labor service, and didn't see anything wrong. For young people there was the Labor Service, that was welcome.

And I never noticed any resistance anywhere.

Do you have memories of the *Kristallnacht*?

I remember that there was a man living in our house, who had been present at the burning of the synagogue. I only heard that from other people. But this man apparently helped set fire to the synagogue. But I never saw it, I only heard that that's what happened.

Do you have personal memories of the *Kristallnacht*?

No. In my circle of friends and acquaintances there were only Nazi sympathizers. We were told the Jews had gone.

And you didn't notice Jewish shops plundered and destroyed?

No. We thought all the Jews had emigrated. Also when we were told the Jews had been "deported," we didn't think that anything bad would happen to them.

Did you experience anything sad between 1938 and 1945?

No, nothing in particular. I was in Styria at the end of the war, finally in Schladming.

How would you behave today? The same as in 1938?

Looking back I reproach myself for not being interested in the other side. My son often "grumbles" at me about that. He rightly points out that there were many people who, despite the terrible times, took note of what was happening to the other side and behaved accordingly. And that's right! I must admit that's true!

Could you have helped someone?

No one asked me to help him. But I have to admit, I didn't want to hear or see; I just wanted to swim with the wave.

". . . The *Anschluss* made us feel lost, betrayed, and scoffed at. . ."

Interview with *Hans J. Thalberg* in December 1989.

Hans J. Thalberg, born 1916 comes from the upper-class Jewish society, which played an important part in the economic, cultured and social life during the pre-World War I period. He managed to survive the Nazi persecutions and was very active first in France, secretly, and then in Switzerland openly, for a free Austria. When the war ended, he entered the diplomatic service of the Second Republic and contributed to the reestablishment of an independent Austrian foreign policy, serving in important positions in Washington, Berlin and later as ambassador in Mexico, Cuba, Central America, China and Switzerland. During the periods 1962-66 and 1973-75 he worked in close cooperation with Bruno Kreisky, which afforded him ample opportunities to observe the developments and effects of Kreisky's Near-East policies from close range.

Ambassador Thalberg, you come from that significant upper-class Jewish milieu that had put its stamp on the economic, cultural and social life of Vienna before World War I. You survived the Holocaust but your family perished in it. Yet now you live in Austria again. How come?

After the *Anschluss* in March 1938, tens of thousands of Austrians were forced to leave their country. Those who did not leave were sent to concentration camps and murdered. The memory of these horrible events prevented many from returning. In addition, the Austrian Government did not seem particularly eager to have these persons return to Austria, and the Austrian authorities actually discouraged them from coming back. I belonged to a small group of young, politically interested people like Bruno Kreisky, Ernst Lemberger, Walter Wodak, and Martin Fuchs, who at the end of the war spontaneously and optimistically turned their efforts towards rebuilding the ravaged and morally knocked-out country. I wrote a book about my experiences in postwar Austria.

Yes, you devote a long chapter in that book to the description of your happy youth, the feeling of security in the warm atmosphere of your parents' home. And then all of a sudden. . .

In March 1938 everything abruptly changed within twenty-four hours. When we heard Schuschnigg's farewell address, with the famous conclusion: "Gott schütze Österreich!" (May God protect Austria), we were paralyzed. We had been a respected family for generations, and now? Vienna suddenly was a totally different city! The *Anschluss* made us feel lost, betrayed, and scoffed at. . . . Yet, we had no idea of the horrible things waiting for us. . . .

Let us return to your youth. Did you get a religious education? Did your parents have Zionist leanings?

My family had lived in Vienna since the end of the eighteenth century. My grandfather was a liberal, assimilated Jew. Both liberalism and freemasonry were established family traditions. In later years my grandfather served as president of one of Vienna's large Lodges. Neither family from either my father's or mother's side was religious, and Zionism was not taken seriously. This was best left to the *Ostjuden* (the Jews who came from eastern Europe), who generally were looked upon with contempt. Judaism was something which at best lived in our memories but which we seldom gave any thought to. We believed in total assimilation. . .

Yet in 1933 Hitler assumed power in Germany; how did your parents react to the handwriting on the wall?

No one wanted to see those threatening indications! The Jewish bourgeoisie simply had totally identified with Austria and felt it belonged there with equal rights. One simply would not accept the position that in the tolerant climate of law-abiding Austria the Jewish people there could be deprived overnight of all their rights.

Mr. Ambassador, when did you first learn of your Jewish descent?

This we learned, my sister and I through the educational effort of our nanny Margarete Sperling, who had come from the Froebel Institute in Dresden. On a dusky afternoon she suddenly asked my sister and me: "Do you know that the two of you are different from the others?" On learning that we were Jews we felt as if we had been told that we were Chinese. . . We were totally unprepared for the coming events. An experience comes to my mind: one day my sister Marietta and the nanny were waiting for me at the Catholic school in the Bräunerstrasse. In front of the school there was a crowd of boys who asked my dark-haired rather Jewish-looking sister: "Say, girlie, are you Jewish?" To which my sister, laughing innocently, answered: "By no means, I am Viennese!" Such was our naive attitude in those days.

Well, Mr. Ambassador, so gradually you were made to notice that to the average Austrian you appeared to be evidently "different"?

The recognition of the true attitude of our Austrian environment came gradually. One day the mother of my closest school friend revealed to my mother that on the orders of her husband, who was a major in the Austrian army, their son no longer was permitted to have social contacts with me. To them we were the "rich Jews" and their envy knew no limits. I was simply shattered and unable to understand the world of the adults. . .

How did your life and that of your family develop in Vienna?

The first harbinger of many serious events to come was my father's loss of part of his fortune. Beginning in the early thirties we had to give up our high standard of living—servants and a sumptuous apartment—and adapt to more modest conditions.

You were born in 1916, so you may remember the events of 15 July 1927? What significance did this day have for you and your family?

Our apartment was right behind the Rathaus (City Hall), near the center of the bloody confrontation. In spite of being forbidden, we children could not resist the temptation to watch the events through the window shutters; police, armed with rifles, came storming out of the Rathausstrasse, and all of a sudden we saw the nearby Palace of Justice go up in fire!

My father was unable to control his feelings: for him, a lawyer, the Palace of Justice was the symbol of the law-abiding state. He never like Social Democracy, for it had abolished the Monarchy and created the unbeloved Republic. The bourgeoisie never favored Social Democracy, and for father his bourgeois descent meant more than his Jewish roots. He had abandoned religious Judaism long ago, feeling himself an agnostic, a free citizen of the world, devoid of all ties with Judaism. A friend of ours, a devoted Social Democrat, once remarked: "One day you Jewish liberals will kiss the soil on which a Social Democrat once tread. . . ." This friend of ours, who was so disappointed with my father's political views, turned out to have been right in the end. . . .

For generations your family had contributed to the establishment of a prosperous and widely respected Austria, shared with the population the good as well as the bad times; now came the *Anschluss* and Hitler's troops marched into Austria. . . what did you actually feel at this situation? What happened to your family? Your friends? Did they survive?

The dramatic transformation after the *Anschluss* put its mark on our immediate surrounding. Our neighbor was "Professor M.", a world-famous figure in ophthalmology (who in his youth had been a friend of Georg von Schönerer, a leading figure of radical Austrian anti-Semitism). He instantly stopped greeting any member of our family. Other acquaintances and so-called friends did that too. When I met my former teacher, Prof. Bon in the street, a classical philologist, who had visited our house quite often, a man who shared my father's enthusiasm for Latin and for the Classics, he turned his face, pretending not to see me. . . .

Please don't ask me how we survived the next few weeks. . . I don't know any more. . . . I kept running from one consulate to another. . . the embassies of the various countries had of course been closed immediately. . . . Everywhere you saw long lines of people trying to apply for visas, but without success. . . help and assistance were extremely hard to find in those days.

Thinking of the refugees in western Europe today. . . .

I am happy that they get a totally different treatment today. Yet at the same moment I have a feeling of shame and depression when I recall the inhuman treatment which we candidates for certain death had to suffer from the so-called civilized world!! England, France, America, the small western European countries, the Vatican, not to speak of the overseas countries, the International Red Cross. . . . They all watched silently as the Jewry of Central Europe was chased into the gas-chambers.

In your book you speak of the "amputated life." You survived, yet. . . .

Yes, I remember that in September of 1938 I had finally managed to obtain a visa to Yugoslavia. My parents thought that I as a healthy, strong young man was in the greatest danger and consequently that I should leave immediately. Yet to this very day. . . again and again. . . . I am tormented by the thought: perhaps my parents, but surely my sister Marietta should have applied for a visa too?? They had remained so inactive, both my delicate mother and my almost 70-year-old father. . . could they have survived all those hardships of the next years? These are tormenting questions, a most painful thorn in my flesh, which will continue to hurt till the end of my life.

Then in your book you also describe your last days with your loved ones. . . and the parting. . .

My mother held me in an embrace and wept! Father too was weeping. . . he looked so helpless. . . I had to hurry, the taxi was waiting. . . . Once more I turned to see my parents standing in that entrance door, which I knew so well. . . Mama was waving goodbye. . . I have never seen either again. Marietta accompanied me to the railway station, then. . . In 1942 she failed to return from an errand; she was apprehended on the street, thrown into a truck and deported to a death camp in the East. She was only twenty-two. You can imagine how my parents felt. . . In the summer our domestic help had left my parents to look for an "Aryan" house. . . Soon after, my parents were evacuated by force to a small apartment, one room and kitchen—the Aryans had become interested in our spacious yet cozy apartment. . . Then came the brief censored messages from Theresienstadt: "We feel well," and in 1942 Mama announced in a short note that Father had died. Later, indirectly, I heard from a friend that Mama had been sent to Auschwitz. . . .

Finally, how do you, with your experience of the past, feel about German unification?

I believe that Austrians in general and Austrian Jews in particular have good reason to watch events very carefully. German unification may mean a strengthening of German-nationalist emotions in Austria. And German nationalism in Austria—as distinct from Germany—means right-wing radicalism, means anti-Semitism and Jew-baiting, and in the last analysis means a trend toward a new *Anschluss*. I am deeply disturbed that people in this country seem so complacent and refuse to consider the serious consequences that may arise for their own country.

". . .My father saw the handwriting on the wall . . ."

Interview with *Eleasar Weissbrot* in Vienna on October 19, 1990.

Eleasar L. Weissbrot, raised and educated in Vienna, left the city after the "Matura" in 1935 to go to Jerusalem, where he graduated from the Hebrew University in Natural Sciences. He directed a major adult educational organization (The British Institutes) for 40 years. A soldier in the Israeli war of independence, he was among other things later president of Rotary and Bnai-Brith. He also assumed an active role in art and music education and management through engagements with the Jerusalem Symphony Orchestra, Jerusalem Music Centre, and the Israel Festival. He has also served since 1980 as president of the Israeli Austrian Friendship League, in which capacity he is responsible for the establishment of good relations with Austria by means of exchanges of study groups and official delegations.

Professor Weissbrot, you live in Israel and today you are visiting Vienna with a group of young people under your guidance. What are you doing here?

I came here to show a group of young Israelis some institutions, universities, and many other features of present-day Austria, in order to improve the blemished image of Austria in Israel today; I wish the young people to see the real Austria and not the

picture of it handed down to them by distorted media presenta-
tions.

Quite; you are Viennese, aren't you? Then why do you live in Israel today and not in Vienna?

This is a question I could write a whole book about! Well, my father already suffered mistreatment from his Viennese fellow citizens at a time when we should have been able to lead a normal life in Vienna, to which he had returned from World War I. He felt the anti-Semitism in Vienna even before the time of the Austrofascism! This was the period when war-ravaged Vienna suffered misery, malnutrition, lack of dwellings, a city swamped with poor refugees from the eastern provinces, a bleak city that bordered on hopelessness for Jews in an atmosphere of growing xenophobia. He hated the thought that I could be brought up in an atmosphere of "Jews not wanted" and he left for a country where I could "belong." Hence we left Austria long before Hitler came marching in.

So your father had realized so early how things stood?

Yes, he saw and read the handwriting on the wall!! When Hitler came to power in Germany in 1933 father felt it would not be long before he would come to Austria. He prepared his emigra-tion, leaving me behind with relatives, so that I could graduate from high school with the *Matura*. In 1935 I registered at Hebrew University in Jerusalem as the first student from Vienna.

Did you encounter any language problems, difficulties?

Fortunately, none whatsoever! I had studied for eight years at the Chajes-Real-Gymnasium where Hebrew was a compulsory (fourth) language. On arrival in Palestine I mastered the language fully and was prepared for life there, all thanks to my Zionist upbringing.

Well, you and your parents left Vienna in time; did you lose relatives due to the Nazi period?

Look, my father had fourteen uncles and aunts in Vienna, all with their families; they all were middle class, pretty well assimilated here. They must have totaled about 100 people, of whom 11 managed to make it to Palestine, 2 to Cuba, 4 to the U.S.A., the rest simply perished in concentration camps. . . You know, just 2 younger cousins were Zionists like my father; the others, well-established as lawyers, doctors, and merchants felt like assimilated Austrians, for whom Hitler and his Nazi hordes came as an unexpected shock. . . .

By 1938 your family was already well established in Palestine. Why did you not bring more relatives from Vienna?

Oh, you seem to forget the British policy of appeasing the Arabs by curbing Jewish immigration to Palestine; we managed to obtain only one "Certificate" to bring our grandparents here, after Grandpa had been sent to Dachau. . . In the first stage of his activities in Vienna, Eichmann aimed to make it "judenrein" (free of Jews) at all costs, so he made emigration possible for those who could show that they had visas, affidavits, certificates, etc. So he let some Jews get out, naturally not before he had robbed them of all their earthly possessions. . . .

Then, in 1939, the infamous "White Paper" was published by the British, limiting Jewish immigration still further, so that when the need was greatest, the gates of Palestine were closed!! Yet the Jews fortunately did not give up; they came as illegal immigrants on small Danube steamers, old Romanian cargo boats, Greek freighters, and anything that could keep afloat as far as the shores of Palestine. From here the Jewish authorities took over so that the British could not trace the refugees. I know of several Viennese families that had made this journey of three to four weeks, but no one from my family managed to join this venture. On reflection I must honestly say that my parents, even if they had managed to get a place on such a transport, could not have survived it. They were not aggressive enough, nor were they capable of adjusting quickly to the horrible conditions of such ventures, on which people simply died of exhaustion. Moreover can you imagine what endurance, skill, and even selfishness it took to decide to flee, to save your own life leaving behind your loved ones?

Were you a religious family?

No, my father had lost his religious feeling during the bloody battles of World War I. "There cannot be a God," he said, "if such unnecessary carnage takes place. And if there is a God watching all this, then I do not wish to know him!" No, father found another inner belief: Zionism. This was not limited only to immigration to Palestine, but referred also to a new moral standard for the newly reborn Jewish worker, professional, intellectual, and official in all spheres of life in Palestine, as opposed to the oppressed Jews in the Diaspora. He dreamt of better human relations, tolerance, modern education among the Jews in their own country—well, father was an idealist, and I am happy he was able to instill some of those values in me. . . .

How did you view those horrible times from your vantage point in Palestine? Had you still maintained some contacts with Vienna?

My only contacts with Vienna were with family and friends who were eagerly looking for an escape route to Palestine from the Nazi hell. We were about 400,000 Jews here, under British rule, pretty powerless apart from the illegal immigration which became more and more complicated with the shifting of the theater of war to the Mediterranean Sea. All that remained was to view with growing desperation how civilized countries like Switzerland, France, England, etc. erected border barriers against Jewish refugees. . . You know, it was Switzerland that proposed to Nazi Germany to imprint the Huge *J* on the passports of Jews!?! We arranged huge demonstrations of protest against the restrictive immigration policy of the British government, sent urgent pleas and petitions, but all was in vain. Well, the Allies even refused to bomb the railway tracks to Auschwitz, though it certainly was technically possible! Yes, we were desperate.

You have lost relatives through the Holocaust; because of anti-Semitic Austria your family left Vienna. Now, as president of the Israel-Austria Friendship League you came here to Vienna again. What do you feel while working for this cause, and why do you do it?

Well, it took me twenty years to overcome that antagonism and the trauma of revisiting Vienna. I still tremble, when I think how I first set foot again on Austrian soil in 1955. I do not forget what the Austrians did to us Jews, nor do I forgive them their barbarism and cruelty to us when we were helpless. But since 1950 there has been a new generation there, and we have to build a bridge to those youngsters; I feel that they seek the contact with us. The "positive" aspect of the Waldheim affair is the awakening of the awareness of guilt and responsibility in the young generation in Austria. Not they are guilty, they feel, but their parents and grandparents and they start asking some delicate questions, which often lead to family conflicts. I claim it is essential to foster contact with such enlightened and intelligent young people and I gladly serve as their contact in Israel.

Do you as a Jew encounter anti-Semitism in Austria today? Do you find it here more than in other countries?

Yes, there is latent anti-Semitism in Austria on many levels; I am able to distinguish between xenophobia and economic anti-Semitism on the one hand, and inborn prejudices and religious anti-Semitism on the other. That means there is definitely religious-sociological anti-Semitism in Austria, but not that based on economic issues, since there are practically no more Jews left. I often encounter occasions when an Austrian, unaware of my Jewishness, makes a blatant anti-Semitic statement, simply because it is deeply ingrained in his environment, even though he himself has never met a Jew in his life. There is moreover nowadays the new stream of "Anti-Isrealism," which very conveniently blends with the trend of classical anti-Semitism. No, I do not reckon that Austria tops the list—I have the same feelings in France, Germany, the UK, and Switzerland, but not in Italy or Dalmatia. . . .

On reflection, do you think you would have established your career or have developed professionally in Austria, had the Nazis not come?

I cannot say. All I know is that the reestablished Jewish state in part of Palestine has diametrically transformed Jewish life all over the world. Before 1948 we were unprotected, so that the Nazis could butcher us like sheep. No more now. We have a recognized state and everyone who feels persecuted in the Diaspora can come home to Israel. It often is pointed out that 200,000 Jews had lived in Vienna (apparently peacefully). Well, father told me of the chicanery he had continuously suffered, as owner of a bookshop, on the part of the Viennese municipal authorities (Magistrat), only because he was Jewish. For generations Jews were used to being treated badly, to say the least, by the Christian authorities in Europe; and Austria certainly was no exception. By accepting this as their fate, the Jews somehow managed to muddle through, by petty bribery, submissiveness, and insult-swallowing. Father was a proud Jew and Zionist and as an ex-soldier expected to be fully recognized as such in Vienna; well, at that time this was a tall order, and since it was not filled, he drew the right conclusions and left for Palestine. He was right in his assessment that there was no future for me in Vienna at that time; well, there is no such blatant anti-Jewish sentiment in Vienna anymore. Yet how many Jews have returned there? 200? 300?

Do you look toward the future optimistically?

Definitely yes!! Not only about Israel, where life never has been easy, but also about Europe and the Arabs. Reason will prevail, even if it takes more than we are used to. In the past we survived Haman in Persia, Hadrian in Palestine, Hitler in Europe, so it augurs well for our future. . . .

"... Thanks to Cardinal König a lot has happened. . ."

Conversations with *Simon Wiesenthal* on 24 June and 20 August 1987.

Mr. Wiesenthal, who was born in 1908 in Galicia, is the head of the Jewish Documentation Center in Vienna.

Mr. Wiesenthal, you survived the odyssey through no fewer than twelve concentration camps, including Buchenwald and Mauthausen. Now you are dedicated to the pursuit of justice and through your efforts it has been possible to track down and capture Nazi criminals all over the world.

You were brought up in an atmosphere in which anti-Semitism and the persecution of Jews was an everyday occurrence. It's now fifty years since the *Anschluss* in Austria. Do you think people have learned from history?

I would say, in Germany yes, in Austria no. And I'll tell you why: because the Germans knew that they would have to pay for an entry card back into the civilized world. This entry card was the moral and material compensation they paid. The Germans bought this entry card. If there hadn't been the Cold War after 1948 and if this hadn't lasted twelve years, then more would have been accomplished in the establishment of German democracy. But in these twelve years only the Nazi criminals won and nothing took place. This fact was simply ignored and Austria ignores it today. This will doubtless be avenged one day in the historiography.

Austria was the so-called "first victim" of Hitler's aggression, and in this way Austria got its entry card free. Of course big efforts were made to pay compensation, but then the Austrian Jews lost everything. The fact that the plague (of Nazism) originated in Austria is played down. Hitler, Kaltenbrunner, Eichmann, and many others were Austrian. Don't forget that 80% of Eichmann's staff were Austrian, and three quarters of the commanders of the extermination camps were also Austrian. Globotschnig, for example, was the chief of Jewish extermination in the General-Gouvernement (Poland), and with a staff of sixty-five people from Carinthia (the region in southern Austria around Klagenfurt) they were responsible for over two million dead. They were Nazis from Austria. And I call them that deliberately because the word "Austria" was always a thorn in the flesh for the Nazis. Remember that the Austrian population composed only 8.5% of the population of the Greater German Reich, yet the proportion of Austrians among those who committed crimes was many times greater than that percentage.

It's not possible to argue on the one hand that the Austrians only served Hitler under pressure, and on the other hand that they defended their homeland. That is a kind of dualism with which one cannot live. I can still remember well, how Gorbach, who was in a concentration camp himself, often said, "Wiesenthal, you keep reopening the old wounds."

I replied: "The fact that you call them wounds is the proof that they are still bleeding. They stuck plaster over wounds but underneath they're still suppurating. . ."

And that's the way it was. The whole state was built upon a lie. The state as such was certainly a victim, but not the people.

What do you think about Hitler's invasion of Austria in March 1938?

Not one shot was fired! It was a "Blumenfeldzug" (flower campaign)! The Germans were not armed like the Austrians. The Austrian Army could have held them, but the Nazi *Soldatenbund* had prepared the way before Hitler marched in.

Of course there were the 100,000 people in the Heldenplatz, but then there were also those people who stayed at home and wept.

And I can tell you, if there was a fiftieth anniversary demonstration today *a g a i n s t* the *Anschluss*—as young Marboe proposed—then you wouldn't get 100,000 people to come.

Do you mean Peter Marboe? The business manager of the ÖVP (the People's Party)?

Yes. He recently wrote a very good article with the title "Shalom for 1988," which appeared in the *Wiener Journal.* I liked this article very much.

What did he write about?

He wrote that it should be possible, 50 years after the *Anschluss*, to organize another big demonstration in the Heldenplatz, this time for justice, freedom, and human dignity, and against suppression and fascism of every variety. Marboe also expressed the view in this article that one should be able to mobilize well-meaning people from different backgrounds: young Socialists as well as young Catholics, representatives from the Scouts, the Viennese Jewish community, and Christian organizations, simply to show that they are all in the same camp. He spoke above all for the postwar generation when he said, "we want to know what it was like." And he meant that young people are entitled to the truth! Because a self-confident Austria can only be built on the truth.

And I have to tell you, this article really pleased me—even if I have my doubts about Marboe's intentions. In fact, I called Bochskanl, the chief editor of the *Wiener Journal,* to let him know that I greatly valued its basic ideas.

If I can ask one or two contemporary questions. I know you were very unhappy about some remarks made by Bronfman and Singer of the World Jewish Congress. Now President Waldheim has received an invitation to an audience with the Pope, and there's a lot of discussion about it. What are your views on the subject?

Look the Pope received Kadafi and many other people. It's a Vatican ritual. If a king or a president of a country seeks an audience with the Pope, then he gets one. You can of course delay it.

As you know, on 22 June I gave a personal declaration to Mr. Ettore Peta, which was published in the *Corriere della Sera.* I can show you this and make it available to you for publication, and then you'll know my opinion of this visit.[1]

What do you think of the letter that the Linz deputy Mayor Hödl sent to Bronfman?

I wrote immediately to Deputy Chancellor Mock to convey my deep concern, but Mock didn't answer the letter.

Why didn't he answer your letter?

I don't know. I received a letter from him six weeks later, but that was in answer to another letter.

In June I gave you a copy of the controversial book, *Standrechtlich gekreuzigt* by the German attorney Weddig Fricke, who as a defense lawyer and layman, addressed the question of Jesus's trial for the first time in the German-speaking

---

[1]"I give this declaration in my name only, and with it I wish to establish that:

In this century no Pope has said so many good and important things about the Jews as the present Pope, John Paul II. Moreover no previous Pope has spoken out as he has done with such firmness and clarity against Nazism. If there are disagreements between the Jews and the Church, these should not lead to a break in dialogue, but to resolution through further talks. Now the Historical Commission is a fact and capable of bringing clarity into the Waldheim case, perhaps the Vatican should consider delaying the (Waldheim) visit until the results of the Commission's deliberations are known. That would contribute to the calming of emotions and be in the interest of all."

(23 June 1987, the text was in Italian).

world.[2] Do you have any ideas on the motivation of the author?

Yes, I know that the book's intellectual origins lay in a legal case in which the author was involved. He was appointed to defend a policeman, an honest fitter, who in 1942 in the Jewish ghetto of Tschenstochau had shot eight Jews for some trifling reason. You've spoken with the author, haven't you?

Yes. He wanted to know how a respectable family man and grandfather could be convinced that he was doing the right thing by murdering people. The author proceeded from the assumption that in countries with a strong Christian culture there is strong anti-Semitism, and his purpose in publishing this book is to destroy the intellectual basis for Christian anti-Semitism by showing that the allegation that the Jews murdered Jesus is historically false, theologically superfluous, and morally pernicious.

Did you read this book and what is your opinion of it?

Of course, I studied the book very closely. And you'll be surprised to hear that I can even remember the page which I wanted to talk about, namely page 145, which needs correction. It's about the Temple money. Religious Jews were forbidden to make human likenesses of any kind, because that amounted to idolatry. So their money only had palms or flowers on it. When pilgrims came from the Roman Empire they brought with them money with heads of the Emperors embossed on them, and so they had to change this money before they could go into the Temple. And that was the reason for money-changers in the Temple—to exchange Roman coinage for Jewish money.

This book has a strong contemporary value, does it not? According to Hödl, Bronfman's remarks about Waldheim are the same as those of his "co-religionists two thousand years ago, who allowed Jesus Christ to be condemned to death in a

---

[2]Weddig Fricke, *Standrechtlich gekreuzigt. Person und Prozess des Jesus aus Galilee* (Freiburg i.B, 1986).

show trial, because he didn't fit in with the plans of the
gentlemen of Jerusalem. . ."

Yes, of course! Even in view of the book's weaknesses and
the fact that the Church has itself certainly contributed to
enlightenment on the subject in the last twenty-seven years—
nonetheless, it's an important contribution to understanding
between Jews and Christians.

**How is all this possible despite the efforts of the Catholic
Church? For example, the declaration of the 1964 Council on
the Jews, that we have not only to "wipe away these imaginary
blood stains of God's murder with our tears," but that we
must also learn to live with Abraham's children. Don't these
reforms reach the people?**

I'll tell you something. The change in the attitude of the Church
toward the Jews in the last decades has only been accepted by
a few Catholics. Developments in the Church often reach the
people very late—it often takes three hundred years.
    Even when Cardinal König says that there's no theological
basis for anti-Semitism, he's correct in the sense of the Second
Vatican Council, but he overlooks the fact that a practice of
centuries is not going to be overcome by a decree in twenty
years. The Council's declaration on the Jews by no means era-
dicated anti-Jewish teachers in the Church, and anti-Semitic
passages were not immediately stricken from official Church
texts—it would have been impossible anyway.

**What do you think of Tabori's controversial production "Das
Buch mit den sieben Siegeln" in the Salzburg Kollegienkirche?**

A Jew came to me and asked, "were you in favor of erecting
scaffolding in the Seitenstettengasse," and I replied, "No, not in
the synagogue."

**On 8 June 1987 there was a so-called memorial service organ-
ized by private Austrian citizens for Austrian resistance
fighters in the Stephansplatz in Vienna. It was intended to**

give pause for thought, that history could not be forgotten, or suppressed. What do you think of it?

Basically, I welcome it. It reminds Austrians that 1945 was not a collapse but a liberation. Because Hitler's defeat was Austria's victory and the basis for the establishment of the Second Republic.

There's only one thing I would add: I'm not entirely happy with the date. It should have been on 13 March, otherwise it's too much connected with Waldheim, and its real purpose— showing that 2,700 Austrians were executed as resistance fighters and 16,493 Austrians were murdered in *Gestapo* prisons, apart from the 69,459 Austrian Jews who were killed—all that gets lost in the polemic over Waldheim.

I read in your book, *Krystyna*, that anti-Semitism in Poland was so widespead in 1938 that the Polish government invalidated the passports of Polish Jews living abroad and thereby affected the 17,000 of them living in Germany.[3]

What were relations like between Poles and Jews at the time of the *Anschluss*?

You know, there was hatred between the Poles and Jews, and it had largely to do with collaboration. After the German invasion of Poland some Polish fascists believed that they could strike a deal with the Nazis. In 1933 when Hitler came to power, the right-wing of the Polish National Democratic Party thought they had a model to follow, by which they could use anti-Semitism to come to power in Warsaw. They followed the Nazi example and were able to win over a considerable number of Polish students to their ideas.

Why did you write this book?

The fate of this twenty-year-old Polish girl moved me very deeply. She had joined the resistance movement after losing all

---

[3]Simon Wiesenthal, *Krystyna. Die Tragödie des polnischen Widerstandes* (München, 1986). English translation: *Krystyna. The Tragedy of the Polish Resistance* (Ariadne Press, 1991).

her family and after Poland's occupation by Nazi and Soviet forces. Her companion, Anja, who survived and whom I met many years later in Geneva, instructed me to bring the guilty ones to justice. I put a lot of my heart into this book. . . as you know, I haven't put the fate of this girl in the book, but I was very moved by it, I told you.

We have spoken about 1938. Today, in 1988, we know every-thing that is happening—if we want to know. History has served a purpose there. The last year and a half was rather stormy—how do you see the situation in Austria?

I do not hate. No judgments without proof. I think there are so many important problems which are not addressed. It seems like there's just the Waldheim case. I really can't stand it when people try to tell me who and what a Nazi is. I've dedicated my life to justice and not to hatred. There are some people in the USA and in Austria who want to make a career out of it. And important problems of the present are forgotten. We have to wait for the results of the Historians' Commission (on Waldheim) and then draw conclusions afterwards. I believe anyway that Wald-heim will resign because he can't deny being an accessory.

Where do you think this painful "Waldheim Affair" began, Mr. Wiesenthal?

Look, the people in Austria really have to accept that the "Waldheim Affair" began in Vienna. People just have to believe that members of the Socialist Party were getting worried that they could lose an election and therefore got in touch with the World Jewish Congress. I wrote an extensive article about it at the time in my newspaper. My position is laid out clearly there.

Did people come to you at that time in search of documentary evidence against Waldheim?

Yes, they tried all kinds of ways to get material. They even wanted to prove that Waldheim was in the SS, on the basis of his service in 1941 with a cavalry division, which was so decimated in 1945 that it was merged with the SS Cavalry. They wanted to use this fact to prove Waldheim's membership in the SS.

How did that work out?

Well, Waldheim wasn't with this division for very long, and at the end of the war he was with a completely different outfit.

How is it that the World Jewish Congress spoke of Waldheim's personal guilt?

Look, that mistake was soon cleared up, but Mr. Singer immediately took it as a sign of guilt, without having any documentary evidence.

What does the World Jewish Congress consist of?

That's a voluntary organization composed of representatives from Jewish communities from all over the world, with the exception of Israel.

Does the World Jewish Congress have good relations with the Jewish Community in Vienna?

The Jewish Community in Vienna was not consulted in the Waldheim Affair. Nor was the Documentation Center.

What do you think of the collective threat from the World Jewish Congress?

To make a collective threat against a whole people (the Austrians) is indefensible. Particularly when it comes from a Jew, whose people have themselves been the victims of collective threats for two thousand years. I consider this threat to be a very undiplomatic tactic on the part of the World Jewish Congress.

It's given the old anti-Semites precisely the kind of ammunition that we've been working for years to stop. Ammunition that only serves to influence young people and that says, "You see, that's what the Jews are like. They are even threatening you young people who weren't even born during the Nazi period and had nothing to do with it." Personally I can only regret that very much.

Didn't Singer also attack the Austrian press, and compare it to the (Nazi and virulently anti-Semitic newspaper) *Stürmer*?

Well, no Austrian newspaper has deserved this label. You know of course that not every newspaper has philosemites on its staff and that the *Kronenzeitung* ran a series which annoyed all Jews, but there isn't a single newspaper in Austria that should be attacked in this manner. Singer acts as if he's a spokesman for Jews in the whole world, but so far as I know, no Jews have appointed him to that post.

What do you think about guilt?

Guilt is always an individual thing, it's never collective.

In many conversations, I've noticed that Austrians often don't know what the World Jewish Congress does. Can you say something about its role?

The World Jewish Congress is based on four principles: firstly, to help Jews, secondly, to combat anti-Semitism, thirdly, not to interfere in the internal affairs of sovereign states, and fourthly, not to follow any party political line.

Do you think Mr. Singer has always behaved correctly?

It's clear that Mr. Singer wasn't concerned that his remarks might make difficulties for Vienna's Jews.

But "Mr. Singer" is not "the Jews"?

Look, it's always the same: generalizations are never valid. Of course, Mr. Singer cannot be seen as a representative for all Jews, but that's the problem—people don't understand that. It's the same as if one made the whole German people responsible for the Holocaust after the collapse of the Third Reich.

I've often been asked whether it was possible for Waldheim not to know about the deportation of Jews from Greece. What's your opinion?

Look, he served in General Löhr's headquarters, about five kilometers from Salonika. We know that. We also know that the deportation of Jews took place from Salonika. Waldheim personally told me that he didn't know about the deportations, and I told him that I didn't believe him. A transport of 50,000 people—only five kilometers away—can't take place without being noticed! I simply don't believe that! Moreover, deportations that were looked after by the Army? These transports comprised around two thousand people and were carried out in railroad cars which also brought military equipment to Greece. I'll say it again: not to have known—that I don't believe!

Why do you think that there are so many negative voices abroad? If you read the foreign newspapers you get the feeling that they sound partly sympathetic, partly malicious and often very concerned. What's your opinion?

I can only repeat, it's all in the language. The word "liberation" is for export only. You've heard the argument that "we were defending the homeland." Especially if it's about the military aspects, then they talk about "defending the homeland," regardless of whether this "defense of the homeland" was taking place in Norway or any other theater of the Second World War. They speak of the war generation in Austria, of a "forced fulfillment of duty," and that strikes a certain note abroad.

And apropos abroad, it occurs to me that the Mayor of Stuttgart (in West Germany) said on a recent trip to Israel that he "belonged to the many Germans who say: it was better to lose the war than win it with Hitler." I think that's a clear and unmistakable statement.

What do you associate with the date 1938? What do you immediately think of?

1938 was not only a year of suffering for the Jews, it was also a year of great disappointment with neighbors and acquaintances. . . Many years ago I wrote an article about the situation of the Austrian Jews. The idea I expressed then was of an invisible curtain between Jews and non-Jews, a curtain created by both sides; by those who could not forget and by those who didn't want to be reminded.

One last question: what do you think of Cardinal König?

Thanks to Cardinal König a lot has happened. Thanks to his work many prejudices have disappeared. Here more than in any other country. He knows better than anyone else and recognizes the Christian roots of anti-Semitism. He works constantly for a better understanding between Jews and Christians. He recently declared that the interpretation and commentary of the New Testament through the Christian centuries has contributed in no small measure towards the heightening of anti-Judaic/heathen prejudices. And he points out that from the early Middle Ages until modern times this interpretion has led to the suppression and killing of Jews. And he says openly, as you know, that this contributed towards preparing the ground for *Auschwitz*.

"... the ground was well prepared..."

Conversations with *Grete Windbrechtinger* on 2 and 4 October 1987.

Mrs. Windbrechtinger was born in Vienna in 1900 and was in Ramingstein in the state of Salzburg in 1938. She died in November 1987 a few weeks after her interview with the author.

Was 1938 a sad year for you? What were the years before like?

This year wasn't sad, it was terrible.

In 1922 I went to Ramingstein, where my husband, a professional soldier, was employed as secretary and bookkeeper to Prince Schwarzenberg. Because I lived in the country after 1922, I naturally missed a lot. My husband joined the *Heimatschutz* (militia), but I didn't have any interest in politics.

We read the *Freie Presse* to keep in contact with the big world outside. We, my husband and I, had long conversations there with the teacher, who was very nice but an incorrigible Nazi. He saw in Hitler prosperity and work. But my husband always said that it would mean war if Hitler came to power, because the enormous rearmament with which he reduced unemployment in Germany was purely unproductive and led inevitably to war.

That's how we spent the days and evenings before the *Anschluss*, talking long into the night.

Can you remember the day of the invasion?

I can remember that the teacher, with whom we were always in discussion, called my husband and told him that he would be arrested. It was all very adventurous; we usually lay down after a meal and we did so on this day. Someone knocked at the door but we didn't open. We said to ourselves, we'll sleep a bit longer. The next day two men from the "black" SS came and accused my husband of being in the *Heimatschutz*. He managed to avoid arrest, however, by buying his freedom with a few hundred Schillings "contribution".

It's interesting that suddenly everyone in this community revealed his illegal (Nazi) party badge. You could say that the ground was well prepared before the *Anschluss*. It was no surprise to anyone.

Were you liable for service?

I was soon called up for Labor Service. There's a story in this that I'd like to tell you. There were people then who behaved in a decent fashion, even when they had high positions. There was a girl who had a child by a French prisoner. I was working then as the right hand of the head of the Welfare Office, and in this capacity I dealt with this girl's case. We were asked by the (Nazi) District leadership to confirm whether it was true that a "German woman"—this girl—had had an illegitimate child "with a French prisoner" who was working on the farm. My boss knew that if such a confirmation reached the District leadership, both of them would be sent to a concentration camp. He acted humanely and told the District that the file was being processed —that was in 1944. In other words, my boss, Mr. K (his name must remain anonymous), who had been transferred for disciplinary reasons from Graz to Murau (he was not a Nazi), just let the file collect dust until the end of the war. In this way he saved the woman and the man from a concentration camp.

Did you make other observations at this time?

Yes. I noticed things about the Nazi bosses which I'll tell you about. For example, there was a butcher who had to deliver great quantities of meat when the District leadership had some sort of celebration. The wine they needed was provided by the pharmacy. In those days the cough syrup was made from wine, and so the pharmacist needed a stock of wine. And this wine was used for the Nazi celebrations.

Even after the war I experienced the Nazis' dishonesty. The driver of my husband's boss had been Deputy District Leader. Among his duties was the receipt of relief packages for the French prisoners (of war). Of course, he should have given these packages to the prisoners, but he didn't do that.

Then after the war, as I was cultivating his garden—he killed himself and his family immediately at the end of the war—I struck something hard. I was shocked and didn't know what it could be. When I dug further I unearthed a five-kilo cocoa container stuffed full of the prisoners' relief packages. I was very upset because they had been meant for the prisoners and certainly not for Mr. Deputy District Leader!

Can you think of anything else?

Yes, something which shocked me to the core. One evening —it was around 1943—the pharmacist couldn't let her employee go early for a planned social evening. She needed her. That was reason enough to have the pharmacist arrested and the poor woman paraded through the town by an SS man with a placard hanging around her neck reading, "I am a Christian sow." What a humiliation!

Are you Jewish?

I am not a Jew. I am a Catholic Christian, but I've many Jewish friends. I grew up among Jews as a young girl. My father had a coffee house in Vienna, the Cafe Kaiser-Wilhelm, in the Weihburggasse. He rented it to the Nafta-Jews (they came from Galicia, in the region around L'vov). I was sixteen then and I learned chess from a very nice guest. I still play it to this day.

Did anyone from among your close acquaintances go to a concentration camp?

I can tell you how easy it was to get sent to one. I had a colleague whose father was sent to a concentration camp because he bought meat on the black market. The District leader had ordered the meat for some feast, and the small, insignificant man was sent to a concentration camp because he'd ordered a bit for himself.

There was one more sad story. A White Russian had fled to Austria during the First World War. He was from Kiev. The father had a meat factory and arrived in Austria after a very adventurous flight from Russia. He spent two years in Vienna and later moved to Graz. This man had a very beautiful baritone voice. He helped the Russians who had fled from the Ukraine and who had been gathered in the factories. He gave them bread coupons, and for that he was arrested and sent to *Dachau*.

He reported terrible things from there. He told us, among other things, that he and his comrades were sprayed with cold water in winter in freezing temperatures and that they had to stand like that all night. They formed living "iceblocks." This man—I can still remember—was called Paul Graf, and he was an opera singer. After a few months he returned from the camp very ill. He died after the war from one of the ailments he contracted in the camp.

You are eighty-seven years old and have seen a great deal in your lifetime. Would you perhaps like to say something, looking back on 1938, of relevance to today?

Yes, I would like to appeal to the media since they bear a great responsibility: you can influence the people. Only through lack of information and poisonous propaganda could a "1938" be accepted by the people without resistance. Only a few people recognized how dangerous the situation was. Many could not see the true position and just followed blindly.

I remember saying to a fanatical supporter, "For once, call the Nazis what they are: the National Socialist German *Workers'* Party, and not simply NSDAP." But they don't want anything to do with the workers. And I didn't just say that to one, I said it to many people.

You dared to do that?

Yes, I did. I often told people, you should pronounce the word exactly as it is in German, and think about it. Whether it corresponds to what it really means, whether the Nazis are really a "Workers' Party." These poor females, these Alpine dairymaids, who came smiling the next day with "Heil Hitler" and hadn't the faintest idea what it was all about.

I often asked them, "Have you any idea what you're doing? Do you know what it all means?"

You talked politics to ordinary people?   Weren't you afraid that these people could report you to the authorities?

No, I have to tell you, the NSDAP, it sounded good, but these simple people had no idea what it really meant. They were seduced. Even if they were German Nationalists they didn't realize the full implications of the thing.

Did you notice anti-Semitism in your environment?

I only know that they would have liked very much "to have had a Jew."

How do you mean?

Every village wanted to have "its Jew." Like this teacher I told you about, who had the pharmacist paraded through the town with "I am a Christian sow" around her neck. They needed their "substitute Jew."

And I'd like to tell you something else in conclusion because perhaps I won't live to see this book come out and won't be able to stand as an eye-witness later. Writers and teachers and artists and everybody who works in public should be reporting and discussing what really happened—and always with reference to today.

You mean especially in the schools?

Yes, the training of teachers—particularly history and religion teachers—should be closely watched. Because these people have a responsibility, an enormous responsibility! They are able to influence and, if they want, to manipulate people.

How was your son taught religion?

Ask him! It was catastrophic! They spoke of nothing else but "the Jews murdered our Christ." Ask my son, he'll tell you all about it.

Young people should get a proper sense of history. Then they can say, we don't know how we would have behaved then, but we know how we would behave now, how we must behave now. . . !

"... couldn't tempt me to join the Hitler Youth..."

Conversations with *Wolfgang Windbrechtinger* on 6, 13, 20 October and 6 November 1987.

Mr. Windbrechtinger was born in 1922 and spent 1938 in Graz. He lives today as an architect in Vienna (he was responsible for the pedestrian mall there).

You were 16 in 1938. What memories do you have from this year and the years before?

I'd like to go back a little further. I grew up in Lungau (Salzburg) where I had early contact with country people as well as the urban working class. I knew the sufferings of many different people. My father was a professional soldier, an officer, and he drummed into me at an early age the importance of defending one's homeland. Even if it meant putting one's own life at stake, and irrespective of the prevailing political conditions. That was my upbringing.

I didn't come into contact with the phenomenon of anti-Semitism when I was young in Ramingstein. What it meant to be a Jew, that I didn't appreciate until after the *Anschluss* in Graz.

My father was a member of the Lungau *Heimatschutz*. As his son, I was in the *Heimatschutzjugend* (the youth branch of this militia). *Heimat* (Home, or Homeland) and *Heimatschutz* (Defence of the Homeland)—these were concepts that were driven into me very deeply. For me, *Heimat* was something to be protected, and something which was scandalously abused by Hitler later on.

I went to Graz as a *Heimatschutz* leader. In this town I had my first clash with the Nazis. It was around 1936. Even then the Nazis had their gangs of storm troops.

Did you have Jewish friends?

In my class there were no Jews. But there were already anti-Semitic slogans at school. The history class was the worst. I had a professor with whom I couldn't avoid getting into loud arguments. He was openly anti-Semitic.

Then there was the religion class—that was unbelievable. "The Jews killed Christ and they'll never be rid of this stigma . . ." I had discussions with the religion professor too, but they always ended unsatisfactorily. . . it all contributed to my confusion as a thinking human being!

Do you think that people already knew what was happening to the Jews after Hitler's seizure of power in Germany?

People knew what Hitler had planned, but they were blind and just saw their own desperate economic situation. And they probably didn't want to believe the things they heard. It was different with me because all too soon I belonged to those who had experienced Nazi violence. I learned soon enough about their brutal methods.

What was it like on the day of the *Anschluss*?

I was very depressed on this day and I wrote in my diary, which unfortunately doesn't exist anymore:

"The Heimat is lost. . ."

My *Heimatschutz* friends and I held a "Meeting of Mourning." We had the feeling that all around us everyone was delighted about the *Anschluss*. We seemed to be the only ones who were concerned about it.

I soon had big problems because I wasn't prepared to go in the Hitler Youth. My mother was very anxious and feared that there would be repercussions for me at school. But even that couldn't tempt me to join the Hitler Youth. I rejected it quite fundamentally. Most of my school comrades were enthusiastic. However, despite the fact that I didn't share their fervor, I didn't get into trouble.

What happened to your father?

My father was imprisoned for a short time. The elementary school director was a big Nazi, but he liked my father nonetheless, and he made sure his imprisonment didn't last too long.

Your parents were in Ramingstein in the state of Salzburg. You yourself were in Graz. Can you remember the *Kristallnacht*?

I was there when they burned the synagogue, and I watched the SA as they arrested the Jews. These SA people wore armbands and funny caps, the sight of which however I did not like. Nobody can say he didn't see how people were dragged out by the SA and how they were carried off in trucks and cars.

I didn't have any Jewish friends then, but what concerned me was the apathy with which people accepted the discrimination against the Jews. As far as I could see, most people just shrugged their shoulders. For them the only thing that was important was that things "would get better". . . economically from now on "it would be better."

To what do you attribute this lethargy on the part of most people?

The anti-Jewish propaganda had had enormous success. It seemed natural when my school colleagues said, "it serves the Jews right. . ."

How were you brought up?

I was brought up as a Catholic. But I was rarely in agreement with what was taught in the religion class. "Jesus was killed by the Jews, murdered, that's a fact. . . etc. etc."

That was the tenor of religion classes. I'm convinced that this anti-judaism that was instilled into children in school, formed an important basis for racist anti-Semitism. There's no doubt about it.

And I'm shocked that there's still talk of the "worship" of "Anderl of Rinn."

When you look back at 1938 and now in 1988, what do you think of?

That I'm proud I never allied myself to the Nazis. We were all afraid, that's obvious, but my father and my whole family were good Austrians, even in these difficult times, and never for a moment did they sympathize with this criminal system.

You fought as a soldier in the German Wehrmacht. Did you "fulfill your duty?"

Well, I have to say, and it's also relevant to the whole discussion over Waldheim, that I fought with the German *Wehrmacht* and certainly thought at the time: I must do my duty. I must defend my *Heimat*.

What seemed important to me—the way I'd been brought up and what my father had instilled into me, was that the soil of the *Heimat* had to be defended against the "Red Danger."

Pretty soon, however, and that was during the war still, I became aware that I was "fulfilling my duty" under an illegitimate ruler. We were working under a fallacy—yes, even I.

There are continual discussions about the "uniqueness" of Nazi crimes. Recently there has been an intense debate among West German historians as to the "singularity" of the Holocaust. Some of these scholars seek to "relativize" Hitler's crimes by comparing them to those of Stalin. What's your opinion in this regard?

For me *Auschwitz* is such a satanic crime that no argument can support its "relativization." I often ask myself how we are all going to cope with this burden. We can only try and ensure that nothing like it ever occurs again.

Do you mean that something like it could happen again?

I'm afraid so because we live in a totally materialist world and the latest development (the Waldheim Affair) has given me cause for thought. I didn't think such a thing was possible anymore.

How do you mean?

I know so many people who've given me the feeling in the last few years that there wouldn't be anti-Semitism anymore. What really struck me was the fact that, during the election campaign, emotions surfaced which suddenly reminded me of that terrible time before 1938. The campaign itself used methods which instrumentalized anti-Semitism, and I am thinking of particular mottos of the ÖVP (Peoples Party) and their tasteless election posters.

Since Waldheim there is a situation again in Austria where many people think that "the Jews" are to blame for the fact that we have a Federal President who does not command the respect abroad which his office would seem to require.

The trouble is these people don't look to the causes of this situation, and that's of great concern to me. There's one thing we can't avoid: Waldheim's clumsy behavior and his claim "to have known nothing" and seen nothing—that must make him unbelievable. Or not? At least it does with those people who live according to the principles of truth and humanity, rather than mere opportunism. And by humanity I mean the unfolding of man's true nature, a striving towards the ideal of "human nobility."

Those who seek explanations shouldn't be deemed "guilty," rather there should be a desire to accomodate them.

In conclusion one more question: what do you as a Catholic think of Cardinal König?

Cardinal König was an extraordinary Christian Cardinal and not a Church representative. He was a man of world vision. Over the centuries the Church has been responsible for some terrible things. The merciless burning of witches for example and the unbelievable brutality towards dissenters in the Church. This retreat of the Church, which is taking place now little by little, is not welcome.

How do mean?

Krenn and Groer are Church officials for me but not Christians. I see in their appointment a real step backwards for the Church and the endangerment of all the good work done by the old Cardinal.

". . . They are the strong ones in this country, who laugh under the tears, who conceal their suffering and make others happy. . ."

Conversations with *Ernst Florian Winter*
on 23, 24, and 25 January 1988.

Dr. Winter was born in 1923. He is a former professor of political science and director of the Diplomatic Academy. In 1938 he was in Vienna, today he lives in the East Tyrol.

Your father was the Third Deputy Mayor of Vienna during the Corporate State period (1934-1938) in Austria. His colleague Karl. H. Heinz has already told me a great deal about him.
How did you as a youngster experience this difficult time for your family?

We lived very modestly, almost in poverty, in a two-room appartment in the Ladenburggasse 58/12—today it's Thimiggasse, Gersthof. Mother was a practical and careful woman. Most of what he ate we grew in the garden. Beggars were never turned from our door. My father's income came from his work as a publicist, mainly in Switzerland and the United States. And so a circle of friends developed around us, pro-Austrian people who helped us even in the worst days.

Later my father began publishing. As children we helped pack books and carried the *Wiener Politischen Blätter* to different post offices before the censor got them. My parents' bedroom was also the publishing office! The central theme of my father's work was support for Austria's national identity, political justice—above all for the workers—and the renewal of Catholic conviction.

All this certainly contributed to the fact that after 12 February 1934, my father, who was a political person without being a politician, was appointed by the Dollfuss government to be the Third Deputy Mayor of Vienna. In its first phase the "Action Winter" was concerned with bringing about a reconciliation between the workers and the state. But in October 1936 Schuschnigg brought this activity to an abrupt end. In its second phase it was more concerned with the defense of Austria against the aggression of National Socialism.

Without income, we survived by selling anti-Nazi literature that aimed to uncover the truth about the concentration camps, the anti-Christian course of Hitler's policies, and the tremendous danger represented by German expansionism. At the same time my father sought to mobilize his many friends abroad in the struggle for Austria's survival. This brought him to the USA in 1937. When he returned from there he gave a lecture on 8 December in the Kleine Konzerthaussaal entitled "Roosevelt Is Reforming America."

His thesis, that democratic reforms could be successful in an oligarchical country even without an authoritarian regime, excited the audience so much that the police felt obliged to stop the meeting.

This was how I was introduced to my father's "Austrian Action."

Did your father have grounds for his faith in his individual action?

Yes! There was an increasing number of Austrians of all political persuasions who were gathering around a program that sought to mobilize and strengthen Austria. There were several such groups.

I'd like to recall in honor the memory of some of the close colleagues of my father: Brendel, Father Cyril Fischer OFM, Fleischer, Grauer, Häuslmayer, Kogon, Katona, Sebba, and many more. . . . victims of the European Holocaust, which my father foresaw.

All this pressure of activity resulted unexpectedly in a hopeful sign from Schuschnigg on 12 February 1938. On the way back from Berchtesgaden he saw my father and said, "Ernstl, you were right, Hitler is a fool! Austria must be saved."

Within a day my father had written "Austrian Warning," in which he called for mobilization for self-defense, drawing the working-class into the political process, and economic self-sufficiency. Above all, it depended upon military resistance, the establishment of a provisonal capital in Windisch-Matrei in the East Tyrol and the symbolic unfurling of the Red-White-Red flag of Austria on the Grossglockner. The Austrian-patriotic Catholic Youth group to which I belonged was greatly encouraged and ready to dedicate itself to the defense of an independent Austria.

But it never came to that. As we know today Schuschnigg was never prepared to break loose from his authoritarian and pro-German course. There were various signs of a common front against the Nazis, but its coordination was foiled by Nazi infiltration on the one hand, and by the rejection of a common all-Austrian action on the other hand.

How do you remember the days immediately before and after 11 March 1938?

Dr. Schuschnigg convinced my father that he was serious about winning the workers for an independent Austria. He was officially appointed. We had a visit then from a young American Ph.D student named George N. Shuster. He had an American car and a chauffeur called Schneider, and he accompanied my father on his speaking tour through Austria. Although father wanted Schuschnigg to change his mind about the planned plebiscite because he found it provocative, he conducted an astoundingly successful election campaign. The majority of Austrians were prepared to vote "YES." Even the Socialists were in favor although they had been granted none of their demands.

I was attending the Neulandschule High School then. The atmosphere there was typical of Austria and was already infected with Nazi thinking. The provocative history books of Professor Schliers contributed to the general confusion of values. There was a lot of "concealed nazification," but nevertheless Austrian patriotism was growing among students and teachers alike.

There was an atmosphere of growing hope and self-assertion among our circle, so you can imagine that Schuschnigg's resignation speech hit us like the Apocalypse. Betrayed, disappointed, shattered, and deeply worried, some of the guests took mother and the older children in their arms and wept bitterly. Father was not at home. Was he in danger? What would he do? His worst predictions had been exceeded. My second reaction was to burn the lists of Socialist representatives and Monarchists—true Austrians all—who had been our friends and colleagues. Correspondence and pamphlets followed them onto the fire. I had finished by midnight.

Now we were faced with the situation that my father had always predicted and for which he had prepared for months— flight! But where was he? Mother stayed prudent and calm and told me now to burn all my father's diaries. I didn't have the heart to do it and sat before the little stove and began for the first time in my life to read his first diary. He'd begun it at the same age as I was at that time.

By dawn everything was burned. It was the most terrible experience of my life, for which my father—the very personification of kindness and understanding—never reproached me. Then when we were already pretty tired, Mother and I got the idea of burying as quickly as possible my father's valuable documents, books, and manuscripts. What a panic I was in! Father had always stressed, particularly after his dismissal, that we'd have to go into exile but would come back to rebuild a new Austria.

After the war these documents were discovered unscathed, among them was the "Austrian Warning."

If we can return to the diaries, were you able to take in some of the essence of these valuable notes of your father's before they were burned?

Since my father and I had had some of the same high school professors, I was actually reduced to laughter during this terrible night over some of his schoolboy observations. Humor helped relieve a tense situation, mother came in and tears of laughter rolled down our cheeks. My father had written in verse the exact character traits of the chemistry professor, the German professor and even the geography professor, who'd apparently been telling the same jokes for decades.

But a key to my father's character lay in his war diaries, which presented a lasting impression of a volunteer soldier fighting on the Russian and Italian fronts, and developing a passionate love for his country—Austria. In quick prayers he repeatedly asked God to protect him from having to take the life of one of the enemy.

I get the impression from what you are telling me, that you remember other details from these diaries that all too quickly had to be destroyed. Is that so?

You'll laugh now, but a few days later I bought a Hitler Youth diary and I decided to create a new alphabet with which I could smuggle secret information during my flight. In this way I was able to record some of the battles and events, and above all the duel, the conversation with Emperor Karl on the Isonzo front, and the discovery of the intact body of Bishop Josaphat. Even if they'd caught me, none of the Nazi thugs would have been able to decode it.

Where was your father then actually?

We heard nothing from him throughout Saturday. But the telephone rang practically non-stop and delivered awful news about the arrest of friends and colleagues, relatives and godparents, and also the danger in which Baron Zessner-Spitzenberg found himself—the first Austrian martyr, who died in *Dachau* on 1 August. It seemed like a miracle to us that we weren't touched. Apparently our miserable apartment, without even a piano to be "Aryanized," and the absence of any jealous people in our neighborhood, allowed us to escape the notice of the local liberators.

Around midnight I was awakened by an embrace. It was my father with his mustache shaved off and dressed as a farmer. He said mother and I would have to watch out and to do everything we could to get out of Vienna as quickly as possible. Above all we were to trust no one who asked us any questions; not to lie to anyone, but to stay taciturn. He said that Austria was not lost and that, God willing, we would meet again soon abroad. He'd already prepared everything. He agreed on a code with mother, blessed us, and left the house.

It turned out later that he'd been giving an election speech in Graz before an enthusiastic crowd, when SA men closed in on them from two sides. Schneider got Shuster and my father out and led them to a waiting car behind the City Hall. Father wanted to get to the Hungarian border, where there was a cemetery in the care of a priest who was a friend of his. But they didn't make it. Soon after Maria Trost they were stopped by an SA patrol. The leader gave the order to search Shuster, Schneider and the car very carefully.

He took my father to one side and said, "I'm gonna let you go. I'm XY from Donawitz, you got me out of Wöllersdorf back then."

We learned later that father got on a pilgrim train that stopped all over the place. From Vienna it went to Melk (St. Leopold), St. Florian, Lorch (St. Severin and St. Maximilianus), Linz (the Blessed Rudiger), Salzburg (St. Ernst), Rattenberg (St. Notburga), Thaur bei Innsbruck (St. Romedius) and finally to Feldkirch (St. Fidelis von Sigmaringen).[1] The postcards we got from these places in the next few days strengthened my mother in the worst week of her life. Particularly as on Monday the *Gestapo* came.

---

[1] See Hartmann Melzer and Otto Wimmer, *Lexikon der Namen und Heiligen* (Innsbruck, 1984).

Your mother now had to look after you and your six brothers and sisters aged from two to fifteen, alone and without any money?

It was a school day for us. The atmosphere was tense because some of the less friendly kids and some of the teachers were fanatical and overbearing with their swastika signs. Pity that they all had Slav names! They suddenly started acting like Hitler Youth Quex.[2] Some of the teachers gave unenthusiastic declarations of support (for the Nazis). But a disgracefully large number of others cried "Heil Hitler."

Only a few comrades refused to do so; among them was my friend Hansl Dragosits, our poet, who disappeared on the West Wall shortly afterwards. Also the burning patriot Alfons von Stillfried, who had to give his life in Russia for a despicable and criminal cause.

Classes were postponed and a Hitler Youth meeting was announced for all of us that evening. When I got home the apartment was in chaos. My mother was calmly clearing up the mess. The *Gestapo* had taken my father's library, his filing system, and the contents of practically every cupboard. Apparently everything was burned later in a great big public bonfire. Mother thought that I should hide because the *Gestapo* had asked about me.

My sponsor, the director of the Tyrolia Publishing house in Vienna, Dr. Josef Leeb, took me to his place in the Seilerstätte. One or two student colleagues thought that if only we could just get our hands on a few carbines we could do something about the wretched situation. I ran into a crowd of people who had been forced by SA thugs to clean off the election propaganda from walls and sidewalks with brushes and water. I noticed that many of those standing around were laughing and making rude remarks, but more important, some of them were quiet and gloomy. Personally, I'd never seen such an awful spectacle! What was I to do? On the one hand it strengthened my desire to steal a rifle. On the other hand I had the impulse to find people who felt as I did and doing something there and then. I must have stood around there for long time, flabbergasted, until two Hitler

---

[2]"Hitlerjunge Quex" was the title of a feature film produced by the Nazis, a screen apotheosis of a Hitler Youth martyr named Heinz Norkus.

Youth kids grabbed me and shouted, "Don't look so dumb, yer wanna clean too?" and threw me to the ground. Everybody laughed at me. It was at the ditch by the Dreifaltigkeitssäule.

For the first time in my life I was scared and I swore I'd leave that city as fast as possible.[3]

---

[3]After many adventures the Winter family reached Switzerland. They were received there by a Christian group, which had formed around the progressive Catholic journal *Die Entscheidung*, edited by Architect Stöckli and like-minded friends. They provided asylum for many refugees. Attempts to found a Committee for Austrians-in-Exile failed. The next attempt in France, under the patronage of Minister Paul Boncour, was equally unsuccessful. The English organization, Quaker Help for Loyalist Spain, brought the totally impoverished, nine-member Winter family to Swinburn Manor near Oxford in England. There was then a drastic improvement in their lives and soon afterwards they emigrated to the United States. The work of achieving recognition for Austria as the first victim of Hitler-fascism could now begin. For both father and son that was a field of great activity leading to the establishment by E. K. Winter of the "Committee for Central European Reconstruction." It comprised the twelve nationalities of the Danube basis.

". . . I must stop now, it's all too much for me. . ."

Conversations with *Anni Zerkowitz* on 18 and 21 September and 25 October 1987 in the company of her son Dr. Klaus Zerkowitz.

Mrs. Zerkowitz was born in 1905. She was in Graz in 1938 and still lives in the city.

Were you in Graz in 1938? Did you foresee how bad it was going to be then?

I was in Graz in 1938 and felt the danger even before 13 March.

In 1937 a bomb was placed in the cashier's office of the Margarethenbad.

What happened?

Everything exploded. The cashier's building was destroyed. I was with my husband at the time in the Café Humboldt, which doesn't exist anymore. We heard a terrible bang, heard people shouting, a great crowd gathered—fortunately nobody was hurt.

Who was responsible?

We investigated, of course, and it turned out that it was the Nazis who had planted the bomb.

Were there signs of anti-Semitism even before 1938?

I didn't personally experience any anti-Semitism, so far as I can remember now after fifty years. I spent a lot of time in nationalist fraternity circles because I'd been brought up like that.

So, your parents were nationalists?

I come from a very right-wing nationalist family.

When and to whom did you get married?

I married a building contractor in 1933. He was Jewish, but not religious. He was a cultured, liberal Jew—a free thinker.

Did your parents agree to this marriage?

My parents agreed, and I can't remember that there was even any discussion about it.

My husband spent his youth in Graz and had no special contact with Jews. My husband's family were absolutely not religious. They celebrated Christmas and gave presents to their employees. I never had the feeling that I was in a Jewish home.

What was 1938 like? Did your husband benefit from his good contacts with nationalist circles?

My husband was happily married and always a decent human being and could never imagine that anything could happen to him. Also, of course, he never spent any time with other Jews.

But in 1938 everything changed.

How did it change?

You see, my husband never spent any time with Jews—well there was a certain T who as far as I can remember was Jewish —but otherwise he just had a happy family life. Right up until the end he just couldn't believe that anything could happen to him through Hitler.

And I was completely uninterested in politics. I did embroidery and was completely engrossed in it. So I experienced 13 March and what followed like an innocent child. I suppose, when I think about my husband's fears because I wanted to have a child immediately after we got married—I was already over thirty—and he thought that in "such times" one shouldn't bring a child into the world. But because he moved in nationalist circles and these people were naturally for the *Anschluss*, my husband probably didn't recognize the danger, or didn't want to recognize it.

On the day of the invasion I was at home. When he came home he was very upset and very sad.

And his friends? His nationalist friends?

They were all very happy of course. . . there were no sad faces among them.

What happened to your husband?

He didn't say anything after this date, 13 March 1938.

Didn't he want at least to emigrate at this point? Didn't he realize from then on that it was dangerous for him?

Yes, I think he'd talked about it, but as far as I remember he kept convincing himself that he had nothing to fear and it was all right to stay because he was a respected man that had never done anyone any harm. . . he just couldn't imagine that anything could happen to him.

What happened to you both then?

I can't remember the details before the *Kristallnacht*. But this night I remember well, firstly, because it was my son's birthday—his second—and secondly because it was a decisive moment in my life: at four in the morning there was a knock at the door and my husband was taken away by the *Gestapo*.

He was sent to *Dachau* for three months, and what he experienced there is indescribable. For example, he had to stand a whole day and night in pajamas in the open in icy cold weather —that was New Year's Eve! He wasn't allowed to move.

After three months and with great effort I managed to get him out. His hands were bandaged because they'd been frozen in the terrible cold.

How was it possible to get him out?

After my husband's arrest during the *Kristallnacht*, I went to the Police President. I said everything that I thought could help, including the fact that my husband had been wearing his gold Schaffhausen wrist watch when he'd been arrested. This watch was probably the first possibility for contact. I told the Police President that when he was arrested he hadn't thought that his watch would be taken away. The Police President promised to come personally to our apartment. I was very happy.

He came too because he didn't have an apartment and he wanted to have the "Zerkowitz Apartment."

You succeeded in getting your husband out of Dachau. What happened then?

I only saw my husband after this point for a few hours. As you know, he was sent to the concentration camp on the *Kristallnacht* and he got out only by agreeing to emigrate to Yugoslavia.

In 1940 he went to Yugoslavia and then he was put in a concentration camp again. And it was there in 1942 that my husband was killed.

Did you marry again after the war?

No. My family life ended with his death. I never married again. I had such a wonderful husband, and we had such a harmonious marriage and happy family life—there's no substitute!

I've lived alone for fifty years with my son and I don't want to hear or see anything about politics. We lost everything then and we didn't have a penny during the war. I got DM 100 for my son from the Commissariat. I kept everything from my child. I never cried in front of my growing son. I only spoke about it with my son in 1945. Even then I didn't mention the "causes of death." I haven't even spoken to my best friend, Mrs. Gebell, about our fate. Not during the war and not after. Everybody knew what happened, but nothing is said!

It's the same today, I can't and won't participate in discussions because I get too upset. I must stop now, it's all too much for me.[1]

---

[1]Mrs. Zerkowitz's son, Dr. Klaus Zerkowitz, added the following: "I also get very upset when I hear generalizations about the Jews. I have never felt any anti-Semitism in my fifty years in Graz. But my eighteen-year-old son has heard remarks like—ah, so your name is Zerkowitz—they complained about him and also beat him. That was six months ago. I have to add that he was moving in fraternity circles. He's matriculated and wants to go to a fraternity. I think that the present generation is more anti-Semitic than mine, but perhaps it was suppressed then. . ."

". . . a brown plague. . ."

Conversation with *Richard Zigeuner* on
18 September and 22 October 1987.

Dr. Zigeuner, a neurologist, was born in 1920. He spent 1938 in Klagenfurt and lives today in Graz.

How do you remember 1938?

In 1938 I was with my father's family in this town. He was the president of the Klagenfurt District Court, so I experienced the so-called "upheaval" in Klagenfurt, where there were at least as many fanatical Nazis as in Graz. In my opinion that state of affairs has hardly changed even today.

Did your family suffer from the Nazis?

My father was arrested after the German invasion. Our apartment was searched without any legal authority, and several thousand Schillings and my mother's jewelry disappeared. The search was on account of my father's anti-Nazi views, of which he had never made a secret, although he presented himself as a "Greater German" liberal. My father was extremely awkward for the Nazis. They accused him, interestingly enough, of failing to give the death sentence to any of the "July-Putschists," because of which they were deprived of any Nazi martyrs in Carinthia.

My father openly described the Nazis as a "brown plague," and during his period under arrest he was dismissed from the civil service. In the *Tagespost* newspaper of that time there was an article about it. The dismissal was in accord with the rules of the so-called New Order of the Civil Service in National Socialist Greater Germany. In consequence we had to live for a long time on a small welfare payment and what was left of my parents' savings in Graz.

From what date were you in Graz?

I lived from the summer of 1938 in Graz. I studied medicine here and then I was called up for military service. I did not have any particular difficulties with the Nazi authorities.

Did your father survive?

My father returned from *Buchenwald* concentration camp after an absence of several years—from 1938 to 1942 in fact. Apart from his strong physical constitution, he had the Carinthia Nazi Gau (District) Chief R.v.P (this person remains anonymous) to thank for his survival. This man was a German nationalist but not really a Nazi. My father was a close friend of his.

Where did you go to school? What memories do you have of this time?

I took four classes at the elementary school and four classes at the Lichtenfels High School here in Graz. My father was judge in Graz from 1925 to 1934, so my family also lived in the town. From 1934 to 1938 he was president of the District court in Klagenfurt.

I made my first contact with anti-Semitism in 1933. Up until then nobody bothered whether there were Jewish kids in the class or not. But then suddenly thanks to the Nazi terror and its propaganda, there was a dividing wall between "Aryans" and "non-Aryans." And of course between Nazis and non-Nazis.

The essence of the Nazi terror was: whoever is not a Nazi is "a Jew"! Everyone who did not subscribe to the National Socialist philosophy was defamed as "a Jew."

Even before 1938 I thought the Nazis were false. They knew my views and showed a certain caution and restraint. Comrades with whom I had been friends brought their anti-Semitic and anti-Austrian views unmistakably to my notice. Today these people are sitting in important positions again.

Are you a Jew?

No. But in order to malign me as a non-Nazi, Nazi party members described me as a Jew. I remember having had verbal and non-verbal clashes with Nazis in 1933—both vocal and physical rows, Most of my school colleagues were fanatical Nazis, but I have to admit that after the "upheaval" they didn't make any difficulties for me.

What sort of a relationship did you have to the Nazis later?

After 1944 several acquaintances came to me, some of them from my school days. They had been enthusiastic Nazis up until then, but now they told me that they hadn't really been Nazis and I could confirm that. They knew the regime would be defeated and they wanted to get some "insurance" in time.

Out of good-naturedness I stupidly helped quite a few of them. They believed they were "eternally healed" and were now upright Austrians. For the last ten years I've seen these same people boasting that they are Austrian National Socialists, and they haven't the slightest intention of doing anything for Austria. Absolutely nothing's changed.

The mistake they make abroad is to think that Waldheim is the big Nazi. In fact there have been Nazis in all the parties, among the "blacks" (Christian Socials) as well as the "reds" (Social Democrats), since Lueger and even before him.

Can you remember 13 March 1938?

I can even remember the day before. There had already been various Nazi demonstrations in Klagenfurt. I was traveling with friends and had brought posters for Schuschnigg's attempted plebiscite, which meant that we had continuous fights with Nazi groups who ripped the posters down as soon as we had put them up.

After Schuschnigg's visit to Hitler in February 1938 there was unrest, fear, and tension, and it was getting stronger every day. The climax was reached when we heard Schuschnigg's radio announcement on the evening of 11 March 1938, that the government had to resign because of pressure from Germany, and the famous words with which he ended his address: "God save Austria!"

From this point on we merely waited, either for the arrest of my father, or of the whole family.

I experienced this period very intensively. I listened to Radio "Beromünster." It was the station I listened to throughout the war (of course it was forbidden to listen to it, but it was the only way one could be objectively informed). I heard over "Beromünster"—I can't remember which day it was—that in the British House of Lords a member had declared that they did not want to provoke any trouble with Germany over Austria, on the contrary, Hitler should be thanked, since, with the invasion of Austria, a source of unrest in central Europe had been taken care of.

That was natural, the Nazis controlled the mass media from the beginning and the people.

What do you mean by that?

Every appearance by Goering or Hitler was prepared. Whole trains were organized for them. I was also invited on such a trip to the Heldenplatz, where Hitler gave a so-called "Report to History," about the *Anschluss* of his homeland to the German Reich. There were not only Viennese there, but also umpteen thousands brought in from outside.

I was asked to go, but I just said, "Leave me alone!"

How do you see Hitler's invasion of Austria?

The German invasion of Austria was, from a purely military point of view, a disgrace.

I would like to refer to a good book by Schuschnigg.[1] In this book he mentions the concerns of the German generals con-

---

[1]Kurt Schuschnigg, *Im Kampf gegen Hitler. Die Überwindung der Anschlussidee* (Wien/München/Zürich, 1969).

cerning the invasion of Austria. Although no resistance was offered, the German troops got into difficulties with the steep passes and the snow, and if determined resistance had been made, they would have been in great trouble. However, there never was any resistance! The Nazis betrayed everything!

1938 is for me the greatest ignominy there's ever been!

Have people learned from history? How do you see things now, fifty years later? Is there a revival of National Socialism?

The blame for any revival of National Socialism belongs to a large degree to our corrupt democracy. It began with the Socialists and with the reawakened Freedom Party, which was known then as the VDU. The purpose was to split the middle-class and make Nazism respectable again. In 1945 the Socialists tried immediately to get all the Nazi academics on their side and got them good posts. Through the Socialists, incorrigible Nazis came into leading positions in health organizations, trade unions, etc. On the other side the "blacks" also brought unreformed Nazis into important positions.

Another refuge for National Socialism and anti-Semitism has been the student body. There, pure National Socialist thought is passed on from former arch-Nazis to young people. "Blood and Soil" is quite normal there!

Then you mean, Dr. Zigeuner, that we haven't learned anything from history?

No. We haven't learned anything from history. Least of all the National Socialists, the Nazis!

But how do you explain that? After the Holocaust?

Nobody believes that! The extermination of the Jews, six million? The Nazis treat this figure as libelous, for them it didn't happen! They still say the Jews were responsible for the destruction of Germany and provoked the First World War.

What should one do? What should one have done in your opinion?

I can't answer that. Everyone can think what he wants.

Let us go back to 1938, to Graz: were you in Graz during the
Kristallnacht?

Yes. I was in Graz during the *Kristallnacht* and having been
alerted by acquaintances, witnessed the burning of the synagogue
and the funeral parlor at the Jewish cemetery. A great contingent
of SA tried to blow up the pillars of the building—an exercise
that did not succeed; it was a pathetic attempt! All this was with
a fanfare and before a great crowd of people who had apparently
gathered to see the "show."
It was also reported that during this night Jewish citizens
had been thrown out of windows and there were several dead.
No one had sympathy for the Jews—that shocked me.[2]
It was the same in Carinthia.
And of course during the War on the various fronts: nowhere
where I was stationed, was the Jewish problem discussed, because everyone was scared of being arrested and possibly shot.

What sort of people were at the cemetry and at the syna-
gogue?

It was a mob.

Did the situation for the Jews in November 1938 get worse
still? Were the Nazis scared of war?

Yes. The situation for the Jews became increasingly
threatening.
In November 1938 there was fear of war even among the
super-Nazis. They didn't know at that time how militarily

---

[2]"In Styria, where SD and Gestapo only received knowledge of 'a
forthcoming action' after the SA and the Gau leadership, 350 Jews were
arrested in the night of 10 November. They were brought initially to the
cells of the District court, from where they were taken on the evening of 11
November by train to a concentration camp. The synagogue and the funeral
parlor of the Jewish cemetery were 'reduced to ashes.' Some shops in the
Annenstrasse were destroyed. But 'violent actions against the Jews did not
take place.'" See Erike Weinzierl, *Zu wenig Gerechte*, p. 60.

incapable were Germany's enemies. Only Russia was under-estimated. In 1939 there was certainly no enthusiasm for war.

Can you remember, were people taken away from your own circle of acquaintances?

In our house in the Auersperggasse, a Jewish family had lived on the first floor since 1927 or 1928. Both of them were taken away in 1938, the man who was an amputee and diabetic, as well as his wife who was still sprightly. They had to leave all their furniture behind, and their apartment was assigned to a well-known Graz business family. It came at a convenient time for this family since the son had spent all his father's savings; and so at least their "accommodation problem was relatively easily solved." The Jewish couple died a few weeks later. I don't know where these people were taken to, whether they were deported to a concentration camp. I only learned that they died shortly afterwards. They were very old, around seventy.

Do you know whether other people were arrested?

I know that many loyal Austrians were deported to concen-tration camps and many were murdered. That happened after 1938.

When did you learn of the concentration camps?

Since the thirties, I knew what it was like in German concen-tration camps. I got hold of literature on it. I believe the books were published in Switzerland.

Was there at this time a lot of anti-Semitic literature?

I knew about anti-Semitic literature. My father had a copy in his library of the best-seller, *The Foundations of the 19th Century* by Houston Stewart Chamberlain, and I also read Gobineau, who introduced the notion of the blue-eyed Aryan race that was superior to all the others.[3]

Why was there anti-Semitic literature in your family?

In our library there was literature of all kinds because we were a cosmopolitan and intellectual family.

How long were you in Graz?

With some breaks, until 1944. Then I was in Poland and France.

Were there changes in Graz up till 1944?

I had the impression then that everybody in Graz was a Nazi. I can remember only a few friends and acquaintances who were good Austrians. Otherwise I can think only of Nazis.

Were there people of your acquaintance who returned after 1945, who had been driven out in 1938?

I can only remember that people immediately criticized the former Nazis, and that I was accused of having attacked Nazis.

Do you know if every Jew received compensation?

---

[3]Houston Stewart Chamberlain was the son-in-law and a great admirer of Richard Wagner. An Englishman, he became a German citizen in 1916. In his massive *The Foundations of the 19th Century* (1899) he put forward a racial view of human history that later influenced the National Socialists, although he died in 1927, before the Nazis came to power. *Der grosse Brockhaus*, Vol. 2, (Wiesbaden, 1980).
Comte Arthur de Gobineau, (1816-1882) was a French writer and diplomat. In his work, *Essai sur l'inegalité des races humaines* (4 volumes), he presented the view that there were not only physical, but also spiritual and intellectual differences between the races, and he sought to prove the superiority of the Aryan race over all others. *Der grosse Brockhaus*, Vol. 5, (Wiesbaden, 1980).

I know that there were Jews who did not succeed in getting back those businesses, which had been stolen from them by Nazis.

My father helped many Jews. He couldn't help them all, that was simply not possible.

What did you father do after the War?

My father was in the end President of the Graz District Court and President of the Constitutional Court in Vienna.

Do you know when the persecution of the Jews began in Germany?

I learned that the massive persecution in Germany began only after the invasion of Austria. It has to be said that, in relation to their population, the Austrians were over-represented among the murderers of Jews in comparison with the Germans. People won't hear of that in Austria! But then who likes to admit that he's made a mistake!?

How do you think things will carry on in Austria?

I only know that there won't be any more National Socialism. But I also know that there are officials of the Freedom Party who called out to Haider at some function, "We'll march with you to Russia. . ." They also sang "Deutschland, Deutschland über alles," and the Horst-Wessel Song. . . . those are things that I find questionable. That is also Austria!

So, there won't be any more Nazism, but if these people carry on like this, the state could be divided up. The state is in danger, really in danger!

Let's return once again to 1938. What was the most essential thing for you about this time? Which day?

11 March 1938 was for me the most important, with the threat of the German invasion and the forced resignation of Schuschnigg. I spent 13 March at home with my family. The schools were closed for the week. The masses on the street were

in a state of great excitement. The few, the good Austrians, quickly found out by telephone from each other who was still free and who had already been arrested. Then came the telephone calls that so-and-so had been arrested.

Did you have Jewish friends?

In my class there were two Jewish students, they took their examinations for graduation with me. That was in 1938 when, interestingly, the big Nazis in the class, without Hitler, could never have gotten their certificates because they were such bad students.

A super-Nazi had received a "4" (failed) in his exams and was dismissed as "insufficient." Then he was pardoned, so to speak, by the Reichsminister for Education for his "activities on behalf of Nationalial Socialism" and permitted to enter medical school! I learned after the War that my two Jewish colleagues went abroad after a few months. However, I think they were killed during the War.

We had a good acquaintance in Klagenfurt who had been an officer in the Austro-Hungarian Army. He'd been decorated with the Golden Bravery Medal and had lost a leg. We advised him without a second thought to emigrate before the final catastrophe, but he thought that nothing could happen to him because he was a severely wounded officer from the First World War. He stayed in Klagenfurt and thought he was "sacrosanct;" he was killed by the Nazis in a concentration camp. There was a law in the "Third Reich" which should have protected severely wounded Jewish veterans from persecution under the Nuremberg Laws, but the Nazis didn't uphold it.

Back to 13 March: what was the atmosphere like?

13 March began with an end-of-the-world atmosphere. There was a feeling that there was no future because at this stage there didn't seem any likelihood that this "Third Reich" would come to a quick end. And if the leadership had not been so weak, then we'd still have it today. Yes, really, without the failure of those incompetents we would still have the Third Reich today!

Do you mean that in connection with popular mentality?

Yes. Even the Americans were indifferent to what was happening to the Jews in Europe. It is a historical fact; the
Americans took the reports over mass exterminations in the
concentration camps to be horror propaganda. They said: that
simply isn't true. And therefore I think the whole discussion over
Waldheim is ridiculous. In Austria there are hundreds of thousands of Nazis.

Do you mean that worn-out phrase, "fulfilling one's duty"?

Yes, some of the "blacks" have talked themselves into
believing that, without considering. . . .

**And you think an immediate solidarity grew up with the "in-
curables"—the ones that live eternally in the past?**

Yes, that is exactly the case with the Veterans' Associations.
These organizations should be placed on the "watch list."

**What do you think of the "watch list" action of the Austrian
Veterans Association?**

It reminds me of Kreisky's remark: "The greatest achievement of the Austrians is that they declared Hitler to be a German
and Beethoven to be an Austrian."
But one thing we know, anti-Semitism emanates from National Socialism. Leading "black" groups are, as successors to
Lueger, clearly anti-Semitic. And thanks to the mistakes that
were made after the War, these convinced Nazis rose to high
positions through the Socialist Party, and they are still there
today.

**How did it go with your circle of friends from 1938? Did you
you all remain friends?**

I noticed only one thing, that many of the friends whom I
thought I had, suddenly didn't recognize me anymore.

I don't understand that. How do you mean?

I simply did not exist for them anymore! Quite simple! Then they recognized me again in 1945! And I must say, it is a similar situation now: people who I know are old Nazis, doctors, lawyers, judges, behave in a very reserved, if not hostile manner in my company.

What sort of family background do you come from, Dr. Zigeuner?

I come from an Austro-Hungarian civil service family. I have proof of ancestry back to the time of Maria Theresia. There was a forefather of mine who was ennobled, he was a member of the Imperial Court—I think the Bohemian Court.[4] My grandfather was an Austro-Hungarian officer and company commander in the Battle of Koeniggrätz (1866).[5] My family's anti-Prussian attitude stems from this experience. But in order to defame my family, Nazi circles say even today, behind my back, that I am a Jew!

Is it possible that people in 1938 and afterwards during the War did not know anything about the persecution of the Jews? Especially if they had no Jewish friends or acquaintances for example?

The notion put forward today by people whom I know to be Nazis, that they knew nothing about the fate of Jews and

---

[4]The Court Chancellory was set up in 1620 as the central authority of the Austrian states for foreign, internal, and legal administration; it was also the Supreme Court. Later, independent Chancellories were set up in the separate states. In 1742 the Court and State Chancellories were removed from the Austrian Court Chancellory. The Austrian and Bohemian Court Chancellory was united in 1749 in the "Directorium in publicis et cameralibus" and reorganized in 1761 as the "Directorium in internis." (*Brockhaus*, Vol. 5).

[5]"In the battle of Königgrätz (known as Sadowa in Britain and France) on 3 July 1866, the Prussian victory (v. Moltke) over the Austrians and the Saxons (v. Benedeck) decided the outcome of the 1866 German War." (Brockhaus, Vol. 6).

opponents of National Socialism during the War, is totally groundless in my opinion and is based on their inability to accept the truth.

I knew before the War through Radio "Beromünster" what dreadful things the Nazis had done in *Dachau, Buchenwald* and other places in June 1934, at the time of the so-called "Röhm Putsch."[6] Typically, the leader of the Hitler Youth in Klagenfurt, who up until then had been a "good friend" of mine, told me after I had made a critical comment about conditions after the *Anschluss,* "One more outburst like that and you'll go to *Dachau!*" And I ask you—the Nazis claim now they didn't know about the concentration camps?

Incidentally, during the War I was posted to the area around *Auschwitz*; the German-speaking population there had known for years that Jews were burned in *Auschwitz* and pointed to the smoke coming out of the crematoria. I spoke to people myself about it because I had no idea about *Auschwitz.* That was in 1944.

How did these people there behave? How did they talk about it?

The people who showed me the smoking chimneys were completely indifferent! At the most they feared reprisals from the Nazis. But I never saw any sympathy.

How do you explain that as a doctor? You are a man who has dedicated himself to humanitarianism. You are a nerve specialist and understand the human psyche. What was going on inside these people? Can you explain that scientifically?

---

[6]"Röhm Putsch": Nazi term for an alleged conspiracy of the SA leadership around Ernst Röhm, and taken by Hitler as a pretext for murdering this leadership in a three-day operation carried out by the Gestapo and the SS. At the same time other unpopular personalities were eliminated, i.e., K. v. Schleicher, G. Strasser, Ritter v. Kahr, E. Jung, E. Klausener. On 3 July 1934 Hitler justified his action on the grounds of a threat to the security of the state (*Brockhaus*, Vol. 9).

Stupidity of the masses, and the incitement that Hitler had been stirring up for years, i.e., the Jew is the deadly enemy of the German and only has one purpose: the destruction of the German people!

Do you think that today one can still succeed with this kind of propaganda?

Of course. You can see it. The reaction to the whole miserable Waldheim affair shows clearly that one can succeed with such slogans. People need a scapegoat. The Jews murdered Christ.

Do you think that anti-Semitism, I mean its roots, goes back to Christian anti-Semitism?

I think that the roots of anti-Semitism go back to the thesis of the murder of God. Of course, certain additional factors which are always important with persecuted minorities play a role. I mean a minority—if you observe this phenomenon—"must be exterminated." In other words, find a scapegoat and a diversion from the contemporary economic crisis. That has been the case for thousands of years. Whenever a prince in France or Spain got into difficulties, then he unleashed a pogrom against the Jews. It's just that there has never been such an absurdly extreme case as the "Third Reich."

Do you know about the violent controversy last year in the Federal Republic of Germany? Jürgen Habermas accused some German historians of apologistic tendencies. Are they encouraging the demoralization of the past? The Hamburger "Zeit" reported on it. Do you know about this debate?

I'll tell you, I believe these Nazi crimes are so serious because this theory of "misfortune" has succeeded in driving a cultured and hard-working people into a mass psychosis.

Do you mean therefore that the singularity of the crimes lies in the fact that they were committed by a highly civilized people in a hysteria of persecution induced by their respon-

sible leaders, and that they were directed at totally exterminating a particular group of human beings, including the old, women, children, and babies, and that they were carried out with all the available power of the state?

Yes. These crimes were unique! It's beyond discussion!

Afterword

In "times like these" contemporary historians are very busy. For this reason I was quite hesitant to accept the invitation of Dr. Elfriede Schmidt to write a brief *1938. . . . and the Consequences* epilogue to her anthology in awareness of my work overload, despite the publisher's courtesy of sending me a complete set of proofs.

Then, however, I became increasingly interested as I read the forty and more interviews which Dr. Schmidt has conducted since the summer of 1987 and which have obviously been prepared by correspondence. Her interview partners were contemporary celebrities like Cardinal König, Ex-President Kirchschläger or Ex-Chancellor Kreisky as well as female and male Austrians who are not yet known publicly, individuals mainly from Vienna and Graz, persecuted for political or "racial" reasons during the National-Socialist rule over Austria, survivors of concentration camps, and emigrants. I have known some of them personally for many years. Still I have learned more about their lives from the interviews.

Dr. Schmidt has long been studying anti-Semitism. The incentive to publish this book, however—as indicated in her introduction—came from aggressive, anti-Semitic exclamations made by debaters during the "admonition watch" in front of Vienna's Stephansdom in the summer of 1987. The "admonition watch" had been organized by the group "Neues Österreich" (New Austria).

This group's intention was to fight the anti-Semitism which had become manifest during the presidential election campaign won by Dr. Kurt Waldheim on June 8, 1986, and to call to mind the Austrian resistance against the Nazi rule.

After the separate groups had joined together, they chose 05 as its symbol, representing Austria, as *E* is the fifth letter of the alphabet. Young and older people associated with various political parties kept watch in front of this symbol around the clock, to bring back to mind the "other" Austria.

It is a particular merit of the book by Dr. Schmidt, a convinced Catholic, not only to interview her partners with respect to their experiences in the past which—as it turns out—is not yet overcome, but also to ask for their opinion on present events, up to the end of 1987, that is, on the long tradition of the religious anti-Semitism which is still not extinct.

In this epilogue I need not quote the harsh und clear answers. Anyone may read them in the preceding pages. They report several instances of anti-Semitic aggression and discrimination that Jews have been exposed to long before 1938, particularly in renowned tourist resorts such as in the Salzkammergut.

Elfriede Schmidt concluded her introduction expressing the desire that her work might "be seen as a modest contribution to the dialogue between Christian and Jews." It is more than that: in itself it is testimony of the "other" Austria.

—Erika Weinzierl
Professor of History
University of Vienna

Appendix I

Interview with Walter F. Mondale, Former Vice President of the United States, May 11, 1990 in Minneapolis.

What do you think about the unification of East-West Germany? There is a certain consternation about the situation particularly under the Israelis. Israel Foreign Minister Arens has said: "People must understand that the German unification must be very troublesome for the Jews around the world. Jews have trusted the democratic tradition. . . for more than 40 years. . . and the extension of this tradition in connection with a unified Germany should be seen as a positive step." But there is another opinion on this subject. I am thinking about the correspondence between Rabbi Marvin Hier and Dr. Helmut Kohl. Rabbi Hier speaks about "the fears" which are real because those who bear the scars of the last "unified Germany" do not see their concerns being addressed in the current reunification discussion between world leaders.

I think the fears about the reunification are important, and they have to be dealt with. The German reunification is a thing that's almost done. But I think we should be pressing the Germans and the leadership to confront the issues. For example, let's settle the Polish boundary problem or let's agree not to have nuclear weapons, let's agree to bring Germany into a Western structure, including being in NATO and in the European Economic Community. I thought it was good when East German Parliament declared their guilt about the holocaust. The President of West Germany von Weizsäcker is a fine man.—I think we need to encourage more of that.

There were other stories about anti-Semitism the other day. . . What do you think about this new anti-Semitism?

Oh, it's very severe they tell me! A delegation headed by Rabbi Raskos is leaving from Minnesota on Monday for the Soviet Union to try to convince people to confront the tremendous anti-Semitism going on over there. So I think it's very serious, it's the Pamyat and not just only the Pamyat, it's found in more serious circles. So I think we have to be very mindful of this.

Do you believe in the ability of Poland to achieve economic recovery in the future? I know that you visited Poland recently. What major problems do you see in the economic recovery process for Poland?

I am hopeful, but Poland has also deep problems. The economy is terrible, the leadership is "green" and divided, the environmental mess is horrible, people may get tired of all the sacrifice needed in order to open the economy. I think the West has to help them to get through this "hard part." A lot of things to worry about.

I am an Austrian. What do you think about Austria's role now in this "changed world?" Is there a chance for Austria?

I would like to see Austria be of help here. I am sorry about the President of Austria. I think that's it.

What do you think of the President of Austria?

I think, it's terrible. It's disgraceful. The record is clear. . . more evidence the other day. He clearly has not been telling the truth. I knew him. But it's horrible. Clearly he was a Nazi, he clearly was heavily involved in those areas where Jews were killed and rounded up.

Do you think he was involved?

Yes, well I do. And I think that's exactly what this document shows that I have read. he was listed as a probable participant.

Are you convinced that he was involved?

I saw all the documents in the U.N. I read almost all of them. They sure thought he was. This is not 1944 and I was not there in 1944. But with that record I think he should not be President of Austria!

What should Austria do now? Change their President?

Absolutely! I think, he shouldn't run again. He should step down.

Step down?

Right! I have to go now. . .

Thank you for the interview. . . .

The author with former Vice President Mondale.

Manfred Rommel, Mayor of Stuttgart

Appendix II

Interview with Manfred Rommel, Mayor of Stuttgart, Germany on 14 January 1991. First elected in 1974, he was re-elected for a third term in 1990, receiving 71.7% of the popular vote.

Young people have been proclaiming in Germany's streets, "Ami, out of Arabia!" and "No blood for oil!" Given your historical background, would you say there is a parallel situation between the occupation of Kuwait in 1990 and the occupation of Austria in 1938?

I would say there was a parallel to Hitler's march into Czechoslovakia on September 1, 1938 but not when Hitler marched in Austria earlier. Most of the Austrians were happy when he marched in. Of course, I can say there is a parallel between Hitler in 1938 and Saddam Hussein today, but Hitler was more powerful and more dangerous than Saddam Hussein. S. Hussein has a "big mouth."

The United States Congress authorized George Bush to use force in line with the United Nations Resolution. Do you feel the United Nations should stop S. Hussein by war or by economic sanctions? And what is your opinion in general concerning the present situation in the Middle East? War or no war?

I prefer not to have war, but I don't know if it is realistic. It's absolutely necessary that Mr. Saddam Hussein understands that he must leave Kuwait. He cannot confuse the invasion of Kuwait with the problems concerning Israel. S. Hussein has no sense of realism if he thinks he would be able to fight against the biggest power in the world. I think also there is a "must" to react! Concerning the point of view of history, it is also important to make clear that there is no chance to occupy countries one by

one. . . otherwise we should have a dark future. . . in the next
century.

**According to an article in *Der Spiegel* twenty German firms
are still doing business with Iraq. What is your view concerning German military deliveries to Iraq? Is Germany
sharing responsibility for a potential war against the Jews fifty
years after the holocaust?**

It's really not our business in Germany to provide the whole
world with weapons. And we are not doing this. But I also know
there are "fools," and there were German firms delivering weapons to Iraq and Libya. But I don't know if it happened after the
embargo. If so, then those firms must face up to the consequences. But S. Hussein obtained weapons for a long time from
all parts of the Western powers because they were content that S.
Hussein was against Iran and Khomeni was considered more dangerous than S. Hussein. That direction suddenly changed: the
aggression of S. Hussein against Kuwait and Israel.

**What is the German policy concerning Israel today? Has there
been a change? Will Germany maintain friendly relations towards Israel now that it is united?**

We had a good relationship with Israel. We have a good relationship with Israel today, and maybe we will have an even better
one in the future—I hope so.

**What do you think about the demonstrations in the streets of
Bonn, Munich and Stuttgart. "No blood for oil!" "Ami out of
Arabia!"**

It's not a question of oil, but a question of power, liberty, and
security. In terms of the saying "Der Klügere gibt nach" (the
wiser submits) it would raise the question of how much longer
would it be before Saddam Hussein would occupy Saudi Arabia.
When a man like Saddam Hussein has power over raw-materials,
he has political power and can also buy military power. The consequences of that would be very bad. He would become a "major
power." Therefore you have to oppose him!

And no appeasement policy?

I think it was a big mistake for the British and French to appease Hitler fifty years ago. That was the reason for the tragedy that followed.

Now do you think that George Bush is right to attack Iraq?

I don't want to say "to attack," but I would say that I have a great respect for his resolute attitude. I think George Bush is saving the "world peace!"

Appendix III

A Letter of 12 May 1987 from the Deputy Mayor of Linz,
Dr. Carl Hödl, to Edgar Bronfman,
President of the Jewish World Congress.

Mr. Bronfman!

It is customary for Austrians to use some pleasantry when addressing others in writing but with you I cannot bring myself to do so. Your uncalled-for, unqualified and altogether infernal attack on our Federal President, represents an attack on all Austrians, and therefore I, as an Austrian, a Christian, and a qualified jurist, must defend myself.

When you claim, as you did in Budapest in your latest attack on our President, Dr. Waldheim, that he was part of a killing machine, then I ask myself whether you even understand the nature of war. What happens in every war? Killing and more killing. And therefore your claim applies equally to millions of soldiers from every country. You probably spent the Second World War in a safe country, Mr. Bronfman, or perhaps you were only just out of diapers, otherwise you would know that millions of innocent people, especially in the German city of Dresden, were the victims of senseless air raids.

We know from our President that he was never a Nazi—and you have not been able to prove it but have merely claimed it—and that as a lieutenant in the German Army, he was such a small cog in the machine that he could never have given an order to kill anyone. You, Mr. Bronfman, should know that, either that or you have made this claim against your better judgment. Because these charges are on the same level as those of your co-religionists two thousand years ago, who allowed Jesus Christ to be sentenced to death because he didn't fit in with the plans of the gentlemen in Jerusalem. But allow me another comparison. Just as the pronouncement of that unjust verdict was left to a Roman, so this time you have left it to the American Justice Department to put Dr. Waldheim on the "Watchlist."

So that you can see what I think of the injustice of your action, I invite you to use your not inconsiderable influence to get me put on the "Watchlist." Then it won't be your fault but that of the Justice Department.

There was much about your behavior as President of an "association," as Dr. Kreisky always called it, which was unclear to me until I read the American book *The Source.*

I hope that you have enough decency left to appear before an Austrian court of law, because only such a court has jurisdiction in this case. Our courts are recognized to be fair throughout the world. However I am certain that you will not do this when I recall what you said in Hungary.

I should also like you to know, something I deeply regret, that with your unqualified and unsubstantiated charge you have done great harm to your co-religionists in Austria, in Germany, in Hungary and I don't know where else. I only hope that the members of your association hold you responsible. An eye for an eye, a tooth for a tooth, is not our European belief. You and people like you try to preach this Talmudic notion throughout the world. I can only say that I realize this with profound shock and dismay.

You probably don't know what humanity is, but it might still be possible for you to learn, because it is never too late to gain new and enlightening knowledge.

Dr. Carl Hödl
Deputy Mayor of Linz, Austria

Appendix IV

*Letter of Elfriede Schmidt to Deputy Mayor Mr. Carl Hödl
on 28 July 1987.*

Dear Mr. Deputy Mayor,

You have as a "Christian" and in your capacity as deputy mayor written an anti-Semitic letter. On the one hand you have no regrets for the remarks in your letter, on the other hand you regret "that we have released something which did not exist in Austria, namely anti-Semitism."

"We have not released anything," dear Mr. Deputy Mayor! You have written an intolerable letter and therefore you are responsible!

The interpretation and commentary on the New Testament through the centuries has contributed in no small measure to the creation of anti-Semitic and heathen bigotry. From the Middle Ages to recent times it has led to the oppression and death of Jews, to the expulsion of Jewish communities. Consider Auschwitz.

Christian anti-Semitism then reappeared as racist anti-Semitism.

The Jews were made responsible for everything that went wrong.

It is not a weakness, but a strength of our belief to recognize our guilt in relations with the Jews.

In 1965 the Second Vatican Council decreed that Jews neither in the time of Christ nor today are guilty of the death of Christ. In 1986 the Pope asked for forgiveness in a synagogue in Rome for the crime of accusing the Jews of killing God and causing them so much pain as a result.

But you don't seem to know what anti-Semitism is! You talk about things about which you have no idea.

You use divisive tactics. You reject anti-Semitism yet you use anti-Semitic stereotypes.

What counts for progress in the Church, you seem to ignore. Instead you reproduce what you can remember from your Bible class at school.

You call yourself a lawyer. Then perhaps you would be interested in Wedding Fricke's *Standrechtlich gekreuzigt*. He is a German colleague of yours, who has written on the trial of Christ, and he shows that the accusation of decide against the Jews—should be dropped because it leads to generalizations, and it should be applied to us Christians, that we Austrians should learn the meaning of remorse.

Cardinal König has declared that anti-Semitism in Austria must be fought.

If you had read Wedding Fricke's book you would have spared yourself this embarrassing infamy!

Elfriede Schmidt

Appendix V

Letter of the Austrian Bishops to Gauleiter Bürckel.

(Edited by the delegate of the Führer for the plebiscite of Gauleiter Bürckel. Responsible: Karl Garland, Vienna. With a preface on the Solemn Declaration by the Austrian bishops concerning the plebiscite, Vienna 1938)

Solemn Declaration!

From inner most conviction and of our own free will, we, the undersigned bishops of the austrian ecclesiastical province, on the occasion of the great historical events in German-Austria profess: We joyously acknowledge that the national socialist movement has achieved in the past and is still achieving outstanding results in national and economic reconstruction as well as in social policy for the German Reich and people, and particularly for the poorest strata of the population. We are also convince that the peril from all-destructive and atheist Bolshevism has been averted by the activities of the national socialist movement.

To these activities the bishops add their best blessings for the future and shall admonish their faithful in this spirit. On the day of the plebiscite it goes without saying that it is a national obligation for us bishops as Germans to stand by the German Reich, and we expect all faithful Christians to know what they owe to their nation.

Vienna, 18 March 1938.

Appendix VI

Sermon of Cardinal Innitzer in Vienna's St. Stephan's Cathedral on October 7, 1938:

Catholic youth!
Take the happiness and the thanks of your bishop for accepting the invitation!
You have come to regain strength, to stand strong in great and difficult times.

You have lost them this last year:
Your associations, leagues, and unions have been battered, your banners have been taken from you, you may no longer join in merry, young groups. And yet you have gained much: learning of the solid community of young Christians, of the community in parish and church.

Do not lose your courage!
Stand strong and faithful to God, to parish and to church!
Live a vigorous parish life.
Christ is victor!
He is what it all is about, today more than ever!
But He cannot be taken from this world.
He must conquer!
And this is your mission: to carry His victory into the world with your youthful strength.

Let us stand even stronger and steadier!
Christ is our leader and king.
This is not easy these days.
It is made very difficult for you.
But do not be misled!
Do not be intimidated!
Guard the precious faith!
Retain your faith and remain steady!

For only faith makes one blissful!

Give my regards to your parents, and I thank them for the avowal they have given these days when they were asked whether their children should continue to get their religious instruction in school.

Stand strong in your faith, come what may!
Trust your bishop!
And pray for him, that the Holy Spirit shall guide him in difficult times. You may perhaps not have understood everything lately, you know, what I mean (alluding to his excessive co-operation: acclaim of the "union" and appeal to vote: March/April 1938, to secure the church and the faithful). But it happened out of great responsibility.
Pray for the bishop!
And display your faith openly.
Bravely and steadily.
Influence others, wavering ones, by words and by example, by your example.

This is my great joy, to see you there, side by side: there still exists an ideal youth, despite all slogans!
Team up with like-minded fellows in close association.

Retain the living faith in your hearts!
God does not desert us.
God bless you and give my regards to all!

(In: Georg Wagner, *Österreich. Zweite Republik*. Vol. I, p. 114. Thaur/Tirol-Vienna 1983.)

Bibliography

Adamovich, Ludwig K. und Funk, Bernd-Christian: *Österreichisches Verfassungsrecht.* 3rd edition. (Verfassungsrechtslehre unter Berücksichtigung von Staatslehre und Politikwissenschaft). In: *Springers Kurzlehrbuch f. Rechtswissenschaft.* Wien 1985.

Ahrendt, Hannah: *Eichmann in Jerusalem.* Ein Bericht von der Banalität des Bösen. München 1964, 1986.

1938 - Anatomie eines Jahres. Ed.: Thomas, Chorherr. Wien 1987.

Andics, Helmut: *Der Staat den Keiner wollte.* Österreich 1918 - 1938. Wien 1962.

Baltl, Hermann: *Österreichische Rechtsgeschichte.* Von den Anfängen bis zur Gegenwart. Graz 1982.

Bein, Alex: *Die Judenfrage.* Biographie eines Weltproblems. Vols. I, II. Stuttgart 1980.

Binder, Dieter A.: *Das Schicksal der Grazer Juden 1938.* In: *Historisches Jahrbuch der Stadt Graz 1987.* Graz 1987.

Brenner, Hildegard: *Die Kunstpolitik des Nationalsozialismus.* Hamburg 1963. Der grosse BROCKHAUS (Vol. 12) 18th edition. Wiesbaden 1980.

Broder, Henryk M.: *Der ewige Antisemit.* Über Sinn und Funktion eines beständigen Gefühls. Frankfurt a. M. 1986.

Botz, Gerhard: *Eingliederung Österreichs in das Deutsche Reich.* Planung und Verwirklichung des politisch-administrativen Anschlusses. 1938 - 1940. Wien 1974.

Bruckmüller, Ernst: *Sozialgeschichte Österreichs.* Wien 1985.

Bunzl, John: *Der lange Arm der Erinnerung.* Jüdisches Bewusstsein heute. Wien-Köln-Graz 1987.

Antijudaismus - Christliche Wurzeln. In: *Der Entschluss.* Spiritualität, Jesuiten, Gemeinde. Vol. 42, No. 7 - 8, 1987.

Frankl, Viktor E.: *. . . trotzdem Ja zum Leben sagen.* Eine Psychologie erlebt das Konzentrationslager. München 1981.

Franzel, Emil: *Das Reich der braunen Jakobiner.* Der Nationalsozialismus als geschichtliche Erscheinung. München 1964.

Fremd im eigenen Land. Ed.: Henryk M. Broder, und Michael R. Lang. Frankfurt a. M. 1979.

Fricke, Weddig: *Standrechtlich gekreuzigt.* Person und Prozess des Jesus aus Galiläa. Freiburg i. B. 1986.

Gamm, Hans Jochen: *Der Flüsterwitz im Dritten Reich.* München 1979.

Glaser, Hermann: *Das Dritte Reich.* Anspruch nach Wirklichkeit. Freiburg 1961.

Grenzfeste Deutscher Wissenschaft. Über Faschismus und Vergangenheitsbewältigung an der Universität Graz. Ed.: Verein Kritische Sozialwissenschaft und Politische Bildung. Graz 1985.

Haslinger, Josef: *Politik der Gefühle.* Ein Essay über Österreich. Darmstadt 1987.

Heer, Friedrich: *Gottes erste Liebe.* Die Juden im Spannungsfeld der Geschichte. Frankfurt a. M. 1986.

Heinz, Karl H.: *E. K. Winter.* Ein Katholik zwischen Österreichs Fronten, 1933 - 1938. Ed.: Franz Reiter. Wien-Köln-Graz 1984.

Herzl, Theodor: *Der Judenstaat.* Versuch einer modernen Lösung der Judenfrage. Augsburg 1986.

Hindels, Josef: *Hitler war kein Zufall.* Ein Beitrag zur Soziologie der Nazibarbarei. Wien 1962.

Hirsch, Leo: *Jüdische Glaubenswelt.* Basel 1982.

Holl, Adolf: *Religionen.* Wien 1984.

Die Juden als Minderheit in der Geschichte. Eds.: Bernd Martin und Ernst Schulin. München 1981.

Das jüdische Echo. Zeitschrift für Kultur und Politik. Ed.: Jüdische Akademiker Österreichs und Vereinigung jüdischer Hochschüler in Österreich.

Jüdische Lebenswege. Gespräche mit Nahum Goldmann, Simon Wiesenthal, H. G. Adler. Ed.: Karl B. Schnelting. Frankfurt a. M. 1982.

Kardinal König. Ed.: Annemarie Fenzl. Wien 1985.

Karner, Stefan: *Die Steiermark im Dritten Reich 1938 - 1945.* Aspekte ihrer politischen, wirtschaftlich-sozialen und kulturellen Entwicklung. Graz-Wien 1986.

Kirchschläger, Rudolf: *Der Friede beginnt im eigenen Haus.* Gedanken über Österreich. Wien 1980.

Kreisky, Bruno: *Zwischen den Zeiten.* Erinnerungen aus fünf Jahrzehnten. Wien 1987.

Kreiskys gosse Liebe. Inszenierungen eines Staatsmannes. Ed.: Irene Etzersdorfer. Wien 1987.

Kogon, Eugen: *Der SS-Staat.* Das System der deutschen Konzentrationslager. Frankfurt a. M. 1946.

Kolb, Eberhard: *Die Weimarer Republik.* Grundriss der Geschichte. Wien 1984.

Landesmann, Peter: *Die Juden und ihr Glaube.* Eine Gemeinschaft im Zeichen der Tora. Wien 1987.

Langbein, Hermann: *Im Namen des deutschen Volkes.* Zwischenbilanz der Prozesse wegen nationalsozialistischer Verbrechen.

Lanzmann, Claude: *Shoa.* Mit einem Vorwort von Simone de Beauvoir. Düsseldorf 1986.

Lembeck, Fred und Giere, Wolfgang: *Otto Loewi.* Ein Lebensbild in Dokumenten. Biographische Dokumentation und Bibliographie. Berlin-Heidelberg-New York 1968.

Lexikon für Theologie und Kirche. Freiburg 1963 - 1966.

Meisel, Josef: *Die Mauer im Kopf.* Erinnerungen eines ausgeschlossenen Kommunisten 1945 - 1970. Wien 1986.

Melzer, Hartmann und Wimmer, Otto: *Lexikon der Namen und Heiligen.* Innsbruck 1984.

Mitscherlich, Margarete und Alexander: *Die Unfähigkeit zu trauern.* Grundlagen kollektiven Verhaltens. München 1968.

Müller, Ingo: *Furchtbare Juristen.* Die unbewältigte Vergangenheit unserer Justiz. München 1987.

Der Nationalsozialismus. Dokumente 1933 - 1945. Ed. und kommentiert v. Walter Hofer. Frankfurt a. M. 1983.

Obermann, Heiko A.: *Wurzeln des Antisemitismus.* Christenangst und Judenplage im Zeitalter von Humanismus und Reformation. Tübingen 1981.

Österreichische Bundesverfassungsgesetze. 11 edition. Stuttgart 1985.

Österreichs Fall. Schriftsteller berichten vom "Anschluss." Ed.: Ulrich Weinzierl. Wien-München 1987.

Pelinka, Anton: *Unterdrückung, Befreiung, Bewältigung.* Zum Umgang mit Österreichs widersprüchlicher Vergangenheit. In: *Totenbuch Theresienstadt.* Damit sie nicht vergessen werden. Ed.: Mary Steinhauser und Dokumentenarchiv des österreichischen Widerstandes. Wien 1971, 1987.

Pollack, Martin: *Des Lebens Lauf.* Jüdische Familienbilder aus Zwischen-Europa. Wien 1987.

Portisch, Hugo und Riff, Sepp: *Österreich II. Der lange Weg zur Freiheit.* Wien 1986.

Rendi, Otto: *Die Geschichte der Juden in Graz und in der Steiermark.* In: *Zeitschrift des Historischen Vereines für Steiermark.* Graz 1971.

Salzer-Eibenstein, Gerhard: *Die Wohn- und Berufsstandorte der Grazer Juden 1938.* Jahrbuch der Stadt Graz. Vol. 10.

Sartre, Jean Paul: *Réflexion sur la question juive.* Paris 1954.

Schechter, Edmund: *Viennese Vignettes.* Personal Recollections. Vantage Press, New York 1983.

Schenz, Marco: *Bundespräsident Rudolf Krichschläger.* Wien-Köln-Graz 1984.

Schriftenreihe des Steirischen Studentenhistoriker-Vereines. Series 12: Ein Beitrag zur Geschichte des Zionismus auf Grazer akademischen Boden. Ed.: Harald Seewann. Graz 1986. Series 13: Die Jüdisch-Akademische Verbindung, Charitas, Graz 1897 - 1938. Vol. 2 mit einer Auswahl von Beiträgen zur Geschichte und zur Selbstdarstellung des bis zum Jahre 1938 bestandenen jüdisch-nationalen Waffenstudententums in Österreich. Ed.: Harald Seewann. Graz 1987.

Schuschnigg, Kurt: *Im Kampf gegen Hitler.* Eine Überwindung der Anschlussidee. Wien-München-Zürich 1969.

Sichrovsky, Peter: *Schuldig geboren.* Kinder aus Nazifamilien. Köln 1985.

Sichrovsky, Peter: *Wir wissen nicht was morgen wird, wir wissen wohl was gestern war.* Junge Juden in Deutschland und Österreich. Köln 1985.

Spiel, Hilde: *Glanz und Untergang,* Wien 1866 - 1938. Wien 1987.

Der Gelbe Stern. Die Judenverfolgung in Europa 1933 - 1945. Ed.: Gerhard Schoenberner. Hamburg 1961.

Sternberger, Dolf und Storz, Gerhard: *W. E. Süsskind.* Aus dem Wörterbuch des Unmenschen. Hamburg 1957.

Stiefel, Dieter: *Entnazifizierung in Österreich.* Wien-München-Zürich 1981.

Totenbuch Theresienstadt. Damit sie nicht vergessen werden. Ed.: Mary Steinhauser und Dokumentenarchiv des österreichischen Widerstandes. Wien 1971, 1987.

Verjährung? 200 Persönlichkeiten des öffentlichen Lebens sagen NEIN. Eine Dokumentation. Ed.: Simon Wiesenthal. Frankfurt a. M. 1965.

Vertriebene Vernunft. Emigration und Exil österreichischer Wissenschaft 1930 - 1940. Ed.: Friedrich Stadler. Wien-München 1987.

Vogl, Friedrich: *Widerstand im Waffenrock*. In: Materialien zur Arbeiterbewegung (Nr. 7) Ed.: Ludwig-Botzmann-Institut. Wien 1977.

Wagner, Georg: *Österreich*. Zweite Republik. Vol. I, II. Thaur/Tirol-Wien 1983, 1987.

Weinzierl, Erika: *Zu wenig Gerechte*. Österreicher und Judenverfolgung 1938 - 1945. Graz-Wien-Köln 1969.

Wiesel, Elie: *Der Schwur von Kolvillàg*. 1987.

Wiesel, Elie: *Was die Tore des Himmels öffnet*. Geschichten chassidischer Meister. Wien 1981.

Wiesel, Elie: *Das Geheimnis des Golem*. Freiburg i. Br. 1985.

Wiesenthal, Simon: *Max und Helen*. Ein Tatsachenroman. Wien 1983.

Wiesenthal, Simon: *Krystyna*. Die Tragödie des polnischen Widerstandes. München 1986.

Zeitzeugen. Wege zur Zweiten Republik. Ed.: Universität Salzburg in Zusammenarbeit mit dem Historischen Archiv des ORF unter Mitarbeit von Peter Dusek, Hannes Eichmann, Adolf Haslinger, Herbert Hayduck u. a. 358 Abbildungen nach Dokumenten und Photographien. Wien 1987.

Zweig, Stefan: *Die Welt von gestern*. Erinnerungen eines Europäers. Frankfurt a. M. 1970.

Zwischen Diktatur und Literatur. Gespräche mit Marcel Reich-Ranicki und Joachim Fest. Ed.: Karl B. Schnelting. Frankfurt a. R. 1984.

About This Book

I very much welcome the appearance of an English-language version of your book. It is most important that people from other countries receive as comprehensive a view as possible of the important events of 1938—and your book provides that.

> Professor Anton Pelinka,
> University of Innsbruck

The topics that you treat are of the greatest importance for the democratic development of your country. I endorse your efforts and wish you well.

> Jeffrey A. Ross, Ph.D.
> Director, Department of Campus Affairs/
> Higher Education
> Anti-Defamation League of B'nai B'rith,
> New York

Your book is excellently written and covers the subject very well.

> Professor Richard Berczeller,
> Physician and Author
> New York

Your achievement is remarkable and deserves the highest praise.

> Leo Bretholz
> Auschwitz survivor
> and consultant on the Holocaust

The book is a new contribution to our understanding of the Nazi period.

Dr. Wolf Calebow, Cultural Attaché,
Embassy of the Federal Republic of Germany,
Washington, D.C.

With great commitment and courage, using often shocking evidence, Dr. Elfriede Schmidt has written a book which deals not only with the period of the Holocaust, but also with its after-effects today.

We know from this and other books that the victims as well as the "perpetrators" of the Holocaust have great difficulty in speaking about this time. However, in the interest of educating the young people of today, it is necessary that the shocking stories of the victims be made known and be protected for posterity. Dr. Schmidt has done this with a great deal of love and care. We owe her our thanks.

Chief Rabbi Chaim Eisenberg

I read your book with great interest and hope it will find a broad readership. The book's style and format should stimulate discussion on the subject of Austrian anti-Semitism among those not familiar with the academic literature.

Professor Hartmut Lehmann,
Director of the German Historical Institute,
Washington, D.C.

The theme of your book on 1938 is, of course, immensely important. The Anschluss was a major event in the history of modern Austria, and Austrians are just now beginning to come to grips with its significance. I hope that your book is helping Austrians gain insight into their past. . . .

Professor David F. Good,
Director of the Center for Austrian Studies
University of Minnesota

Your book is a very valuable contribution to our knowledge of the events surrounding the Anschluss of 1938.

> Dr. Friedrich Hoess,
> Austrian Ambassador to the United States

Your interviews of a cross section of Austrians, Jews, and Christians represents a significant historical source for future research. Congratulations!

> Joshua O. Haberman,
> Rabbi Emeritus
> Washington, D.C.

I find the book moving, impressive, and informative. It is a document of unique value because it records the memories, reactions, and excuses of so wide a range of Austrians, each of whom seems to have a slightly different view of what happened in 1938. It is to your great credit that you took the time to conduct these interviews and to publish them in book form.

> Fred Hift,
> Journalist, New York

Your work with the interviews is most important today and it seems to me it would bring the world of yesterday vibrantly alive to the young people of today.

> Stella K. Hershan,
> Author, New York

The pointed questions you raise in the interviews evoke a fascinating range of responses and provide a great deal of insight into the historical situation within which political and moral choices were made. The reader is left to draw his or her own conclusions about them. One learns much from the book, and one is challenged to learn more.

> Professor Jacques Kornberg,
> University of Toronto

I have valued Dr. Schmidt's work for years.

> Bruno Kreisky,
> Former Austrian Chancellor

With this book. . . you have, in a decisive way, helped Christians and Jews to see the great tasks that they can accomplish together.

> Cardinal Franz König,
> Vienna

Your book asks the right questions and finds answers; that is the only way we can be kept from sinking into indifference. The world must not be allowed to forget what happened in Austria in 1938, and you have contributed a valuable document.

> Ronald S. Lauder,
> Former U.S. Ambassador to Austria

A touching, shocking, thought-provoking book.

> Franz Vranitzky,
> Austrian Chancellor

The author shows herself to be a knowledgeable and sympathetic interviewer. . . her book is a shocking but necessary contribution to the process by which Austrians come to terms with the past.

> Professor Harry Zohn,
> Brandeis University

Fifty years after the annexation of Austria by Nazi Germany, it is imperative to focus on the fateful year of 1938. Present events indicate that we have not come to terms with what happened when Austria came under the cloak of National Socialism. For many Austria was merely a victim of the Third Reich and there are those who would like to minimize the criminal barbarity of the time.

Elfriede Schmidt has interviewed a selection of prominent personalities and people from all walks of life who had a firsthand view of the events of 1938. Their candid answers to her questions provide us with knowledge that is essential, shocking and moving. Dr. Schmidt has made an important historical contribution to understanding the past. We can only come to terms with the present if we come to terms with the past.

The spectrum ranges from disputing the number of millions murdered to denying that Auschwitz was a death factory. Absurd and malicious statements and slogans by politicians and other public figures have helped foster a resurgence of anti-Semitism. World attention has been drawn to the open conflict that has rent Austrian society.

Roland D. Graham
Attorney at Law
Minneapolis